D1555388

THE RELIGIOUS ROOTS OF
AMERICAN SOCIOLOGY

GARLAND LIBRARY OF SOCIOLOGY
General Editor: Dan A. Chekki
(VOL. 23)

GARLAND REFERENCE LIBRARY
OF SOCIAL SCIENCE
(VOL. 786)

GARLAND LIBRARY OF SOCIOLOGY
General Editor: Dan A. Chekki

THE RELIGIOUS ROOTS OF AMERICAN SOCIOLOGY

Cecil E. Greek

GARLAND PUBLISHING, INC. • NEW YORK & LONDON
1992

Library of Congress Cataloging-in-Publication Data

Greek, Cecil E.
    The religious roots of American sociology / Cecil E. Greek.
        p. cm. — (Garland library of sociology ; vol. 23)
    (Garland reference library of social science ; vol. 786)
    Includes bibliographical references (p.   ).
    ISBN 0-8153-0390-4
    1. Sociology—United States—History—19th century.
    2. Sociology, Christian—United States—History—19th century.
    3. Social gospel. I. Title. II. Series. III. Series: Garland
reference library of social science ; v. 786.
    HM22.U5G74   1992
    301'.0973—dc20   91-38373
                                                                    CIP

Printed on acid-free, 250-year-life paper
Manufactured in the United States of America

Contents

Preface

Within contemporary American sociology the reigning paradigm is that research must be "value-free." Religious beliefs and values are not only suspect, they must be eliminated, lest they contaminate sociological research. Sociology is generally considered solely a secular endeavor.

This work will show that American sociology had origins quite different from its current philosophical underpinnings. American sociology has deep religious roots which, in fact, continue to influence, both directly and indirectly, the discipline today. During the early history of American sociology, between approximately 1880 and 1920, the discipline was understood by many, both those inside sociology and those outside of the field, to be a fundamentally religious undertaking. American sociology was closely aligned with the social gospel movement in Protestantism, which hoped to make use of the new science of sociology to help solve social problems and, ultimately, prepare America for the establishment of Christ's Kingdom on earth. The works of many of the founding fathers of American sociology such as Albion Small, Charles Henderson, E.A. Ross, and Charles Ellwood were based upon such religious beliefs, which they openly stated on many occasions. Sociology, through providing a holistic theoretical perspective to analyze American society, was to supply religiously motivated social reformers with the means necessary to ameliorate the newly industrialized, urbanized, and bureaucratized nation and thus help bring about a heavenly utopia, the Kingdom of God on earth.

Although American sociology was to become overtly secularized after 1920, it retained its ameliorative outlook, hoping to "save" mankind through positivistic sociological analysis and technocratic societal planning. "Applied sociology" in America has to this day retained the discipline's original soteriological aspirations.

In effect, this book represents an attempt to employ a social constructionist model similar to that developed by Blumer (1971) and Spector and Kitsuse (1977) to investigate a historical example of social engineering. While social constructionists have investigated contemporary moral entrepreneurs from the worlds of religion, psychology, business, and politics they have not, to date, explored the moral origins of their own discipline. An informed understanding of contemporary American sociology must begin with an analysis of the discipline's unique American origins and its links to the predominant religious beliefs of that era. This work should also be helpful to those interested in the history of American sociology's long-term fascination with social problems and their cure. It was religiously influenced sociologists who set the discipline's overall direction and initiated sociology's interest in such topics as minorities, crime and delinquency, marital and family breakdown, sexism, labor relations, and urban decay. One of the major reasons that early American sociology rarely investigated religion as a topic or ever produced a sociologist of religion on the scale of Weber or Durkheim was that the entire endeavor of sociology was, in effect, applied Christianity.

This book is divided into three major sections. The first documents the emergence of the social gospel within American Protestantism in the late nineteenth century and demonstrates why "Christian sociology" was needed to aid in hastening the arrival of Christ's earthly utopia. The first chapter briefly summarizes Protestant attempts at social reform in America during the eighteenth and nineteenth centuries prior to the appearance of the social gospel, highlighting the theological differences between the latter and earlier Protestant reform movements. The important leaders of these movements are discussed, as well as some of the major sins targeted for eradication, such as slavery and alcohol consumption.

The second chapter analyzes the origins of social gospel theology in the 1870s and 1880s. The social gospel had five major tenets: (1) a strong allegiance to evolutionism; (2) faith in inevitable progress; (3) an optimistic view of human nature; (4) a belief that the

Kingdom of God was to be an earthly utopia; and (5) the expectation that America was to be the place where the earthly Kingdom first would be established, then to serve as a model for the rest of the world.

The third chapter attempts to explain why the social gospel sought to create a new social science, sociology, to assist it in bringing about God's Kingdom on earth. It seems that the naively optimistic social gospelers were taken aback by the terrible negative consequences of industrialization and urbanization. Nevertheless, rather than reject their optimistic beliefs as being without empirical proof because of the continued existence of these evils, the social gospelers relabeled the evils as obstacles—social problems—that were blocking the arrival of the otherwise inevitable Kingdom. In addition, they believed these obstacles were God's way of testing the sincerity of their faith, and demonstrated that God intended for the church to be His willing partner in helping Him to establish His Kingdom. The social gospelers attempted to redirect the church's mission toward the amelioration of social problems, so that the Kingdom's arrival could be hastened and assured. After their realization that earlier forms of Christian amelioration were now obsolete, the social gospelers called upon the fledgling discipline of sociology to help create new reform strategies, based upon social scientific truths that would be compatible with their theological beliefs.

The second section of the book specifically discusses the type of sociology produced during the 1890–1920 period. In the 1890s, the first flowering of American sociology, the discipline emerged as one closely aligned with religion. Sociology was to take on its primary ameliorative orientation during this period. In addition, early American sociology was to develop a critical—although distinctively non-Marxist—stance toward the status quo in society, directed oftentimes at current ruling elites in government and industry who appeared to be directly responsible for the continuation of certain social problems.

Chapter four analyzes the sociological writings of the first American sociology faculty established at the University of Chicago, and one of their students, Charles Ellwood, in order to discover the social gospel presuppositions that underpinned both their sociological theories and ameliorative methodologies. The four members of the

University of Chicago's first faculty were Albion Small, Charles Henderson, George Vincent, and Marion Talbot. From 1892 until 1904 all four were in the sociology department, uniting Small's concern for creating an adequate sociological theory and methodology with Henderson's and Vincent's advocacy of applied sociology—social reform, social work, settlements, penology—with Talbot's sanitary engineering. Women, such as Talbot, were to play a major role during the 1890s in sociology's development. Closely associated with the Chicago sociology department was Jane Addams, whose settlement house movement attracted a number of middle-class women to sociology with the hope of finding a way to expand the domestic sphere to include the traditional male worlds of business and government. Charles Ellwood was to take Chicago's brand of social gospel sociology to the University of Missouri. Ellwood's approach is particularly important because of his attempt to rid sociology of its biologically rooted Aryanism and ethnocentrism, an unfortunate legacy of sociology's Protestant origin.

Chapter five covers the work of Richard T. Ely, a social gospel economist, and his student E.A. Ross. They were to create another haven for Christian sociology at the University of Wisconsin and succeeded in uniting the university and the state government into an instrument for Progressive reform politics: a model that would later be brought to full fruition in Franklin D. Roosevelt's creation of the welfare state.

The one sociologist who served as the great critic of social gospel sociology was William Graham Sumner. He is discussed in chapter six. While many of the social gospelers' reforms represented attempts to socially control portions of the population that were deemed unsalvageable, Sumner advocated a form of civil libertarianism that would guarantee equal opportunity for all. But, Sumner's sociology can also be reinterpreted to reveal its own fundamentally religious roots. Sumner, a former Protestant minister, can be best understood as a Calvinist Christian who has been cut off from his God and left to find meaning in life solely through success in the world of work and faith in the inevitability of natural forces.

The final section of the book covers the demise of social gospel sociology and analyzes the continuing religious nature of American sociology. In the 1920s, the era of social gospel sociology was to come to a close. The Protestant denominations that had backed the social gospel pulled back from social reform with the emergence of Fundamentalism. World War I brought an end to the optimistic belief that human nature had fully outgrown its animal origins. Chapter seven covers the social gospel's decline.

The final chapter addresses what happened within the discipline of sociology, as the applied side of the field was taken over by positivistic sociologists such as William Ogburn who stressed an objective, value-free approach that would not permit overtly religious, moralistic beliefs to be used in its methodology. However, Ogburn's positivism did not represent the end of "religion" in American sociology, since he merely secularized the conservative version of the social gospel advocated by his mentor, Franklin Giddings. Ogburn's applied sociology incorporated his own moralistic notion of cultural lag into his plan for the employment of a statistically trained technocratic elite who were to cure America's "lags," and thus insure societal well-being. Ogburn had his own vision of a kingdom just as the social gospelers had theirs.

One of Ogburn's ultimate goals was to replace sociological theory as well as other forms of social science methodology with statistical analysis. While the social gospelers had employed statistics frequently, they were eclectic in their methodology, making use of historical, comparative, and case study approaches. Ogburn's predicted demise for sociological theory has to some extent come true, particularly within applied sociology. Except for functionalism, applied sociology seems to have made very little use of the theories which emerged in the post–World War II era, such as neo-Marxian analyses or phenomenological sociologies. Sociology has been reduced largely to a technique but rarely openly asks itself which god that technique is serving, now that the discipline has rejected its original goal of service to the Christian God. It seems that applied sociology has focused its concerns upon solving problems assigned it by our society's secular gods, government and business. Having rejected God, sociology has chosen to serve Mammon instead, performing research for any institution willing to pay for it.

PART I

CHAPTER 1

Social Reform and Protestant Theology From the Colonial Period to the Civil War

Prior to the Civil War, Protestant social reform activity was based on a very different theology from that which inspired the social gospel movement in the closing decades of the nineteenth century. This chapter will focus on the major leaders of antebellum Protestant social reform movements, the issues and causes they championed, and their basic theological perspectives. This is not to say that all of these Protestant leaders were identical in their outlook—as will be shown each was to some extent unique—but general similarities can be found and highlighted. The basic ideas they shared were revivalism, perfectionism, and millennialism. These beliefs were very closely welded together and dominated Protestant thinking concerning social reform prior to the Civil War.

Although most of this section will deal with the period after 1800, the theology of Jonathan Edwards (1703–1758) is a good place to begin because many of his ideas became dominant in the early nineteenth century. Edwards is important because he was one of the first American millennialists. Prior to Edwards the dominant theological interpretation of the future had been millenarian, meaning that the world would grow worse and worse until Christ returned. Since the world could not be redeemed, millenarian saints believed they should separate themselves from this incurably evil world. The majority of those who came to America from England were premillennialists, who believed God would have to send Christ back a second time to bring order to the world (McLoughlin, 1978:76). Edwards initiated the American rejection of the millenarian position, replacing it by a millennialist perspective, one which sees the world as having the potential of becoming a holy utopia. Edwards's millennialism would become dominant in Protestant theology in the first half of the nineteenth century and later would be incorporated into social gospel thought.

Edwards came to his millennial beliefs through his experience with the outpouring of God's spirit during the revivals of the 1730s and 1740s, now known as the First Great Awakening. He felt the Great Awakening might be ushering in the millennium (Tuveson, 1968:23). The Awakening was one of the final ebbings in the ever upward wave motion that Edwards believed history had followed since the advent of Christianity. Historical periods of darkness were followed by periods of spiritual revival that reached ever larger portions of the populace (Miller, 1949). He believed the next revival might bring with it the millennium. Edwards put forward these ideas in his opus, *History of the Work of Redemption* (Tuveson, 1968:27). America was to be used as God's instrument, ushering in the millennium. Edwards argued that the discovery of the New World and the establishment of Atlantic settlements were the final preparation for the beginning of the millennium (Tuveson, 1968:99). The work of spiritually reviving the world for the almighty had thus already begun in America (McLoughlin, 1978:77).

However, the millennium was not to come about solely because God willed that it would happen. Human effort would play an important part as well. Edwards stated that a true saint would be devoted to "disinterested benevolence," a selfless giving of one's time and energy to social concerns (Ahlstrom, 1975, Vol. II:79). Edwards's concept of disinterested benevolence would later be expanded and become the basis of the manifold social reform activities associated with the Second Great Awakening early in the nineteenth century. Disinterested benevolence would be humanity's role to play in bringing about the millennium through ridding society of its impurities.

Among the important figures of the late eighteenth century who followed Edwards's lead was Newport, Rhode Island, minister Samuel

Hopkins (1721–1803). Hopkins, in his 1793 *A Treatise on the Millennium*, outlined a utopian world based on justice, benevolence, and prosperity (Tuveson, 1968:99).

During the first half of the nineteenth century, a period later known as the Second Great Awakening, there were a number of prominent religious social reformers. Among the most influential were Lyman Beecher, Charles Finney, Theodore Dwight Weld, and Horace Bushnell.

Probably the most prominent Protestant leader of the early nineteenth century was Lyman Beecher (1775–1863), a Congregationalist. He spent most of his life in New England and toward the end of his career moved to Ohio to assist in the "Christianizing of the West." Beecher is historically important for two reasons. First of all, he attempted to modify the old Calvinist doctrine of mankind's absolute moral depravity. Second, Beecher was a leading advocate of social reform activity.

Beecher's move away from the Calvinist doctrine of total depravity was an important step because it signified the beginnings of an optimistic Christian view of human nature, which would be developed further by Horace Bushnell, and later adopted wholeheartedly by the social gospelers. Once human beings were endowed by theologians with the potential for doing good, an optimistic view of history became believable. In his famous 1823 sermon *The Faith Once Delivered to the Saints*, Beecher rejected Calvinistic determinism for a theory of free will. Human beings had the ability to choose freely between good and evil, between God and Satan (McLoughin, 1968:70–86). However, Beecher's theology remained for the most part orthodox Calvinism. Fallen humanity was damned by original sin but left with free will either to choose or reject salvation (Cole, 1954).

Lyman Beecher was one of the most active religiously motivated social reformers of his age. Beecher strongly advocated social reform because he believed that God had called America to a special task: leadership in the conversion of the rest of the world to Christianity. However, before this purpose could be achieved, America had first to set itself straight by becoming a moral society. Beecher's social reform activities were aimed at reaching this goal (Harding, 1965). As early as 1804 he published a sermon entitled *The Practicability of Suppressing Vice by Means of Societies Instituted for That Purpose.* Beecher was optimistic that believers could build and maintain a truly Christian American society. This would be accomplished partially through conversions and revivals, but Beecher was never satisfied with so atomistic a goal as the saving of individual souls. Moral reforms had to augment revivalism (Harding, 1965). Beecher's style of reform used clergy leadership to urge congregations toward corporate action in the newly created voluntary reform societies, and direct political involvement through lobbying for the passage of needed moral legislation.

Beecher involved himself in many moral campaigns. Among them were the temperance movement, the anti-slavery movement, attempts to put an end to the practice of duelling, and proposals to prohibit Sabbath breaking. He was instrumental in founding both the American Temperance Society (1826) and the African Colonization Society (1817) (McLoughlin, 1978:112).

Although some temperance writers approved of drinking in moderation, Beecher preached that even moderate drinking was anathema (Walters, 1978). In 1828, Beecher published a book entitled *Six Sermons on the Nature, Occasions, Signs, Evils, and Remedies of Intemperance*, which stated his views on the problems of drinking. In this work he referred to intemperance as a great national sin, one whose remedy called upon the nation to array itself, *en masse*, against it. Beecher raised the possibility of passing federal legislation to stop the making and selling of alcohol, thus separating himself from temperance spokesmen who felt that converting individuals to Christ would solve America's alcohol problem (Walters, 1978). For Beecher, it was ultimately public sentiment which must be swayed before drinking would be stopped in America. This required a threefold program of federal regulation, spiritual conversion, and education about the evils and dangers of alcohol. As with all the reformers of his age, Beecher felt that his campaign against alcohol abuse was an attack upon a sin rather than a "social problem."

Such an attitude is also apparent in Beecher's position on slavery. He viewed slavery as another great national sin, but one that was so deeply rooted in the society that it could only be eliminated gradually. Beecher could not fully support the radical abolitionist position of William Lloyd Garrison, who attended Beecher's Park Street Church in Boston during the 1830s (Harding, 1965). Garrison, on the other hand, saw himself as attempting to put into practice Beecher's vision for the removal of this transgression. However, Beecher cautioned Garrison to be concerned about the consequences of his radical abolitionist policy. One of Beecher's solutions to slavery took form as the organizing of the African Colonization Society in 1817 (McLoughlin, 1978:112). The recolonization of Africa by former American slaves would provide the ultimate solution to the Negro problem (Bodo, 1954).

Somewhat surprisingly, neither Beecher nor his contemporaries considered poverty to be a national sin in need of elimination. Beecher was Calvinistic when it came to the issue of the distribution of wealth in society. The rich were successful because of their moral superiority over the immoral poor (Cole, 1954). He believed the impoverished must overcome their predicament through their own hard work (Walters, 1978). Beecher's stance toward poverty was very different from the one that would develop later in the nineteenth century among the social gospelers.

The most famous revivalist of the first half of the nineteenth century was Charles Finney. However, he was a leading force in social reform activities as well. Finney differs from Beecher in that the former's social reform orientation springs primarily from his evangelical concern for making genuine conversions. Finney's stand on social reform is a combination of four elements: free will, holiness, benevolent activity, and faith in dramatic change.

First of all, Finney broke completely from the Calvinist belief that sinners could be saved only if God first stirred their hearts. Finney argued that God gave men free will to effect their own salvation whenever they chose. He stated this boldly in his famous sermon *Sinners Bound to Change Their Own Hearts* (McLoughlin, 1978:124).

Not only could sinners change their own hearts according to Finney, they also could attain a higher sinless state of "holiness" or "perfection" (Ahlstrom, 1975, Vol. I:557). The idea of perfectionism was not first developed by Finney but by John Wesley in the English Methodist revivals of the eighteenth century. However, Finney's belief in the possibility of holiness or perfection was related to his reform orientation. In his individualistic theology, Finney believed that the way to ultimately change society was to purify the hearts and minds of all society's members. This, of course, was accomplished by mass conversions through consciously applying the revivalistic techniques that Finney himself developed and advocated. Finney had reduced revivalism to laws of cause and effect; the right techniques would produce inevitable results (McLoughlin, 1959; Harding, 1943).

The tie in Finney's theology between holiness and reform activity existed in his notion of benevolence, an idea Jonathan Edwards had earlier employed. For Finney, the true sign of a perfected person was a deep concern for benevolent activity. The reborn were to become genuinely altruistic. Finney defined all sin as selfishness, and thus sin's opposite—holiness—was to take its shape in disinterested benevolence (McLoughlin, 1978:128). The new convert was to become committed to sacrificing his own pleasures in order that God's Kingdom on earth might be advanced. Christian benevolent societies, such as the American Anti-Slavery Society organized in 1834, sprang up and served as outlets for converts to benevolent perfectionism.

The final part of Finney's optimistic theology of social change was his belief in the possibility of dramatic change. As Finney stated:

> If immediate conversion is available by an act of the human will, then, through God's miraculous grace, all things are possible: human nature is open to total renovation in the twinkling of an eye and so, then, is the nature of society. The world is unfettered from tradition, custom, institutions; is unconditioned by history or environment. Society is totally malleable to the power that works in harmony with God's will (quoted in McLoughlin, 1978:114).

Based upon such an optimistic faith, Finney believed that in the 1830s the final millennium could be brought about within a three-year period (McLoughlin, 1959). Thus, the wave of social reform which followed the Second Great Awakening was largely the result of Finney's brand of perfectionist zeal (McLoughlin, 1978:128). With the later social gospelers it would be adherence to theistic evolution and not revivalistic perfectionism that served as a primary impetus to social reform. Finney backed a number of different causes and movements. Among them were anti-slavery, temperance, economic and business reform, prohibition of Sabbath breaking, women's rights, and education (Vulgamore, 1963).

Finney's views concerning social reform in general can best be seen in his attitude toward the abolitionist movement. On the one hand, Finney was instrumental in the abolitionist activities of both William Lloyd Garrison and Theodore Dwight Weld. Finney allowed Garrison to use his church to form the American Anti-Slavery Society in 1833 (McLoughlin, 1978:130). On the other hand, Finney's own approach toward abolition was much less radical than that of Garrison. Finney's reform methods were employed by his most famous disciple, Theodore Dwight Weld. Finney had always considered abolitionism to be an auxiliary to the ultimately significant revival crusades. Involvement in the abolitionist movement was a sign that one was now a convert who had taken on the proper benevolent orientation. Finney urged local congregations privately to reprove members who were slave owners. If they failed to release their slaves, the congregation was then to chastise them publicly. As a last resort slave owners were to be barred from the congregation (Grover, 1957). Finney did not advocate government action to free the slaves. He saw manumission as an individual matter to be solved through exhortation of the individual offenders who owned slaves. Finney never supported laws to restrain men or prohibit them from bad actions. His fundamental axiom was that men must be transformed from within (McLoughlin, 1978:129).

Finney's disciple, Theodore Dwight Weld, also combined evangelism and abolitionism. Weld was a young man when converted at a Finney revival (Barnes, 1973). Weld began his abolitionist activities in 1830 while attending Lane Seminary in Cincinnati, under its then president Lyman Beecher (Barnes, 1973). Weld and a group of students became known as the Lane Rebels for their radical abolitionist stance; they created so much controversy on the campus and in the city that Beecher had them expelled. Weld and the Lane Rebels transferred, *en masse*, to Oberlin College in 1835 to study with Charles Finney (Barnes, 1973). From there Weld went on to become an renowned evangelist for abolitionism. Using Finney's revival techniques Weld would end a rousing sermon by denouncing slavery and calling upon those who wished to become abolitionists to rise, come forward, and sign a pledge (Barnes, 1973). In 1835 and 1836 he preached all over Ohio, western Pennsylvania, and western New York, converting thousands to the abolitionist movement (Barnes, 1973). Like Finney, Weld preached that slavery was a sin, and that the abolitionist movement was a great revival of religious benevolence. Weld's preaching was so successful that seventy other men were appointed by the national society in 1836 to use Weld's methods (Barnes, 1973). Weld personally converted the Tappan brothers, Arthur and Lewis, and James G. Birney to abolitionism (Weld, 1969). By age thirty-three, Weld's voice had given out and he then turned to the printed word. In 1839 he published *American Slavery As It Is*, which sold 100,000 copies in its first year (Weld, 1969). It was to later become the basis for the novel, *Uncle Tom's Cabin*, written by Harriet Beecher Stowe— Lyman Beecher's daughter. However, in the mid-1830s, Weld and Finney got into a dispute over the place that abolitionism should play in regard to revivalism. In 1835 Finney instructed his students at Oberlin College to avoid the abolitionist movement and dedicate themselves to saving the souls of those involved in slavery (McLoughlin, 1978:130). Finney felt that abolition could only be an appendage of a general revival. Weld disagreed and realized he must go beyond Finney's individualistic solution. Weld lobbied in Congress in the 1830s for passage of a law abolishing slavery in the District of Columbia (McLoughlin, 1978:130).

On other social issues Finney demonstrated the same individualistic solution he proposed to end slavery. For example, concerning temperance Finney saw conversion and reproof of the drunk as the way to rid America of alcohol (Vulgamore, 1963). Finney even believed that one of his revivals in Rochester, New York, had lowered the crime rate in that city by one-third because so many drunkards had turned their lives over to God (Harding, 1943).

Finney expressed his individualistic orientation in the area of business and economics as well. Finney's efforts among the poor involved preaching and praying but were never directed at eradicating the social roots of poverty (Cole, 1954). Finney was convinced that all economic and political injustices and discriminatory social practices could be altered by means of revivalism (McLoughlin, 1959). For those with wealth, Finney urged that they use it for general benevolence instead of being selfish (Vulgamore, 1963). Finney exhorted businessmen to make money for the glory of God, but in Finney's mind its only sacred usage should be for redemption of sinners (Grover, 1957).

Somewhat more liberal in his attitude toward women, he favored female education, allowed women to speak up during religious services, and, in 1850, established Oberlin as the first coeducational college in America (Ahlstrom, 1975, Vol. II:86). However, the purpose of female education was to make them more effective in their domestic role (Vulgamore, 1963).

Overall, Finney's reform philosophy reflected an individualistic bent; he had no notion of social forces. Recognition of the extreme importance of social forces would be one of the key ideas that the social gospelers would develop in their own social philosophy.

Individualistic as Finney's theology was, the ultimate outcome of revivalism and benevolent activity would be social, ushering in the final millennium (Cross, 1965). Finney, like Lyman Beecher, believed that through the spread of Christianity the world itself was working toward a state of perfection (Vulgamore, 1963). Inevitably, there would come a one thousand year period of universal peace and plenty that would lay the basis for the return of Christ and the ultimate establishment of God's Kingdom on earth (McLoughlin, 1959). In the 1830s, Finney predicted this might begin in only three years, because of the tremendous numbers of conversions he had himself witnessed. Finney felt that degenerationist theologians like William Miller, who in 1843 predicted that the world was growing so bad that Christ would have to return to save humanity from itself, were mistaken

(McLoughlin, 1978:130). One of the most significant differences between Finney's message and that of many post–Civil War evangelists, was that they adopted Miller's pessimistic premillennialism rather than Finney's optimistic postmillennialism (McLoughlin, 1959). Premillennialism was pessimistic because it was linked with the degenerationist belief that the world would only grow worse and worse prior to Christ's Second Coming. Postmillennialists, however, predicted gradual societal improvement, culminating in a one thousand year period of peace and prosperity followed immediately by Christ's return to earth. The postmillennialists of the post–Civil War era were the social gospelers and the social Darwinian modernists who were akin to Finney with his optimistic outlook, while the premillennialist position was adopted by urban revivalists such as Dwight Moody, and later by Fundamentalists.

Finney's theology was typical of the reform movements fueled by the revivals of the 1830s. The major difference between the revivals of the 1830s and those of the 1740s was that the goal of salvaging the unconverted was supplanted by the objective of saving the world through organized movements (Cole, 1954). While they still aimed their messages at the redemption of sinners, 1830s revivalists invaded a number of fields of social reform (Cross, 1965). In addition to the areas already mentioned, such as anti-slavery and temperance, the revivals of the 1830s also produced missionary societies, Bible and tract societies, a Sunday school movement, and attempts at eliminating vice and juvenile delinquency (Cole, 1954). Among the vices opposed was the theater (Cole, 1954). To help end female juvenile delinquency an anti-prostitution campaign was begun in New York City by John R. McDowell, a Presbyterian clergyman, who set up an asylum to reform prostitutes (Cross, 1965). Reformers in a number of eastern seaboard cities also founded Houses of Refuge to help both male and female delinquents straighten out their lives.

In the 1830s, benevolent societies met annually in New York City for national conventions. Participation grew by hundreds of thousands during the decade, and societies included members of both sexes and all ages (Barnes, 1973). For example, the American Temperance Society, the product of an 1830 revival, grew to two thousand local branches in New York State alone and printed eighty-nine million pages of propaganda a year (Barnes, 1973). Leadership in the benevolent societies was exercised through a series of interlocking directorates, composed of a relatively small number of prominent clergymen and philanthropists (Barnes, 1973). Probably the most famous leaders of these reform societies during the 1830s were Arthur and Lewis Tappan, brothers from New York City (Wyatt-Brown, 1969). They were wealthy capitalists who, inspired by Finney's call for benevolent businessmen, served on the boards of directors of a number of the reform societies (Ahlstrom, 1975, Vol. II:96). As with Finney, their method of reform consisted of exhorting nonpartakers to rebuke those who did take part in the alleged sins. Thus, denunciation of the evil came first, actual reform of the evil was incidental to that primary obligation (Barnes, 1973).

Before moving on to one of the more transitional religious figures, Horace Bushnell, an important exception to this reform zeal should be mentioned. It concerns what was taking place in the South in the antebellum period. As in the North, revivals were sweeping the South during the Second Great Awakening, fostered especially by Methodist and Baptist itinerant evangelists. However, this revivalism did not lead to an emphasis on social reform in the South. Why it did not is an issue which must be addressed.

The answer is twofold. First, in the South, revivalism was channeled into individual pietism and not social reform movements. Second, southern slaveholders did not wish to give up the practice merely because some northerners were claiming it was sinful.

For the first reason, evangelical Christianity in the South was not channeled into reform activities. Instead its emphasis was on transforming individual believers in the context of a Christian community that had rejected the larger world or society. The basis of evangelical Christianity has always been tied to behavior; a convert's life was to be characterized by moral discipline in his own life and missionary zeal in his dealings with others. These energies could be channeled into reform activities as they were in the North, or concentrated on personal holiness as was the norm in the South. In the South, evangelicalism did not develop the sense of civic responsibility that was part of the New England heritage, dating back to the Puritans and their belief in a communitywide covenant relationship with God (Mathews, 1977:41). In the South, evangelicals located the moral struggle in the inner life of the individual believer. However, even in the South, evangelicalism was not a call to individualism, a personal relationship to Christ alone. It was always a call to community, to join a fellowship of believers (Mathews, 1977:19–20). Together, these evangelicals rejected society, calling it the "world," and felt called out of it to communal fellowship. Together, southern evangelists concentrated on personal sins, not reform issues. The kind of perfectionism the Methodists and other evangelical denominations sought was inward and personal holiness, not disinterested benevolence (McLoughlin, 1978:136). Thus, pietistic revivalism on the individual level decreased concern with politics in the South (McLoughlin, 1978:137).

The second reason that southern Christians stayed away from reform issues was because of their adamant refusal to believe that slavery was a sin in need of eradication. However, it would be incorrect to believe that southern Christians never took up the issue of the possible moral problems associated with slavery. In fact, in the late eighteenth century, a number of Methodist congregations in the South discussed the issue of slavery and concluded it was morally wrong. Gradually, however, Methodists receded from this stance. In 1780 Methodist preachers ordered their circuit riders to free their own slaves and advised all Methodists to follow their example (Mathews, 1977:68). The reason given was that slavery was "contrary to the laws of God, man and nature, and harmful to society, contrary to the dictates of conscience and pure religion" (Mathews, 1977:68). In 1784 southern Methodists threatened to excommunicate all church members not freeing their slaves within two years (Mathews, 1977:69). This was a rare extension of the evangelical ethic beyond the internal life of the believer into southern social relationships. However, the slavery debate almost shattered the young church and within six months the act of excommunication was rescinded and replaced by a less confrontational policy of education and moral suasion (Mathews, 1977:69). But southern slaveholders refused to be either persuaded, pushed, or bullied. Gradually, southern evangelical anti-slavery sentiment became limited to the mountain areas of the South, where slaveholders were not very powerful (Mathews, 1977:75). Slaveowners, on the other hand, defended their practice using the Bible as their justification. Slaveholders learned to recite the standard Biblical texts on Negro inferiority—e.g., the story of Noah's cursed son, the patriarchal and Mosaic acceptance of servitude, and Paul's counsels to slaves to obey their masters (Ahlstrom, 1975, Vol. II:104). Even southern preachers argued they could find nothing in the Bible that told them to declare that the institution of slavery was a sin. They stated that taken literally the Bible seemed much more clearly to accept slavery as a sad but necessary condition for some people (McLoughlin, 1978:136). Evangelical preachers continued to withdraw from the slavery question. They argued that the spirit of God could be seen working in their own expansion of converts among the slave population, and were unwilling to place opposition to slavery above the need to gain new members for Christ's Kingdom (Mathews, 1977:77). The first priority was to save souls. During the nineteenth century the dominant southern evangelical policy toward slaveholding was that it was a civil institution and, as such, Christians should not interfere in its workings. The character of civil institutions was governed by politics, and politics was considered to be beyond the scope of the church (Mathews, 1977:157). Personal piety and reform politics did not mix in the South. Of course, there were many notable exceptions, such as the Grimke sisters from Charleston, South Carolina, who published a pamphlet against slavery in 1836 (Mathews, 1977:116). Also, there were socially conscious voluntary societies in the South, but they concentrated their efforts on establishing Sunday schools, promoting foreign missions and domestic evangelism, and establishing Christian colleges, and not on reform activities (Mathews, 1977:88).

The next major theologian to be considered as a key transitional figure in nineteenth-century Protestant thought was Horace Bushnell (1802–1876). His writings set the stage for some of the major concepts of later social gospel theology: the belief in the nondepravity of infants and children, a "Christian theory of socialization," and the use of an organic model to describe the process of societal development.

Bushnell, as early as the 1840s, rejected the Calvinist concept of human natural depravity. Bushnell believed that children were born blameless and, indeed, that the infant soul, like the needle of a compass, pointed unerringly and instinctively toward its maker (Douglas, 1977:161). Thus, there was a spark of the divine in all children. This idea would later make possible the social gospelers' belief in human perfectibility.

For Bushnell, this spark of divinity did not necessarily lead to the development of a Christian adult. To explain why such an outcome was not inevitable, Bushnell developed his own Christian theory of socialization, arguing that one's immediate environment, the family, could either destroy the divine seed in the infant or allow it to blossom. Bushnell referred to his idea as "Christian nurture" (Bushnell, 1975). By Christian nurture, Bushnell meant that given the proper Christian environment, a Christian home with loving Christian parents, a child could grow up as a Christian and never know himself as being otherwise. He believed that the child's mind could be molded and led where the parents willed while the character was still being set. Bushnell's belief in Christian nurture led him to downplay the need for revivalism. The maturing child raised in a Christian home did not need to experience the agonizing crisis of a conversion experience. The child would have always known himself to be a Christian and conversion would thus be unnecessary. As Bushnell (1975) put it: "growth not conquest, is the true method of Christian progress." Bushnell felt that dramatic spiritual changes did not often take place.

At first, Bushnell's view of Christian nurture was attacked by traditional evangelicals such as Finney, but by the end of the nineteenth century it had won wide acceptance, especially in New England. This view would become the predominant one among the social gospelers, because it fit so nicely with their notion of social change as being a slow, gradual process.

Bushnell himself expanded upon his concept of Christian nurture and made out of it a theory about how social change would take place. Although he employed the idea of slow, gradual growth to describe social change, his writings in this area do contain some nondevelopmental concepts. Bushnell (1975) argued that the family unit was the key to the uplifting of society. Since the Great Awakening the spiritual importance of the family unit had been downplayed for a focus upon individual salvation, but he hoped to restore the family to its proper place. Bushnell's first goal was to create church communities of nurturing Christian families as the way of beginning the regenerative process within society (Grover, 1957). Through its families the church could penetrate the other organic social bodies—e.g., politics, business, education, etc.—making them vehicles of this same regenerative process. Through this slow, gradual process, amelioration would eventually include the whole of humanity. Bushnell's social strategy was to foster first the increase of Christian nurture within the church, and then its extension from that center to the periphery of society.

When discussing American society, its development, and the problems it had that need eradication, Bushnell slipped back and forth from gradualist to catastrophic ideas. For example, in his analysis of the growth of America, Bushnell (1975:149) expressed his faith in gradual progress.

The true increase of a nation is not that which is made by conquest and plunder, but that which is the simple development of its vital and prolific resources. Two centuries ago there came over to these western shores a few thousand men. These were the germ of a great nation here to arise and come into the public history of the world, possibly as a leading member. Potentially speaking, these men had in themselves, that is, in their persons, their principles, their habits, and other resources, all that now is or is yet to be of power and greatness in our republic. They went to work with a degree of spirit and energy never before exhibited. Habits of virtuous and frugal industry were unfolded by a wise and careful training. Simplicity of manners, for the first time, appeared, not as a barbaric virtue, but as the proper fruit of simplicity in religion. The mental rigor, produced by the same causes, was further sharpened by the necessities of a new state of existence. Population multiplied, wealth increased, the forest fell away at the sound of their axes, the natives retired before the potent and prolific energy of Saxon life, as before the Great Spirit himself. Cities rose upon the shores, the waters whitened to the sun under the sails of commerce, the civil order unfolded itself, as it were naturally, from the germ that blossomed in the Mayflower, and, behold, a great, wealthy, powerful and free nation stalks into history with the tread of a giant, fastening the astonished gaze of the world—all in the way of

simple growth! We have made no conquests. We have only unfolded
our original germ, the mustard seed of our first colonization. There is
no other kind of national advancement which is legitimate or safe.
The civil order must grow as a creature of life, and unfold itself from
within.

However, in some of his other writings, such as his 1863 *Nature
and the Supernatural as Together Constituting One System of God*,
Bushnell refused to accept a linear theory of progress. He argued that
the road to the millennium could not be a smooth process of
development alone. Bushnell felt that a series of crises or dramatic
reversals must take place before the final millennium could be ushered
in.

The ambivalence in Bushnell's thought is quite evident in his
attitude toward slavery. Bushnell (1839) believed that an "Irreversible
Providence" would lead to the downfall of the institution of slavery.
Bushnell felt the destruction of slavery was inevitable, with or without
the aid of abolitionists. Bushnell argued that this process would be slow
and gradual, and he spoke out against the abolitionists who wanted to
institute radical changes. However, when the Civil War came, Bushnell
regarded it as a decisive moment in America's history. A national sin
had to be atoned for; the country must purge itself from its evil before it
could move on toward the millennium (Cross, 1958).

Another important religious trend of early and mid-nineteenth-
century America, the communal movement, should be mentioned
briefly, because it had a number of similarities to the later social gospel
movement. There were many attempts made in nineteenth-century
America to establish utopian communes. During the century over one
hundred religious and socialistic communes were established, making it
a widespread movement which involved over one hundred thousand
participants (Holloway, 1966:18). Unlike other reformers, they did not
attempt to actively change society, either by moral suasion or political
action. Instead they tried to set up model ideal commonwealths to
provide examples that, in some cases, they hoped the rest of the society
would later follow. Among the more famous communal groups of the
nineteenth century were the Shakers (Andrews, 1963), the Rappites
(Nordhoff, 1966:63–98), John Humphrey Noyes' Oneida community

(Nordhoff, 1966:259–304), and the Owenite socialist communes (Bestor, 1967). All of these communes can be seen as attempts to escape the encroaching mass industrialization of America taking place in the nineteenth century. Communes offered to their members meaningful work rather than dehumanizing machine production. Many of the utopian theories put forward by the communal groups were very similar to the ideas of Christian socialism that later became one strand of social gospel thought and were especially prominent in the labor movement at the turn of the twentieth century. At that point in American history, however, the utopian communal experiments came to an end. Although a full comparison of communal ideology and that of the social gospel is beyond the scope of this work, their basic utopian goals were indeed quite similar.

The major difference between communal utopianism and the social gospel was in its focus. While the communitarians sought to create a separate holy society apart from the world, the social gospel locus of activity was to be within the world itself, ultimately hoping to make all of society holy. Walter Rauschenbusch (1907:346), a leading social gospeler, made this point quite directly. He stated that he was against small scale Christian communistic colonies, because such colonies did not serve to Christianize social life at large. Also, their example did not appear to be widely contagious; it was not influencing the larger society at all, he held.

CHAPTER 2

The Rise of the Social Gospel

In this chapter we now turn to investigate the major ideas that came together in the closing decades of the nineteenth century to form the core of social gospel thought. These major concepts were: (1) the acceptance of evolutionism; (2) faith in inevitable progress; (3) an optimistic perspective on human nature; (4) belief that the Kingdom of God was to be an earthly utopia; and (5) the idea that America was to be the place where the Kingdom would be first established, serving then as a model to the rest of the world.

Faith in evolution was one of the key concepts in the theology of the social gospel. For this reason how evolutionism affected Protestant theology in America in the late nineteenth century needs to be closely analyzed. The time period to be discussed runs from approximately 1865 to 1900.

Prior to Darwin, the relations between science and religion were cordial, since it was taken for granted that the findings of natural scientists would reinforce the revelations of Scripture. Both supported catastrophic assumptions about change. In England, however, new theories presented by the uniformitarian geologists Hutton and Lyell had begun to cast doubts about the Bible's catastrophic assumptions. Around 1800, Hutton argued that the cumulative effects of minute forces and infinitesimal changes could produce results equal to those of any sudden cataclysm (Gillispie, 1959:49). Thus, natural forces could supersede the necessity for any divine intervention in the world. In 1830, Charles Lyell published his *Principles of Geology*. The book was a sustained assault on the prevalent catastrophic assumptions in natural history (Gillispie, 1959:123). The uniformitarian position held that

God's provision for the laws of nature was immutable and that science could prove the divine origin of the laws by demonstrating the self-sufficiency and invariability of their operation, not by finding evidence of miraculous and exceptional interventions. However, many opponents of uniformitarianism argued for a deity who was not only First Cause but also active Governor of His own creation, directly participating in its development (Gillispie, 1959:209).

But the one idea that the new geology had not altered was the prevailing assumptions of biologists concerning the fixity of species (Barbour, 1971:82). In the 1840s and the 1850s, this was the one fact habitually referred to by religious leaders as concrete evidence for the original and continuing interventions of God in the world. This concept was challenged by the appearance in America of Darwin's theory of natural selection, and this, in turn, led to the development of new ideas concerning God's relationship to His creation.

In the 1840s and 1850s, the hypothesis of organic evolution was in much the same position as the Copernican hypothesis in the sixteenth century. Then, in 1859, Darwin intervened, just as Galileo had. Darwin's *Origin of Species* was thought to disprove definitively the dogma of the fixity of species and to assign natural causes for biological "transformism" (Bury, 1955:355). What might before be set aside as a brilliant guess was elevated to the rank of a scientific hypothesis. The idea of natural selection, which Darwin had borrowed from Malthus, made evolution into a scientifically sound theory. Evolution without natural selection might be an interesting philosophical hypothesis; evolution with selection became a convincing scientific explanation. Evolution nullified the argument from design, then used as standard proof of the existence of God, and also threatened the theologians' belief that man was set apart from the other animals (Hofstadter, 1955:25). Because of Darwin's revolution in thought, the world was no longer to be seen as an essentially static structure of immutable forms but rather as characterized throughout by development and change (Barbour, 1971:87). Darwin's ideas challenged traditional Christian thought so fundamentally that the clergy felt they must respond. Darwin could not be ignored.

Americans were first introduced to Darwin's work through the Harvard botanist Asa Gray, who reviewed Darwin's *Origin of Species* in 1860. However, Gray set a pattern that was to be followed by a number of later American theologians, including the social gospelers, when he argued for a "Lamarckian" interpretation of Darwin's work. Gray stated that natural selection, far from being an attack upon the argument from design in nature, might be considered one of the possible theories of the working out of God's intended plan (Hofstadter, 1955:18). Gray's interpretation was Lamarckian in the sense that he defended the idea of a creator working through evolution to produce a gradually unfolding design by providentially supplying the new variations in the right direction (Barbour, 1971:91).

An evolutionary theory can be interpreted as Lamarckian if it allows for some cosmic force to be directing the evolutionary process and does not assume that evolution works on its own because of natural forces. Lamarck, who had written a number of years before Darwin, resorted to a mystical animal will to live in order to explain how evolution had occurred (Russett, 1976:5). Asa Gray and the later theistic evolutionists would assert that God was the immanent force guiding this process of change.

Although Gray set the tone for how many theologians would respond to evolution, the Christian community's response was quite varied on this issue. The diverse reactions to evolutionism can be placed in three basic categories labelled as traditionalist, liberal, and modernist. The modernist position was to become the one that the social gospel would follow.

The initial reaction of American Protestant churchmen to Darwin's ideas was overwhelmingly hostile (Russett, 1976:26). Their response, referred to by Barbour (1971:99) as traditionalist, was an outright rejection of evolutionary ideas, based upon their belief in the Bible as the only source of truth. For example, Charles Hodge (1874:4) of Princeton Seminary, argued that the Bible was the only legitimate source of knowledge concerning human origins. Hodge understood natural selection to imply the denial of both God's design for the world and of His continuing relationship to it through dramatic events. Hodge (1874:173), in his final answer to his book's title, *What Is Darwinism?*, equated Darwinism with the total denial of God or atheism. Later, in the twentieth century, theologians who followed in this tradition accepted the name "Fundamentalists" and continued their attacks not only on evolution but also on modern science and education in general (McLoughlin, 1968:24).

Out of the second major response to evolutionism, the liberal, grew a form of Transcendental Christianity. Liberal theology represented a new methodological approach to religion; the appeal was to religious experience rather than to revealed or natural theology (Barbour, 1971:105). Personal religious feeling was considered the most important aspect of Christianity rather than either a literal interpretation of the Bible as a scientific source book or a belief in evolution. Religious experience became the basis for justifying religious beliefs and could support both the Bible and evolutionism. What one believed was downplayed in favor of belief itself. For example, Theodore Parker, a Unitarian, had no difficulty accepting evolutionary theories and became one of the first sponsors of an evolutionary religion in America because his faith relied on personal experience (Persons, 1950:425). In many of the "inner light" sects, such as Methodism, where religious experience rather than doctrine had traditionally been a major concern, the liberal interpretation became pervasive, especially in the North (Ahlstrom, 1975:775).

Another example of the liberal response appears in M.J. Savage's (1893) *The Evolution of Christianity*. Savage argued that evolution was the chosen method of God. However, he did not see evolutionary science as being antithetical to the Christian faith. Savage defined the Kingdom of God as an internal spiritual condition and argued that love was the supreme value of Christianity. With these beliefs evolution could have no quarrel. Thus, Savage was able to accommodate both Christianity and evolutionism into his experiential theology.

The final response to evolution was complete accommodation; theologians who held this position were referred to as modernists (Barbour, 1971:101). However, the modernists modified Darwin's evolutionary ideas in order to make them more compatible with Christianity. They felt that the element of chance in Darwin's evolutionary theory could not be accommodated to their theology. Darwin's theory stated that organic change is the product of a very large number of random spontaneous variations occurring entirely independently of each other so that the final result is accidental and unpremeditated (Barbour, 1971:89). Darwin's ideas did not seem to require a god and could lead to cosmic pessimism as readily as to optimism. Instead of strictly following Darwin, theologians turned to a Lamarckian form of evolutionism, just as Asa Gray had, because it better suited their theistic purposes. For the modernists, God became the driving force behind evolution. Divine creative activity was depicted not as external and once-and-for-all, but as within the gradual process of evolution. Modernists translated evolution into divine purpose and thus deified the evolutionary process, ultimately making it the means of God's grace and also the source of progress (Barbour, 1971:102). For some of the modernist authors, God became merely an impersonal cosmic force directing evolution; but for most the traditional concept of a personal God was retained, though His relationship to the world was modified. For the modernists, God's principal attribute is His immanence in nature, rather than His divine transcendence. In order to justify their ideas and remain Bible-believing Christians, the modernists made a distinction between the religious ideas of Genesis and the ancient cosmology in which these ideas were expressed. Evolution could be God's way of creating if the Bible were a human document and the Biblical creation account interpreted as symbolic or poetic (Barbour, 1971:97). Biblical criticism had entered into Protestant theology.

Evolution won its chief victories among the intellectually alert members of the more liberal Protestant denominations. Among the prominent theologians who accepted evolutionism were Henry Ward Beecher, Lyman Abbott, James McCosh, and Joseph LeConte.

Beecher and Abbott will be discussed first because they provide good examples of ministers who were converted to evolutionism. Henry Ward Beecher (1813–1887), son of Lyman Beecher, spent most of his preaching career at the Congregationalist Plymouth Church in Brooklyn. Beecher was considered by some to be the most popular orator in America during his day (Clark, 1978). Besides extensive lecturing on the lyceum circuit, Beecher was also a regular contributor to the *New York Ledger*, a paper with a daily circulation of four hundred thousand in the 1870s (Clark, 1978). Early in his career, Henry's theology was patterned closely after that of his father, Lyman. Later, in the 1850s and 1860s, he began to draw heavily on the theology of Horace Bushnell (Clark, 1978). Beecher accepted Bushnell's beliefs that the "irresistible power of God" was carrying the universe upward and onward to its final perfection and glorification, and that the power of religion, if allowed to permeate all aspects of life, would transform the very nature of human relationships. In the 1870s, Beecher became convinced that evolutionism was correct, but he did not speak out on the controversy until the subject had gained a degree of general acceptance (Clark, 1978). In the 1880s, he finally published his thoughts on evolution (H.W. Beecher, 1884). Beecher argued that evolution was a valid theory and that God was immanent in the natural world, ordering the world in terms of natural laws. He also had become an avid devotee of Herbert Spencer, the British social evolutionist, and even spoke at a dinner in Spencer's honor in 1882 (Clark, 1978). For Beecher, evolutionism and faith in the idea of progress were clearly tied together, evolution being the means God had chosen to bring about the world's perfection. This uniting of evolution and progress separated Beecher from such theologians as M.J. Savage, who stressed internal rather than social change.

　　　One of the most important theologians of the era to accept the developmental hypothesis was Beecher's protégé, Lyman Abbott (1887). Abbott was considered the foremost doctor of the Protestant church during his time and represented the main currents of American religious thought (Brown, 1953:vii–viii). Like Beecher, Abbott confessed his conversion to evolutionism early in the 1880s (Brown, 1953:75). Prior to his acceptance of evolutionary thought, Abbott's writings had been quite orthodox. In his 1869 book, *Jesus of Nazareth*, Abbott had stressed both that the Savior was to return to earth and establish His Kingdom and the idea of man's sinful nature. He would later reject both ideas. Abbott's (1897, 1925) two most famous works on evolution were *The Theology of an Evolutionist* and *The Evolution of Christianity*. Abbott (1925:vi) prefaced the latter with this statement:

> I have not abandoned the historic faith of Christendom to become an evolutionist, but have endeavored to show that the historic faith of Christendom, when stated in terms of an evolutionary philosophy, is not only preserved, but is so cleansed of pagan thought and feeling, as to be presented in a purer and more powerful form.

For Abbott (1897:20, 176), evolution was not defined in Darwinian but Lamarckian terms as "continuous progressive change, according to certain laws and by means of resident forces." By "resident forces" he had chosen to identify with an immanent God. Abbott (1925:2, 245) also cited Herbert Spencer's social evolutionism, arguing that social growth is always from lower to higher, from simpler to more complex forms. Abbott argued that:

> God's method of work in the world is the method of growth; and the history of the world . . . is the history of a growth in accordance with . . . evolution (quoted in Russett, 1976:30).

James McCosh (1888:37), in his book *The Religious Aspect of Evolution*, argued that God not only established the initial design of the whole evolutionary process, but continued to work through what appeared to humanity as "spontaneous changes." McCosh's Lamarckian evolutionism was reflected in his belief that God had "stacked the deck" with purposeful variations and thus guided the selective process (Persons, 1950:427).

Joseph LeConte's book, *Evolution: Its Nature, Its Evidences, and Its Relation to Religious Thought*, appeared in 1897. In it LeConte (1897:295) argued that the law of evolution is God's divine process of creation. God was also considered to be an immanent force within nature guiding the evolutionary process through the means of natural selection. Like his contemporary, the sociologist Lester Ward, LeConte felt that with the appearance of human beings a new factor was introduced—the rational—which could supersede natural selection. Thus, natural selection had only a subsidiary role in the evolution of civilized humanity (Russett, 1976:28).

When we turn to the social gospel writers themselves, it becomes plain that they accepted unquestioningly the fact that evolutionary science was the correct way of explaining human origins and social change. Faith in evolutionism appeared very clearly in the works of the three most prominent social gospelers, Walter Rauschenbusch, Josiah Strong, and Washington Gladden.

Rauschenbusch (1861–1918) believed that it was Jesus who first grasped that social change was gradualistic and not catastrophic. As Rauschenbusch (1907:59) states:

> Jesus grasped the substance of the law of organic development in nature and history which our own day at last has begun to elaborate systematically.

Rauschenbusch argued that Jesus was seeking to displace "crude and misleading" catastrophic conceptions about social change with a saner theory about the coming of God's Kingdom. Rauschenbusch also accepted the immanent theory of God's nature expounded by theological evolutionists. He (1945:49) stated that:

> Our universe is not a despotic monarchy, with God above the starry canopy and ourselves down here; it is a spiritual commonwealth with God in the midst of us.

Because of his belief in evolutionary science, Rauschenbusch reinterpreted both human history and the history of the Christian church in developmental terms. Both history and the church had moved through stages in a slow, gradual manner. For example, Rauschenbusch (1945:2) considered the arrival of the social gospel as a stage in the development of the Christian religion. The final results of this stage would be the Christianizing of all of society's institutions. But this would be a slow, gradual process taking many years (Rauschenbusch, 1912:328).

Like Rauschenbusch, Josiah Strong (1847–1916) also acquiesced to evolutionary thought. He stated (1914:6) that evolution was absolutely correct in all its forms: physical, mental, moral, and spiritual. Strong (1915:16) quoted favorably the evolutionary theology of Joseph LeConte. Strong (1902:102) said that God was immanent in nature and therefore active in human affairs. Strong's goal was to reinterpret God in terms of present-day scientific knowledge, thus making God into an evolutionary force.

In 1891 Washington Gladden (1836–1918) stated that one of the burning questions of the day was, "Has evolution abolished God?" His answer was a definitive no. Following Asa Gray and quoting Herbert Spencer frequently, Gladden (1891:1–52) argued that God was behind the evolutionary process, directing it. Gladden (1891:17) declared that there was a note of intelligence in the evolutionary process and a presiding purpose that shaped development. Gladden (1902:6) showed his evolutionary faith when he said, "Society must keep on growing out of its own roots."

These three thinkers were the leading spokesmen for the social gospel movement. Their full acceptance of evolutionism was typical of social gospel ministers. For example, William Adams Brown (1906:218) of Union Seminary, a member of the Brotherhood of the Kingdom—Rauschenbusch's reform organization—asserted that God's method was one of growth or development. Like the others, Brown identified this growth with evolutionary progress.

Very closely aligned with the social gospelers' acceptance of evolution was their faith in inevitable progress. These two ideas were so closely tied together in their thought that it is difficult to separate them analytically. However, belief in progress was not new with the social gospel. As J.B. Bury (1955) has shown, the idea of progress emerged in Western thought in the seventeenth and eighteenth centuries with such figures as Fontenelle and Condorcet. Faith in progress had come to be an important aspect of certain forms of Protestant thought in America in the early nineteenth century. This was especially true for men like Charles Finney and his disciples. However, for Finney progress was always closely associated with both revivalism and perfectionism. Progress was the result of God's working in the hearts of individual men. Perfectionism and disinterested benevolence would lead to the amelioration of social ills. The social gospel's faith in progress would have a fundamentally different source, God's evolutionary direction of nature.

Revivalism after Finney moved away from a faith in progress and toward an acceptance of a degenerationist interpretation of history. This is best exemplified in the preaching of Dwight Moody (1837–1899). Moody believed that until Christ returned none of the basic problems of this world could be solved. For this reason, Moody's sermons, unlike Finney's, usually centered solely on individual salvation. There was none of Finney's appeal to disinterested benevolence; his belief that public good might be superior to private welfare was rejected as well. For Moody, being a friend of Jesus solved a man's personal problems, and once a man was right with God, he would be right with the world. The world could not be saved, nor was it growing better. Moody believed that what went on under the name of progress was satanically inspired, leading mankind away from God and moving society toward inevitable destruction (McLoughlin, 1959). However, Moody thought that acceptance of God by an individual would bring not only spiritual blessings but material prosperity as well. Moody pointed out as evidence the fact that few if any of the poor in urban slums attended church. He continually told his audiences that: "I never saw the man who put Christ first in his life that wasn't successful" (McLoughlin, 1959). Thus, according to Moody's gospel of wealth, poverty could be cured by conversion. Ultimately, Moody rejected evolutionism, which he defined as atheism, and looked discouragingly upon efforts toward social reform which were associated with the social gospel movement (McLoughlin, 1959). Moody found the social gospel's doctrine of universal brotherhood unacceptable because he believed that a person becomes a brother in Christ only after conversion. Revivalists followed Moody's lead and it was not until B. Fay Mills appeared on the scene in the 1890s that a revivalist made a genuine attempt to incorporate the social gospel into his preaching.

However, in the last half of the nineteenth century the overwhelming majority of Protestant ministers and theologians was very optimistic about the possibilities of progress. American Christians played down the importance of the expectation of heavenly bliss in the afterlife, and focused their attention on the hope for a radical transformation of life: in science, art, agriculture, industry, church, and state. The purging of the nation's sin of slavery, the mass benefits brought on by the industrial revolution, and the opening of the West, all helped to foster an optimistic attitude toward progress in the last half of the nineteenth century. But the acceptance of evolutionary science became the final proof of unilinear progress and buttressed the optimistic theological stance of the social gospel. In the late nineteenth century both theological liberals and evangelicals believed in progress. The first group relied exclusively upon evolutionary concepts to prove their beliefs, while some evangelicals attempted to retain certain revolutionary concepts, such as a cataclysmic conversion experience, to buttress their optimistic faith (Niebuhr, 1959:191; Smith, 1952:149).

At the end of his career, Henry Ward Beecher expressed a strong faith in evolutionary progress. His optimistic perspective envisioned civilization as progressing toward higher and more perfect social structures. A theological liberal who was strongly influenced by Horace Bushnell's *Christian Nurture*, Beecher conceived of conversion as a gradual development of character rather than as an instantaneous experience of divine growth. His social philosophy similarly stressed slow, gradual improvement rather than revolutionary change. In 1884 Beecher argued that Herbert Spencer's theory of social evolution complemented Bushnell's ideas, and henceforth he became a stout defender of Spencerian evolutionism. From Spencer, Beecher borrowed the idea that the progressive evolution of society depended upon the efficiency of its members. It was the character of the common people, rather than societal elites, that determined the rate which the nation would progress in the scale of civilization (Clark, 1978). Ultimately, Beecher (1884) believed that the "irresistible power of God" was carrying the universe to its final perfection and glorification. So strongly did Beecher believe in this optimistic faith that he was able to overcome his fears of the labor unrest that was shaking the country in the 1880s (Clark, 1978). Since the destiny of the nation was in the hands of God there was no cause for alarm.

Two other late nineteenth-century figures whose liberal theology incorporates evolution into a developmental theory of progress were John Fiske and M.J. Savage. Fiske's (1899) *From Nature to God* was heavily influenced by Herbert Spencer's beliefs that God was a form of cosmic consciousness and that the loss of paradise set the stage for the beginning of the "rise of man." During its slow evolutionary march, humankind became moral. However, only when moral law became dominant, was humanity fit for an everlasting life of progress

(1899:53). The goal of this process was altruism, and as humanity approached this end the presence of evil would recede into memory (1899:55, 120). Minot Savage (1893:10) went so far as to place all of the major world religions on a progressive evolutionary scale from the most primitive upward to Christianity. The historical appearance of Christianity was itself therefore seen as a proof of progress, the high point in the development of civilized religion. Mankind was now prepared for the final flowering of history. In this romantic conception of progress espoused by men like Beecher, Fiske, and Savage there would be no discontinuities, no crises, and no sacrifices required of humanity. The benevolent, altruistic nature of man would reveal itself inevitably.

When we move on to look at the leading social gospel figures, we also discover a tremendous surge of optimism about the potential for progress. However, what sets the social gospelers apart from the other Christians who had faith in progress was the former's recognition of the negative aspects of modern development. In this chapter, their optimism will be concentrated upon. In the next chapter their ambivalence about progress will be dealt with and explained.

Faith in progress appears very clearly in the writings of Rauschenbusch, Gladden, and Strong. Rauschenbusch's (1912:30) faith in progress can be summed up in this statement: "Progress is more than natural. It is divine." Progress was not only a natural process, it was one that God was directing behind the scenes. Rauschenbusch saw progress taking place in many areas of life: in religion, in modernization, in the common life, and in the development of democracy. On religion he (1945:14) stated: "Every forward step in the historical evolution of religion has been marked by a closer union of religion and ethics." The arrival of the social gospel was regarded as an advanced stage in the development of the Christian religion. Rauschenbusch (1912:63) was also very optimistic about modernity. He argued that the size and complexity of the modern economic system was a good, and not an evil. The division of labor was a forward step in mankind's development. With the Lord's Prayer as his text, Rauschenbusch (1910:18) believed that God's goal was the ultimate perfection of the common life of humanity on earth. He (1912:128–134) saw this very clearly in the "Christianizing of the family." The family had evolved through history to its present near perfect state which was characterized by nurturing mothers and nonautocratic fathers. Finally, Rauschenbusch (1945:146) argued that progress could be seen in the development of democratic political institutions. The social gospel saw progress within the flow of history, in the clash of economic forces and social classes, and in the fall of despotism and various forms of enslavement. With the arrival of democracy, politics had become Christianized (1912:148).

Like Rauschenbusch, Washington Gladden believed that progress was leading the world toward social salvation. Gladden (1902:10) felt that the "law of love" was coming to govern the whole of life. Not only would the home and church be affected, but industry, commerce, and politics as well. Society was to progress because it would keep on growing out of its own roots (1902:235–236). Compassionate activities aimed at the less fortunate, such as those advocated by social gospel, marked man's evolutionary development from earlier more selfish stages.

Josiah Strong (1914:8) believed that progress was changing the nature of the entire earth. He identified this new world tendency as "oneness." Racial and national identities were breaking down. The producers of this trend were industrialization and modernization. Social progress would lead to the kind of metropolitan world envisioned by Strong's contemporary, Lester Ward, whom Strong (1914:57) relied upon for his own analysis. Strong (1914:230) was so optimistic about the human future that he made this prediction concerning the end of war: "Probably never again will a city be laid waste by a victorious army." Such was the faith in progress of the social gospelers in the very year that World War I was to begin.

By comparing the early nineteenth-century theologians discussed in the first chapter to their late nineteenth-century progeny, it becomes apparent that the Calvinistic belief in inherited depravity as the inevitable condition of human nature continued to be replaced by much more optimistic assumptions. A creed based on the innate goodness of humanity would be a cornerstone of social gospel theology.

The Calvinist position held that because of the Fall of mankind through Adam and Eve's sin human nature was inherently depraved. The only hope was for God's elect, whose hearts God would stir through His divine mysterious grace, finally leading them to Him. One of the results of this doctrine was that conversion experiences among the Puritans tended to be long-drawn-out periods—days, weeks, and sometimes months—of anguished contemplation in which the seeker became thoroughly convinced of his own election and salvation. Regeneration of human nature was only possible for the assured true believer, but it was a long and strenuous process requiring strict adherence to rules and dogmas. Ultimately, however, absolute perfection was not attainable, human beings were still destined to failure and sin. The only possibility was to establish an ascetic lifestyle as one's goal and try to avoid sin as much as possible.

The Puritan attitude toward human nature is nowhere more clearly seen than in the beliefs Puritan parents held about their children. Children were believed to be born both evil and ignorant of the good (Morgan, 1966:92). The actions of children were an expression of their ignorance; Puritan children were instructed by their parents concerning what God required of them. In spite of their natural wickedness, children were not seen as incorrigible. Children could be taught good habits even before they were "saved." Children so instructed seemed to have a greater chance at salvation than those left to their natural inclinations. For a people who believed so strongly in predestination and the absolute sovereignty of God, the Puritans placed a tremendous faith in education as an aid to salvation. It was important to teach a child good habits, not because they would save him, but because it was unlikely that he could be saved without them. However, there was no question of developing the child's personality or of drawing out or nourishing any desirable inherent qualities he or she might possess, for children could not by nature possess any desirable qualities. They had to receive any good that might become part of their personality from outside themselves, from education and ultimately from the Holy Spirit (Morgan, 1966:97).

John Wesley (1966), in the eighteenth century, had given to Protestantism a perspective on human nature that was much more positive than the orthodox Calvinist one. Although mired in sin because of their inheritance from Adam, human beings have been left with enough of their residual faculties intact to be able to choose for themselves either the narrow path of salvation or the wide road to destruction. The conversion experience, a cataclysmic event that lifted the final blinders to the truth, became one of the keys in Wesley's attempt to replace Calvin's pessimistic predestination beliefs.

Furthermore, Wesley (1966:28) also believed that at some point after conversion, believers could have a second experience known as sanctification or perfection that would purify them from future sin, or at the least purify the individuals' motives. In the nineteenth century, such optimism about the possibilities of rejuvenated human nature gradually replaced Calvin's position among many evangelical sects in America. For example, Charles Finney's theology concerning the possibilities of social improvement relied upon Wesley's notion of perfectionism. Perfected individuals would inevitably bring about a perfect society. Reform attempts resulting from the Second Great Awakening can be traced to a strong belief in perfectionism. As Timothy Smith (1952) and Donald Dayton (1976:99–119) have documented, in the last decades of the nineteenth century such Holiness sects as the Church of the Nazarene, the Christian and Missionary Alliance, and the Salvation Army became involved in social reform activities. Their involvement was primarily the result of their belief in perfectionism, which they translated individualistically rather than socially. Their desire to save souls and perfect individuals led them into such areas of social concern as alcoholism and poverty.

However, although the social gospel's attitude toward human nature was also extremely optimistic, it was not based upon a belief in Wesleyan perfectionism. For the most part the social gospel movement's perspective on human nature was a combination of Horace Bushnell's benign belief in the pure heart of the infant combined with a faith that evolution was continually uplifting the human spirit toward the divine. According to Bushnell, in the human child was seen the spark of the divine, but it needed to be developed by Christian nurture. This spark could just as easily be extinguished if the child grew up in an unchristian environment. Bushnell's theology marked the beginning of a more social interpretation of human nature: human nature was malleable and subject to environmental influence. (Later, the first generation of sociologists would rely upon a similar social interpretation of human nature to explain how innately good individuals could still end up as evildoers, and require social remedies for individual pathology.)

Two influential late nineteenth-century thinkers who held extremely optimistic beliefs concerning innate human nature were Henry George and Edward Bellamy, both men of strong religious convictions. In *Progress and Poverty*, George (1945) argued that every man and woman shared a common human nature. Among the positive inheritances of birth were a sense of fairness and right, social cooperativeness, creative powers, and a capacity for making a deep religious commitment (Curti, 1980:233). Only environmental factors had held back the full blossoming of humanity's innate capacities. Similarly, Edward Bellamy (1888) in his science fiction classic, *Looking Backwards*, presents us with a future utopia in which innate human nature has been permitted to reach its true potential. Mutual love for all other peoples had the force of an instinct for human beings. But only in a future society which had changed the current economic conditions of life could this mutual love grow and encompass the whole of humanity.

Beliefs concerning human nature that were just as optimistic as these can be found to be representative of the very core of social gospel thought. Not only did the social gospel regard humanity as innately good, it also held that human nature was both improving and improvable. In order to justify such a position, evolutionism was introduced. John Fiske presented just such a theology in his 1884 work, *The Destiny of Man Viewed in the Light of His Origin*. He regarded improvability as the most characteristic, indeed the most essential, feature of human nature. The evolutionary process was gradually creating truly altruistic human beings.

The social gospeler who best represented this creed was Washington Gladden. He relied very heavily on Bushnell's perspective on human nature (Grover, 1957). Like Bushnell, Gladden (1902:24) believed not only that the child was born with a spark of the divine, but that the nature of the young child was extremely plastic or malleable. A Christian family and social environment would produce morally upright individuals, who would realize the upward direction of progress and work to help bring it about through involvement in benevolent activity. Once these positive traits had been acquired by an entire generation, either by proper socialization or Christian education, Gladden naively believed that these acquired characteristics were then capable of being passed on through inheritance. Bushnell had also held this belief (Grover, 1975). Biological evolution was able even to pass on socially acquired characteristics, making human nature quickly changeable, according to Gladden. In the last two decades of the nineteenth century, this position was held by other leading intellectuals as well, exemplifying yet another version of Lamarckianism in American thought (Stocking, 1968). Lester Ward, for one, believed that morals learned through a proper education could be transmitted to the next generation biologically (Curti, 1980:248–253). Such optimism in human perfectibility was the result of this unorthodox interpretation of Darwin's idea of natural selection. For Darwin, biologically beneficial traits were retained by the lower animal species; for humans, socially beneficial traits would be preserved, according to men like Gladden and Ward. Christian education could thus be regarded as a great panacea by the social gospel, one that would ultimately perfect human nature and so speed up social progress.

Walter Rauschenbusch (1945:40–43) strongly argued that Christians could no longer base their understanding of human nature on the Old Testament account of the Fall of mankind. The traditional doctrine of the Fall had caused believers to regard evil as a kind of unvarying racial endowment, carried biologically by all human beings. Rauschenbusch pointed out that none of the Old Testament prophets, or Jesus Christ, or Paul ever made use of the doctrine of the Fall in such a way to suggest that humans are born fundamentally evil. For Rauschenbusch, human nature was innately good. Also, human nature was endowed with an immense latent perfectibility that had been clearly revealed in the swift evolution of America from its agrarian beginnings to its present modern industrialized state (Ahlstrom, 1975, Vol. II:251). Despite his optimistic faith in human nature,

Rauschenbusch remained fundamentally aware of the continued existence of evil in the world. The next chapter will look specifically at his attempt to explain the continued existence of evil while not becoming pessimistic about human nature.

Given their faith in evolutionism, progress, and the innate goodness of humankind, the social gospelers come to the conclusion that history was rapidly coming to a close. The end of history would bring with it a millennial utopia that they identified as the Kingdom of God on earth. Heaven was literally being brought to earth, and one would no longer have to wait until the afterlife in order to live in God's Kingdom.

Even before evolutionism came upon the scene, many influential Protestant theologians already had moved into the millennialist camp, refocusing their concerns principally upon this world rather than the next. Jonathan Edwards had set the stage for later discussion of millennialism in the nineteenth century. Edwards had rejected the millenarian theology that held that the world would only grow worse and worse until Christ was forced to come and rescue his surviving saints. Instead, he held out the possibility of the world's becoming a holy utopia. Samuel Hopkins (1852) in his 1793 work, *A Treatise on the Millennium*, agreed with Edwards that an earthly utopia was indeed God's plan for society. Charles Finney was so optimistic about the possibilities of mass revivalism that, in the 1830s, he confidently predicted the appearance of the final millennium within three years. After a thousand years of peace and plenty Christ would return and bring about God's Kingdom on earth. The ending of the Civil War served as a boost to the millennialist position. The war had put an end once and for all to America's national sin of slavery, and the lives lost by both sides represented a terrible atonement. But, once again purified, American society could expect the immanent arrival of the millennium. Horace Bushnell had held such a belief. All that was necessary was for the already Christianized spheres of the family and the church to engulf the larger spheres of education, business, and politics.

H. Richard Niebuhr (1959) long argued that one of the best ways of understanding nineteenth-century American Protestant theology was by focusing on the concept of the Kingdom of God. Although the term was used continuously by American churchmen, its content underwent considerable modification. Its first meaning, predominant in the eighteenth century and early nineteenth century, can be best translated as the sovereignty of God (Niebuhr, 1959:45–87). God's will was to be carried out in all areas of life. This doctrine was not utopian because it was based upon pessimistic Calvinistic presuppositions about the permanence of human sinfulness. By mid-nineteenth century, the phrase "Kingdom of God" could now be interpreted as the reign of Christ (1959:88–126). Finney's millennialist theology would correspond to this period. Christ's reign was to be one of love brought about by the true benevolence of purified saints. Love was not defined as an emotion, but as a tendency to action, and also as action itself. Christ's actual appearance would follow the millennium.

Finally, in the latter half of the nineteenth century, the phrase "Kingdom of God" was most frequently interpreted as Kingdom on earth (1959:127–163). The Lord's prayer was translated literally, "Thy Kingdom come; thy will be done on earth as it is in heaven." However, the two earlier ideas of God's sovereignty and Christ's reign were not dismissed, but instead incorporated into the concept of the Kingdom of God on earth. In the earthly utopia, God's will would be sovereign and the love of Christ would reign. Theologically, the Kingdom of God on earth was a very powerful doctrine, the culmination of more than a century of Protestant thought.

The Kingdom on earth meant that the focus of salvation must be fundamentally shifted. Social salvation rather then individual salvation would become the primary concern of Christianity. From the perspective of individual salvation, society had been explained in rather static terms, as an affair of institutions and laws. Now that society was seen as a gradually improving entity with a grand destiny for all mankind, God's true intent for social salvation was recognized. Saving individuals for the afterlife was played down, while preparing society for the future utopia was emphasized. It was felt that once again Christians were returning to the convictions expressed by the Old Testament prophets, who dealt almost exclusively with the social or collective aspects of ancient Hebrew society and not solely with individuals (Niebuhr, 1959:139).

By the late nineteenth century, the concept of the Kingdom on earth had moved beyond its roots in evangelical Protestantism. As Niebuhr (1959:162) points out:

> The evangelical doctrine of the kingdom was not adequate for the new situation in which these men found themselves. It could not emancipate itself from the conviction that the human unit is the individual. It was unable therefore to deal with social crisis, with national disease, and the misery of human groups. It continued to think of crisis in terms of death while it had begun to think of promise in social terms. It tended, moreover to become more and more institutionalized. So reaction against the evangelical doctrine of the kingdom needed to arise among its own children. Nevertheless they remained the heirs of its experience and its promise.

Institutionalizing the Kingdom of God on earth was the primary change that the social gospel made in this idea. For the more moderate versions of the social gospel, evolution, growth, progress, development, and the nurture of kindly sentiments became processes of a Christian revolution. The Kingdom was thought to be growing out of the present so that no great crisis or miraculous intervention was necessary to hasten its appearance. In an 1897 work, *Evolution and Religion*, John Bascom argued that social salvation was to be a slow, evolutionary process in conformity to God's laws of nature.

However, a number of social gospel theologians did not reject individual salvation altogether; instead, they sought a theology that would accommodate both individual and social salvation. Walter Rauschenbusch, in particular, stressed both individual and social salvation as essential to the coming Kingdom, and, to a lesser extent, Josiah Strong and Washington Gladden adhered to the necessity for individual salvation.

Josiah Strong firmly believed that the Kingdom of God would be established as an earthly utopia. He envisioned the future society as one that would be in harmony with all the laws of its own being, and that would have realized its highest possibilities (Strong, 1963:56). God, of course, was the author of these laws of society. Strong argued that past civilizations had either emphasized individualism at the expense of society, or vice versa. Hence, progress had been limited by one-sided tendencies. But now, he believed, America was entering a new era, one which would combine the two separate strands of progress into a single cord (Strong, 1893:21). Individuals could express their human potential by contributing to the benefit of the societal organism. A new Christianity with a social emphasis would awaken individuals to their social responsibilities.

Washington Gladden (1902) similarly located the Kingdom on earth and not in the afterlife. The true sign of its coming was not individual revivalism, but benevolence and moral conduct (1891:222, 235–236). Gladden (1891:66) expressed uncertainty as to whether any mortal could know God personally in the evangelical sense. Therefore, Gladden respecified the character of individual conversion. He (1902:14) stated, "No individual is soundly converted until he comprehends his social relations and strives to fulfill them." The fact that the law of love would come to govern all of life, showed clearly that God's intent was for social and not individual salvation. Individual conversion would never be sufficient to bring about social regeneration (1902:7).

Of all the social gospelers, Walter Rauschenbusch was the most effective at retaining important traditional evangelical tenets and combining them with new ideas, such as the social salvation promised by the Kingdom of God on earth. From the Lord's prayer, Rauschenbusch (1910:18) concluded that God's purpose was the ultimate perfection of the common life of humanity on earth. The social gospel restored the doctrine of the Kingdom of God to the original meaning that Christ intended, the redemption of the social organism (1945:21–24). Prior individualistic theological reinterpretations of Christ's message had forgotten Christ's intent. When Christ spoke of the Kingdom of God, he was not referring to the church, as many had interpreted him, but to all of humanity. Christ's distinctive ethical principles were the direct outgrowth of his conception of the Kingdom of God as a future plan for this world (Rauschenbusch, 1945:131–133). Rauschenbusch's (1945:142–143) inner-worldly image of the Kingdom of God is quite clear, as the following quotation suggests:

> The Kingdom of God is humanity organized according to the will of God. Interpreting it through the consciousness of Jesus we may

affirm these convictions about the ethical relations within the Kingdom: (a) Since Christ revealed the divine worth of life and personality, and since his salvation seeks the restoration and fulfillment of even the least, it follows that the Kingdom of God, at every stage of human development, tends toward a social order which will best guarantee to all personalities their freest and highest development. This involves the redemption of social life from the cramping influence of religious bigotry, from the repression of self-assertion in the relation of upper and lower classes, and from all forms of slavery in which human beings are treated as mere means to serve the ends of others. (b) Since love is the supreme law of Christ, the Kingdom of God implies a progressive reign of love in human affairs. We can see its advance wherever the free will of love supersedes the use of force and legal coercion as a regulative of the social order. This involves the redemption of society from political autocracies and economic oligarchies; the substitution of redemption for vindictive penology; the abolition of constraint through hunger as part of the industrial system; and the abolition of war as the supreme expression of hate and the completest cessation of freedom. (c) The highest expression of love is the free surrender of what is truly our own, life, property, and rights. A much lower but perhaps more decisive expression of love is the surrender of any opportunity to exploit men. No social group or organization can claim to be clearly within the Kingdom of God which drains others for its own ease, and resists the effort to abate this fundamental evil. This involves the redemption of society from private property in the natural resources of the earth, and from any condition in industry which makes monopoly profits possible. (d) The reign of love tends toward the progressive unity of mankind, but with the maintenance of individual liberty and the opportunity of nations to work out their national peculiarities and ideals.

Despite his orientation toward social salvation, Rauschenbusch (1907:366–367) did not reject individual salvation, a basic evangelical tenet. He argued that there were two great entities in human life, the human soul and the human race, and that the goal of religion was to save both. A salvation which was confined to the soul and its personal interests was regarded as an imperfect and only partly effective salvation, based on an inadequate understanding of the Kingdom (Rauschenbusch, 1945:95).

The social gospel placed complete faith in its vision of the future. There was no doubt in the minds of its advocates that God intended to turn this world into a holy utopia. Faith in the coming of the millennium and a utopian Kingdom of God on earth was closely aligned with a belief that America as a nation had a very special relationship to God. America came to be seen as a chosen nation, God's new Israel. Once this idea became established, a question emerged that came to plague the American conscience: What are a chosen people to do? Should they become isolationist in order to protect their purity from the tainted influence of less godly nations? Or should they interpret their special blessing as a mandate to save the rest of the world for Christ, to lead all nations into the millennium?

The idea that America had a special blessing from God has had a long history. As early as the 1630s, John Winthrop had called upon Massachusetts's settlers to establish a utopian "city upon a hill" that other nations might see this holy experiment (McLoughlin, 1978:36).

Jonathan Edwards, who fell short of envisioning the colonies as being settled by a peculiar millennial people and who never stated unequivocally that America was a chosen nation, nevertheless felt that God was doing extraordinary things in this new land. The two events that particularly struck Edwards were the Great Awakening and the propagation of the gospel to the Indians. Prior to the arrival of the Christians, the devil had been able to keep a whole continent under his evil influence. Edwards considered pre-Christian America as a heathen nation of devil worshippers. However, with the coming of Europeans to America, and the propagation of the gospel among the Indians, this heathen empire of the devil was to be conquered (Edwards, 1879, Vol. I:468–469). This was one of the certain proofs that the last days were near. Also, the remarkable outpouring of the spirit of God in New England during the Great Awakening led Edwards (1879, Vol. I:470) to believe that the work of the millennium might be starting in America.

During the later portions of the eighteenth century the idea that America might be a chosen nation was on the mind of many leading figures. John Adams wrote in his diary in 1765 that: "I will always consider the settlement of America with reverence and wonder, as the opening of a grand scene and design in Providence for the illumination of the ignorant, and the emancipation of the slavish part of mankind all over the earth" (Tuveson, 1968:25). Timothy Dwight in a 1771 poem, "America," echoed Adams's awareness that America might have a special role in world history (Tuveson, 1968:105).

> Hail Land of light and joy! thy power shall grow
> Far as the sea, which round thy regions flow;
> Through earth's wide realms thy glory shall extend,
> And savage nations at thy scepter bend.
> Around the frozen shores thy sons shall sail,
> Or stretch their canvas to the Asian gale.

The American Revolution only served to prove to Dwight and later leaders that America had God's blessing. In 1783, Dwight compared the American Revolution to the conquering of Canaan by the Israelites (Tuveson, 1968:106). Dwight was stating that America was the modern Israel, God's new chosen people.

Two late eighteenth-century ministers, Thomas Bernard and David Austin, gave assent to Dwight's belief. Bernard, delivering a sermon in Salem, Massachusetts, in 1795, stated that the people of America could say to each other with cheerful countenances that they were a people peculiarly favored of heaven. America was now God's vineyard (Tuveson, 1968:31). While the Old World was abandoned to tyranny, misery, ignorance, injustice, and vice, the New World was innocent of these sins. Many of those who had fought for independence were convinced of this fact. David Austin, a student of Dwight at Yale, went further, showing that God's election could be used to justify future American imperialism. In 1794, Austin wrote the following statement:

> Behold, then, this hero of America, wielding the standard of civil and religious liberty over these United States!—Follow him, in his strides, across the Atlantic!—See him, with his spear already in the beast!—tyranny, civil and ecclesiastical, bleeding at every pore! See the votaries of the tyrants; of the beasts; of the false prophets, and serpents of the earth, ranged in battle array, to withstand the progress and dominion of him, who hath commission to break down the usurpations of tyranny—to let the prisoner out of the prison house; to set the vassal in bondage free from his chains—to level the

mountains—to raise the valleys, and to prepare an highway for the Lord! (quoted in Tuveson, 1968:117).

Of course, the beast referred to in this passage was the Roman Catholic church, which many Protestants felt must be defeated before true Christianity could reign. However, Austin's nascent imperialism was the exception rather than the rule in eighteenth-century American thought, although such ideas would be incorporated almost one hundred years later into Josiah Strong's version of the social gospel.

In the early nineteenth century, the predominant interpretation of the chosen nation theme was one such as held by Lyman Beecher. First, he envisioned a great Christian republic stretching westward beyond the Appalachians and serving as a beacon and exemplar to the rest of the world (Ahlstrom, 1975, Vol. II:80). Beecher left his New England home in the 1820s to help in the Christianizing of the West (Bodo, 1954). He wanted to make sure that Catholics would not gain the upper hand in the new territories. Once America had kept to the right—i.e., Protestant—path, it could take up its special task, leadership in converting the world (Harding, 1965). Much of the impetus for the American missionary zeal of the nineteenth century can be traced to the chosen nation theme. But, Beecher went beyond exporting American religion to faraway lands, he also believed that American political ideas should be sent along as well. In his famous 1835 document, *A Plea for the West*, he stated:

> If the nation is, in the providence of God, destined to lead the way in the moral and political emancipation of the world, it is time she understood her high calling, and were harnessed for the work (quoted in Tuveson, 1968:170).

Not only American Protestantism, but American democracy had been blessed by God, thus sacralizing the new republic's political system. Beecher founded Lane Theological Seminary in Cincinnati, Ohio, and sent forth a stream of preachers imbued with this vision of the church and of America. Josiah Strong was one of Lane's graduates.

The French scholar, Alexis de Tocqueville, while visiting America in the 1830s, noticed and was, in fact, apprehensive about the religious zeal of its people. He (1945, Vol. II:142) observed that

Americans referred to themselves as the most religious people on earth: "Religious zeal is perpetually warmed in the United States."

In the 1830s, it became quite evident to the northern Protestant clergy that the chosen nation had to remove the dark, sinful stain of slavery from its heart if it was to continue to enjoy God's blessing. Lyman Beecher influenced his daughter, Harriet Beecher Stowe, to adopt this perspective. Her purpose in writing *Uncle Tom's Cabin* was to awaken Americans to the fact that they were God's special agents. America was one nation, destined to play one part in the divine plan; it could not be permitted to ignore the evil still in its bosom (Tuveson, 1968:191). During and after the Civil War, Horace Bushnell regarded that conflict as both a condemnation and an atonement for America (Cross, 1958). God's blessing would return with even greater rewards now that the nation was purified.

Even during the war, Bushnell predicted that God would use the nation to rescue the "fallen" peoples of the world. This was clearly expressed in his thinking about race in *Nature and the Supernatural* (1863). Bushnell rejected the thought of his contemporary, anthropologist Lewis Henry Morgan, that humankind had developed from primitive beginnings, through the stages of savagery and barbarism, to full civilization. American Indians, African tribes, and other primitives were, according to Morgan, stuck fast in an early stage. Bushnell regarded this opinion as an example of the errors of a purely secular account of human development. Savages, Bushnell (1863) said, "are beings, or races physiologically run down, or become effete, under sin; fallen at last below progress, below society, become a herd no longer capable of public organization, and true social life." However, some races, while they started at a cultural level equal to that of primitives, ascended rather than descended because they were led by holy seers and law-givers. In these nations, natural progress took over and they were gradually raised to civilization. But those nations reduced to savagery and primitivism would never be able to get back on the march of progress by themselves because they had become tainted by sin. Thus, the mission of the civilized races and in particular, American Protestantism, was clear. God had prepared the United States for the redemption/conquering of these underdeveloped or fallen races.

Bushnell makes racial chauvinism part of the ideology accompanying the chosen nation theme, to go along with its other ethnocentric elements. Not only was American Protestantism regarded as uniquely spiritual, American geography seen as a vastness to be filled with God-fearing people, American inventiveness and initiative praised, and American democracy believed to be the apex of political progress, but the American people or race—i.e., Anglo Saxon or Germanic—were declared to be culturally superior as well. This was the inheritance that the social gospel received. H. Richard Niebuhr (1959:179) summarized it in this way:

> The old idea of American Christians as a chosen people who had been called to a special task was turned into the notion of a chosen nation especially favored. . . . Christianity, democracy, Americanism, the English language and culture, the growth of industry and science, American institutions—these are all confounded and confused. The contemplation of their own righteousness filled Americans with such lofty and enthusiastic sentiments that they readily identified it with the righteousness of God. . . . It is in particular the kingdom of the Anglo-Saxon race, which is destined to bring light to the gentiles by means of lamps manufactured in America.

This is especially true when one turns to the writings of Josiah Strong. His major work, *Our Country*, first published in 1886, was one of the best selling—175,000 thousand copies before 1916—and most highly praised of all social gospel texts. It helped to set the tone for the entire movement. Strong regarded the Anglo-Saxon race in general, and its American branch in particular, as being destined by God to eventually rule the world. Strong (1893:54–65) cited as evidence the following: (1) the Anglo-Saxon race is more spiritual and Christian than any other; (2) it has developed superior political institutions; (3) it leads the world in inventions. In addition, Strong (1893:62) proudly pointed to the fact that English was rapidly becoming the world's predominant language. The Anglo-Saxon race already controlled one-third of the earth's land area and soon would have more (Strong, 1893:67). Strong (1893:64) compared contemporary Anglo-Saxon civilization with the great cultures of antiquity: "The Anglo-Saxon is doing for the modern world what the Greek did for the ancient."

In America, the Anglo-Saxon race had reached its highest point of development. America was growing richer more rapidly than any other nation (Strong, 1898:24). America's expansion from coast to coast, its vast farmlands capable of feeding a billion people, and its continually developing industry and technology all pointed to its people's superiority (Strong, 1898:21–23). In America, the mixing of various strains of the Anglo-Saxon race was creating a new superior race. Strong (1963:209–211) attributed the strengthening of the race to Darwinian natural selection and backed up his claim with an early application of physical anthropology: the fact that the Civil War measurement of soldiers of English, Scotch, and American ancestry found those born in America to be taller and larger than those born in Europe. In America, the Anglo-Saxon race had developed a purely spiritual Christianity and become the great missionary race (Strong, 1963:201). Strong (1963:214) believed that once the race had filled all the territory in the United States, it would then expand around the globe as part of God's plan to people the world with better and finer material. Not only would the aborigines of North America disappear before the all-conquering Anglo-Saxon, but the United States would come to dominate the entire world (1963:215–218). Strong (1963:205) predicted that within one hundred years, fueled by American population growth, the Anglo-Saxon would outnumber all the peoples of Europe, and within two hundred years outnumber all the civilized races of the world. Strong (1963:217) stated: "This race is destined to dispossess many weaker races, assimilate others, and mold the remainder until it has Anglo-Saxonized mankind." In his book *The New Era or the Coming Kingdom*, Strong (1893:81) identified the Kingdom of God on earth with Anglo-Saxon imperialism.

> In the new era mankind is to come more and more under Anglo-Saxon influence, and they are more favorable of any other to the spread of those principles whose universal triumph is necessary to that perfection of the race to which it is destined; the entire realization of which will be the kingdom of heaven fully come down on earth.

But conquering the world for Christ might be slowed down or even halted completely by the mass immigration of inferior races to

America, many of whom Strong (1963:53) argued were from the pauper and criminal classes. Using statistics concerning the percentage of immigrants arrested and in prison, Strong (1963:54) concluded that there was a strong propensity to crime among certain peoples. The fact that most of them were Catholic only added to his apprehensions. Strong (1898:97) believed that Romanism already controlled the large cities in America. "Being Roman Catholics they are Catholics first and citizens afterwards" (Strong, 1898:95). This made them a dangerous political force because they would vote as a bloc, throwing inordinate support to Catholic candidates. And, of course, the Catholics brought with them the liquor traffic (Strong, 1963:55). All of these factors meant that Catholic and other non-Protestant foreigners must be assimilated as quickly as possible. Strong (1963:89–90) argued that assimilation was the ultimate purpose of the public school system, the goal being the Americanization of the children of immigrants. He preached against the establishment of parochial schools, whose only object was to turn out good Catholics, not good citizens. Strong (1963:57) favored restricting the amount of immigration from Europe lest the Anglo-Saxon destiny be thwarted: "Our safety demands the assimilation of these strange populations, and the process of assimilation will become slower and more difficult as the proportion of foreigners increases."

Washington Gladden held a belief similar to that of Strong concerning the religious destiny of the American people. In a 1890 speech, Gladden put forth his ideas about the United States (Tuveson, 1968:128–129). Discussing the great westward migrations in American history, Gladden interpreted them as the working out of God's plan. It was by divine ordination that the great mass of the current inhabitants of the New World belonged to the Aryan race. They had peopled the entire nation, arrived at the Pacific coast, and stood gazing at the Asian continent—countries now crowded with decadent civilizations—from which the entire westward movement had begun many generations ago. Here, in America, the Kingdom of God was to be established. "Here, upon these plains, the problems of history are to be solved, here, if anywhere, is to rise that city of God, the New Jerusalem, whose glories are to fill the earth" (Tuveson, 1968:129).

The influence of the social gospel was one of the factors that led America to its first intervention into a major European war, World War I. Social gospelers believed the war was an opportunity for American Christians to do something important for world salvation. For example, Francis Greenwood Peabody of Harvard University interpreted the war of 1914 as a touchstone for a Christian's faith. As Herbst (1961:65) stated, Peabody regarded the war in the following way:

> For Europe, the war represented the awful Nemesis which follows a long series of moral wrongs. To the United States, however, it offered the singular opportunity to prove the conversion of militarism, the spiritualization of soldierliness, the Christianization of courage, and the enlightenment of good soldiers of Jesus Christ as goals worthy of a Christian nation. Once actively pursued, these goals would strengthen America's moral superiority and enable her to fulfill her task as a judaical and unprejudiced tribunal for the great adjudication which must come. Their traditional idealism would now enable Americans to be the peace-makers blessed by Jesus in the Beatitudes.

Similarly, Shailer Mathews of Chicago Divinity School, strongly supported United States intervention in World War I in his 1918 work, *Patriotism and Religion*. Democracy must be preserved so that God could continue to work through it to bring about His Kingdom.

In summary, the social gospel combined the chosen nation theme, the belief that America would be involved in establishing Christ's Kingdom on earth, with faith in human perfectibility, inevitable progress, and theistic evolutionism. However, this new theology emerged tinged with imperialist, racist, and nativist ideas common to the era. We now turn to the relationship which was to develop between the social gospel and social science in America in the 1890s.

CHAPTER 3

The Turn to Sociology

The underlying presuppositions of the social gospel made it the most optimistic version of Christian theology concerning the possibility of this-worldly salvation ever conceived. However, the true test of the validity of such a doctrine would come only when its adherents compared the social gospel's optimistic theology with the reality of social conditions. When social gospelers actually looked in the world signs of progress could be found everywhere, but theologians were puzzled by the continuing existence of evil, which did not seem to be disappearing gradually as they had hoped. Instead, evil or sin appeared to be further compounded by the forces of industrialization and urbanization that were rapidly changing the nation. However, rather than give up on their theology social gospelers interpreted these evils as a test from God; in order to prepare the way and make ready for the coming earthly utopia the church would have to apply its spiritual energies toward the removal of social problems. At first, faith in the power of religious ethics and solutions was thought to be enough, but the social gospelers soon realized they needed further assistance. Once again, just as they had done with evolutionism, they placed their faith in science and, in particular, called for establishment of a new social science, sociology, to come to their aid in the removal of social evil. Their plea was heard, and soon colleges and seminaries responded with a proliferation of sociology courses, programs, and departments. Sociological surveys and statistics were compiled to benefit the social gospel's program of scientific social reform. Settlement houses and social work received a tremendous impetus from social Christianity during this period as well. Social gospelers attempted to Christianize business, industry, politics, and the city's immigrant populations, all of which they regarded as the major unregenerate spheres of the society. Much of early American sociology can be seen as a response to the influence and energy of the social gospel.

In the social sciences, before any social theory can be believed, it must be tested empirically to see if it does indeed correspond to situations in the real world. While the social gospelers were not in a strict sense social scientists, they believed that their theology had to be tested by looking in the world for verification. Could their optimistic faith in gradual evolutionary progress, culminating in an earthly Christian utopia, be shown to be what was actually taking shape in American society in the final decades of the nineteenth century? The social gospelers certainly hoped to find evidence for their theology in the signs of the times, since the future utopia they envisioned was just beyond the horizon and soon to make its appearance, possibly even in their own lifetimes.

The social gospelers did find signs of progress everywhere. Josiah Strong (1902:195) argued that the growth of democracy, the abolition of slavery, and the elevation of women all documented the fact that America was making steps toward social perfection. Technologically, there were signs of rapid progress as well. The use of steam power, the growth of railroads, mass communications made possible by the telegraph, and the improvement of farming techniques were cited as evidence of advancement (Strong, 1898:18–23, 1963:14). Not surprisingly, for the ethnocentric Strong (1963:209–215), the growth in power of the Anglo-Saxon race both in America and worldwide was evidence of God's special blessing. Walter Rauschenbusch (1945:142–143) had seen signs of the coming Kingdom in America's establishment of religious freedom, the abolishment of slavery, the creation of a nonautocratic political system, and a penal system based on rehabilitation or reform rather than punishment. (See McHugh [1978:32–68] for a discussion of the Christian roots of the reformatory and rehabilitation movements in nineteenth century American penology.)

However, despite all the evidence they amassed showing that American society was moving toward the Kingdom of God on earth, social gospelers were forced to admit that evil was still a very prevalent force in the nation. In fact, they had to acknowledge that industrialization and urbanization were bringing, along with their positive benefits, greater potentials for evil and sin. John Bascom (1883:171) noted that industrialism had brought with it both progress and a new set of problems caused by the unequal distribution of wealth. George Herron (1895:48) pointed out the continuing existence of evil as:

> . . . the failure to apprehend and obey the divine order, to discern and move with history toward unity, that has corrupted institutions bringing them into conflict with progress, causing them to be absorbed in the increase of their own dominion, instead of the increase of life among men.

Josiah Strong (1893:81) accounted for the great evils that vexed modern society by asserting that civilization had been Christianized only partially.

In the writings of Walter Rauschenbusch there can be seen the strongest insistence upon recognition of the continuing power of the "Kingdom of Evil" (Ahlstrom, 1975, Vol. II:268). The progress of humanity had created a potential for even greater depravity than in previous eras.

> Science supplies the means of killing, finance the methods of stealing, the newspapers have learned how to bear false witness to a globe full of people daily, and covetousness is the moral basis of our civilization (Rauschenbusch, 1945:49).

Although the size and complexity of America's economic system could be regarded as a good and not an evil, it had led to injustice and inequality because the powers of control and ownership were in the hands of a few (Rauschenbusch, 1912:163). Rauschenbusch (1945:182) regarded all aspects of society as interrelated, so that when one social class sinned, the other classes were involved in the suffering which followed upon it. Sin was so prevalent because, once established, it was transmitted along the lines of social tradition (1945:60). Rauschenbusch (1945:166) concluded that it would be difficult for the

Kingdom of God to make headway against the social entrenchments of the Kingdom of Evil. Rauschenbusch realized the tremendous potentialities for evil that modernization and technology could bring, yet he did not become despondent or pessimistic and remained optimistic about the future.

Neither Rauschenbusch nor any of the other social gospelers allowed their discovery of the continuing existence of evil to dampen their enthusiasm, and even more importantly, to be used as evidence to disprove their teleological theory concerning the coming utopian Kingdom. They were committed to the assumptions that evolutionary progress was natural and to be expected. The social gospelers came to believe that the iniquities they uncovered were obstacles blocking or preventing the arrival of the Kingdom of God on earth, rather than seeing sin as a permanent part of the human predicament. The critique of developmentalist thought devised by Frederick Teggart (1972:89) can be applied to analyzing why the social gospel refused to allow evidence to disprove its theology:

> . . . modern thought became committed to the assumption that progress is "natural" and to be expected. As a consequence, . . . men have concerned themselves, not with the investigation of the conditions under which advancement takes place, but with inquiry into the obstacles which are thought to have delayed or interrupted the "natural course" of development, and with proposals for the removal of these obstacles.

The social gospelers' response to the continuing existence of evil in a world in which it was supposed to be disappearing followed Teggart's hypothesis. Rather than scrap or revise their optimistic theology, they instead interpreted evil as an obstacle in the path of the coming Kingdom and labelled the new forms of societal evil which accompanied modernization as social problems. Thus the modern American sociological concern with the study of social problems was born. If social problems were obstacles blocking the inevitable future Christian utopia, then the social gospelers could hasten the Kingdom's coming by directing their spiritual energies toward the removal of these obstacles. Once removed, the Kingdom would be clearly visible. Just as John the Baptist had prepared the people for the coming of the Messiah, the social gospelers felt they could prepare the way for His Second Coming by ridding American society of its social sins. Once they had perfected American society, it would be ready for Christ's rule. Thus, although the social gospel never gave up its belief that progress was inevitable, it could be achieved more swiftly if churchmen dedicated themselves to a sacrificial struggle against the entrenched forces of evil. Social gospel leaders were quite optimistic that all the desirable reforms they devised would come to pass through the agency of an enlightened public moral conscience that would embrace their programs.

The social gospel's employment of the phrase, "social problems," to discuss institutionalized evil is a key to understanding the optimism of their theology. The word, "social, " was not a morally neutral one, but instead a word loaded with positive connotations. As C. Wright Mills (1943:173) has pointed out:

> The "social" becomes a good term when it is used in ethical polemics against "individualism" or against such abstract moral qualities as "selfishness," lack of "altruism," or of "antisocial" sentiments. "Social" is conceived as a "cooperative," "sharing" of something, or as "conducive" to the general welfare.

Thus, in social gospel thought, the positively valued word, "social," was paired with one of negative connotation, "problem." The problems can then be seen as the unintended consequences of the otherwise positive social processes of industrialization, accumulation of wealth, modernization, the expansion of technology, and urbanization. Once these unintended negative consequences had been removed, mankind would enjoy the positive benefits of modernization.

The social gospeler's list of social problems was quite lengthy, because the late nineteenth century was a period of intense suffering for such groups as factory workers, immigrants, and Blacks. For Josiah Strong (1914:100–101), many of the major problems were related to business and industry, including low wages, long working hours, job-related accidents, and child and female labor. Moreover, the new urban environment produced such evils as mass poverty, corrupt politics, and alcohol abuse (Strong, 1963:172, 181; 1898:94). From his Anglo-Saxon perspective, Strong (1898:98–99) saw immigration as a major problem because it had brought so many criminals, liquor users, and Catholics to the United States. If the same types continued to immigrate to America, they might postpone the arrival of the Protestant Kingdom indefinitely.

Washington Gladden (1902:34–35) focused primarily on poverty and industrial problems, the two being interrelated. He regarded poverty not as a sign of personal failure—the Calvinist work ethic perspective—but as a consequence of social causes. Industrial depressions, seasonal unemployment, and technological advance that displaced unskilled workers were to blame for poverty, not laziness or immorality. As early as 1886, Gladden (1886:71) had come to the conclusion that the socialist criticism of the present order, with its unequal distribution of wealth, was indeed correct. However, Gladden was less sure about socialism's proposed solution.

Walter Rauschenbusch (1907:217; 1910:51–52; 1912:31, 36) cited a number of social problems including: tenement slums, urban-spread diseases, unsanitary factories, child labor, an entrenched wealthy urban class, and the traditional conservative church.

George Herron (1893:25) also indicted the capitalist economic system as a producer of poverty: "Under capitalism, capitalists are receiving more than a just share of the fruits of labor, and the laborer is receiving relatively less and less of the profits of his toil."

Francis Greenwood Peabody (1900:189) opposed the vast accumulation of wealth by the upper class and the negative view they held toward the poor. Following the teachings of Jesus, Peabody (1900:207) argued:

> Prosperity, he [Jesus] preaches, is no sign of Divine acceptance; on the contrary, it is one of the most threatening obstructions of the spiritual life. The desire of the nation, therefore, should be turned away from the thought of wealth as a sign of piety, or of poverty as a sign of Divine disfavor. Let the poor take heart again.

From Peabody's (1900:226) perspective, the poor should be dealt with compassionately because they were not responsible for their plight. Modern capitalism had created stunted, dehumanized individuals who were in need of help (Peabody, 1900:282).

The social gospelers made a very clear bifurcation of sacred from profane social institutions in their writings on American society. On the one hand, there were social spheres that had already been Christianized, and on the other, as yet unregenerate ones. It was the unregenerate social spheres that were the source of social problems and therefore needed to be redeemed.

The social institution that almost all of the social gospelers assumed was already Christianized was the family. Their ideas concerning the family can be traced back to Horace Bushnell's *Christian Nurture* (Cross, 1958). Walter Rauschenbusch (1912:128, 133) stated that the family had already been Christianized. The proof was in the changing nature of marital roles: the father was becoming less autocratic and more loving while the wife was taking on the role of the nurturing mother. Peabody (1900:138), using evidence from anthropology, argued that the modern Christian family was the final outcome of evolutionary changes in family systems. For example, matriarchal family formations had evolved toward patriarchal ones, and polygyny had been replaced by monogamy, the best possible marriage form.

The social gospel's perspective on human relationships, as derived from Bushnell, pictured concentric spheres that surrounded the individual and radiated outward toward society. This represented their interpretation of social interaction and the individual's place within society. For Peabody (1900:124), the concentric circles that surround the individual were: (1) the family; (2) the community; (3) the industrial order. Christianity was to gradually invade each of these circles in turn and thus eventually sacralize all of society.

Rauschenbusch (1907:189) felt that the expansion of religion in modern life had already encompassed "the ethics of private life, of the family, and of friendly social intercourse, together with the interests of education, literature, and to some extent of art within this circle." The as yet unchristianized spheres of industry, commerce, and politics lay outside this inner circle. Half a decade later, Rauschenbusch (1912:148, 152, 156) had changed his opinion about politics and now moved it within the inner circle as an already Christianized institution because of America's democratic heritage. However, politics still retained a vestige of evil and was prone to backsliding, a consequence of the evil influence of the business establishment in America. If only business could be Christianized, the source of all the country's current troubles could be eliminated. Business was declared to be the most significant unregenerate institution within the American social order.

Action against the unregenerate spheres would have to be taken quickly, lest they start to spread their iniquities into the previously sacralized inner circle of the family. Peabody (1900:164–168) saw urbanization and industrialization as forces that would weaken the traditional family unit. The fact that divorce rates were rising in cities was cited as evidence. Many urban dwellers lived in tenements and pursued nomadic life styles, so that children were not being raised in a real home. For Peabody, suburbanization and the expansion of mass transit provided a solution to the family problems of urban living because they offered opportunities for children to live in a genuine home environment. He suggested that if the urban family could not afford such a move, urban ghetto children should be placed for adoption in rural or suburban homes. Rauschenbusch (1912:264) argued that forcing women to work outside the home threatened to destroy the family because it altered the mother's nurturing role. So important was preservation of the role of the nurturing mother that the social gospelers regarded the women's suffrage movement with ambivalence. Gladden (1888:96) was critical of the women's movement because it seemed to be being carried out by persons who had no respect for the family. "There are some who speak of marriage and maternity as if they thought them bondage and degradation, and openly counsel women never to marry." One of the reasons Gladden (1888:98) saw the family as so crucial was that it shielded men from the temptations of the world. Gladden identified with the nineteenth-century belief that the woman's role as wife and mother was to morally govern the more base instincts of both husbands and sons.

Having identified the social problems blocking the coming of the Kingdom, the social gospelers began to propose solutions that would purify American society. Purification and social redemption became the new goals for which the Christian community had to strive. "The church must accept her commission to prepare the way for the full coming of the kingdom, and become the champion of needed reforms" (Strong, 1893:242). Strong (1963:xvii) believed that Christians had the power "to hasten or retard the coming of Christ's Kingdom in this world by hundreds, and perhaps, thousands of years." Christians could not be complacent and wait for the arrival of the Kingdom. They had to act in order to accelerate its appearance. The required actions were to become involved in social reform activities aimed at ridding American society of its institutionalized evils. However, reform did not require demolition of the present order, only Christianization of its yet unregenerate elements (Gladden, 1888:98). Iniquity could be diminished and eventually eliminated because it was regarded not as a permanent feature of the human condition, but rather as a temporary impediment to the realization of the true life of humanity (Rauschenbusch, 1945:43). Sin could be eliminated by conscious social action directed toward the final goal of the Kingdom (Rauschenbusch, 1945:60).

From the start, the social gospelers made a distinction between collective social reforms and changes that could be accomplished through individual evangelization and conversion. Although their zeal to redeem society was as earnest as the evangelists' to save souls, the social gospelers rejected individual evangelism as an adequate reform strategy. Individual salvation would not be capable of solving our social problems (Strong, 1902:xiii). Unlike Charles Finney, the social gospelers did not feel that social reform could be successfully grafted onto personal evangelism. In the 1890s, urban revivalist B. Fay Mills had attempted to link personal evangelism and social reform and discovered his ministry to be a failure (McLoughlin, 1959). Mills was a friend of Washington Gladden and well versed in the social gospel writings of George Herron. However, Mills argued that revivalism could be used to bring about the Kingdom on earth. Early in his career, Mills had preached a traditional evangelistic message, but in the 1890s he began to exhort his parishioners to correct social as well as individual sins. Mills's social gospel sermons were forceful but led to little action by church congregations who wanted to oppose old-fashioned vices like gambling and drinking, but did not wish to become involved in reorganizing business practices or reforming politics. Other evangelical ministers rejected Mills and his social gospel stance, and he became so discouraged that he quit evangelism altogether in 1899.

Walter Rauschenbusch (1907:65) was also strongly opposed to individual salvation as the sole solution to America's social ills.

> The kingdom of God is not a matter of saving human atoms, but of saving the social organism. It is not a matter of getting individuals to heaven, but of transforming the life on earth into the harmony of heaven.

Rauschenbusch (1907:349) felt that the traditional evangelical camp did not understand adequately the social forms which evil takes; they did not clearly comprehend the nature of corporate sin.

> If our exposition of the supernatural agents of sin and of the Kingdom of Evil is true, then evidently a salvation confined to the soul and its personal interests is an imperfect and only partly effective salvation (1945:95).

Social salvation could not be based upon an individualistic theology of conversion and proselytization. Rauschenbusch even attempted to explain why the Christian church had up until the present day not taken on the fundamental task of social salvation. Rauschenbusch made use of a teleological argument, including a doctrine of obstacles, to explain this conundrum.

> We set out on this discussion with the proposition that the failure of Christianity to accomplish that task of social regeneration to which it seemed committed by its origins, was not due to the conscious and wise self-limitation of the Church, but to a series of historical causes. . . . It follows that the failure of the Church to undertake the work of a Christian reconstruction of social life has not been caused by its close adherence to the spirit of Christ and to the essence of its religious task, but to the deflecting influence of alien forces penetrating Christianity from without and clogging the revolutionary moral power inherent in it.
>
> In primitive Christianity the failure is sufficiently accounted for by the impossibility of undertaking a social propaganda within the hostile Empire, and by the hostility to the existing civilization created through the persecutions suffered by Christians. The catastrophic element in the millennial hope was an inheritance from Judaism. The

belief in demon powers ruling in heathen society was partly Jewish, partly heathen.

The other-worldliness, the sacramental and ritual superstitions, the asceticism and monastic enthusiasm, were all derived from contemporary religious drifts in heathen society. The dogmatic bent was acquired mainly from Greek intellectualism. The union of Church and State was likewise a reversion to ethnic religion. The lack of political rights and interests among the mass of Christian people, and the disappearance of the original democracy of church organization, were part of the curse of despotism which lay upon all of humanity. The lack of a scientific comprehension of society was in the main inevitable in the past stages of intellectual progress (1907:198–199).

Thus, for Rauschenbusch, the nineteenth-century Protestant focus on individual salvation was only the most recent of an elaborate series of historical incidents that had blinded the church to the original social message of Jesus. Rauschenbusch's theological doctrine required that he negate the entire history of the Christian church in order to explain why social salvation had never been the dominant Christian view.

Having rejected individual salvation as alone sufficient to solve social problems, the social gospelers needed to devise an alternative method of bringing about social change. At first, they believed that by applying Christian ethics to social institutions, rather than only to individuals, the social problems could be solved. Although they never gave up their hope that society could be improved through the application of Christian teachings about brotherhood, they very quickly recognized that social reform efforts needed to go beyond mere moralizing. This realization eventually led them to discover sociology.

But, initially, the power of Christian love was conceived of as the great panacea for America's social ills, especially for its industrial problems (Hopkins, 1940:31). Love could smooth the relations between capitalists and labor. Equally simplistic was the belief that good stewardship could be the ultimate solution for capitalist abuses of wealth and power, and that government regulation was only to be used as a last resort (Hopkins, 1940:102). Social gospelers sought to insure that their reform theories had a valid scriptural basis. They argued this could be accomplished through the application of the "social teachings of Jesus" to social problems (Hopkins, 1940:205). For example, Rauschenbusch (1907:70, 87) argued that Christ's ideal society involved the abolition of rank and the extinction of the badges of rank in which inequality is encrusted. The only title to greatness must be like Christ's, distinguished service to others at a cost to self. Instead of a society resting on coercion, exploitation, and inequality, Jesus had desired to found a society based on love, service, and equality. Josiah Strong (1898:123–127, 1902:102) agreed that the major social teachings of Jesus were the laws of service, sacrifice, and love.

The social gospel very definitely represented an example of Weber's (1963:166) inner-worldly asceticism. For example, Strong (1902:105) argued that there could be no separation of life into sacred and secular aspects and sought to resacralize the mundane world. Jesus, he alleged, held the same view and His struggle was to remove all evil from the world (Strong, 1902:80).

Washington Gladden (1905:7) felt that the Sermon on the Mount must become the basis for any social reconstruction. The New Testament spoke of justice, equity, love, and self-sacrifice as the basis of society. This was in stark contrast to the contemporary world of business, which is based on market values, profits, supply and demand, and self-interest (Gladden, 1888:167–168). The wage system was both anti-social and anti-Christian in Gladden's (1886:33) view and the only solution was to incorporate the golden rule, "Thou shalt love thy neighbor as thyself," into the organization of management and labor. Gladden (1905:111, 154) opposed going the socialist route because "true socialism" could only come out of an application of the golden rule, and not by revolution or political mandate.

George Herron (1893:30, 36), although he did later come to advocate socialism, also regarded the Sermon on the Mount as Christ's key social document: Christ's "social constitution." Herron viewed that the relationship between employer and employee as sacred; to treat it as a money relationship was the root of all the strife between the two. Herron (1893:37) stated:

> It lies within the power of the American capitalists who call themselves Christians to create a new and divine civilization by

> taking the Sermon on the Mount and patiently working it into the
> foundations of industry.

Besides business and industry, the state must also adopt this social constitution of Jesus (1893:30). J.H.W. Stuckenberg (1893:309–310) called for an end to the church's ignorance concerning social problems, and argued that the church must study and master the "sociological teachings of the New Testament," such as the duty of property—i.e., stewardship—and the necessity of adopting a servant orientation. Francis Greenwood Peabody (1900:20–21) summarized the social gospel's attitude toward humanity:

> The gospel of Jesus was a gospel for the poor, the blind, the
> prisoners, and the brokenhearted. . . . The solution to the social
> question can be found . . . in the principles of the Christian religion.

Besides rejecting individual evangelism and moral suasion, the social gospelers were also convinced that other traditional forms of social amelioration practiced by the Christian church, such as charity, were not the ultimate solution. As a result, they were left to develop a novel approach to social reform. Peabody (1900:29) stated that traditional Christian philanthropy such as alms-giving to the poor was not the answer. Rauschenbusch (1907:346) was critical of the Christian communal movements of the nineteenth century because they attempted to escape from the evils of the contemporary world rather than actively work to reform the larger society (see also Bliss, 1898:683–684, on this point) In addition, the traditional Protestant church was itself seen as a conservative force in society preventing reform (Rauschenbusch, 1912:36). Shailer Mathews (1927:377) argued that the church had made little attempt to change the economic or social status quo, and was thus part of the very problem it sought to solve. Mathews pointed to such post–Civil War revivalists as Dwight Moody as major culprits because they attempted to cure poverty through instilling the Protestant work ethic among the urban poor.

One of the first steps that would have to be taken to insure the success of reforms advocated by the social gospel was to awaken the church to its forgotten social mission. Because social gospelers were already hard at work reshaping mainstream Protestant theology, the immediate task was to convince the rest of the church, particularly the more conservative denominations and ministers, to accept social gospel tenets and then to take action. Rauschenbusch (1910:10) even went so far as to write new social hymns and prayers to replace those that were individualistic in orientation in order to provide the church with a liturgy appropriate for reformism.

However, what ultimately made the social gospel theology intellectually tenable and acceptable to the newly emerging middle-class church was its link to rational scientific thought and methodology. Social gospel concepts could not be dismissed as mere subjective moralizing once they were grafted onto emerging scientific orientations and procedures. But could basic Biblical principles such as the social teachings of Jesus—e.g., the Sermon on the Mount—be made into scientific principles concerning society and social reform? The social gospelers became convinced that they could and expressed a very strong faith that science and religiously inspired reform could be accommodated. What was needed was a newly created "social science" that would assist them in their mission. Early in the 1880s, social gospelers began searching for a way to unite their theological principles with a relevant and applicable science, one they would call sociology (Hopkins, 1940:54).

But why should the social gospel turn to science? For one, gospel ministers had already rejected earlier Christian policies concerning reform such as communal socialism. They needed a new method to bring about their envisioned social salvation. For another, they had already announced their acceptance of Western science, including two of its major tenets, the evolutionary model and the idea of progress. Their attitude toward science had been positive from the start. If God's design could be seen in the laws of nature, laws subject to verification, social gospelers intended to look for that design in scientifically measurable terms. They were in general agreement with such leading theologians as Lyman Abbott who argued that he would accept scientific conclusions and realign his theology to fit them (McLoughlin, 1978:155). Thus, the social gospel would not be founded solely on religious sentiment, but also on scientific knowledge. William

Visser 'T Hooft (1928:148–149) has summarized the social gospel's dependence on modern science:

> . . . it is one of the outstanding characteristics of the social gospel that it believes not only in the compatibility of science and Christianity but also in the indispensability of their mutual interpenetration. This is a conviction that often leads to a further belief that through the contribution of modern science humanity is being enabled to understand Christianity and Christ himself much better than any preceding generation.

The social gospelers' need to have dominion over nature and the world in order to bring about social salvation, depended so heavily on a knowledge of God's scientific laws that they soon became virtual captives of science. This was especially the case in the areas of economics and sociology.

This positive attitude toward science can be seen in the writings of all major social gospel theologians. Walter Rauschenbusch (1945:57) stated that "theology ought to be the science of redemption and offer scientific methods for the eradication of sin." He (1907:209) believed in "the possibility of so directing religious energy by scientific knowledge that a comprehensive and continuous reconstruction of social life in the name of God is within the bounds of human possibility." Rauschenbusch (1907:91) argued that he had uncovered the key area of overlap between Spencer's scientific theory of the organic nature of society and Paul's description of the body of Christ in 1 Corinthians 12. Rauschenbusch stated: "We need a combination of the Kingdom of God, and the modern comprehension of the organic development of human society." Lack of a scientific comprehension of society prior to Spencer's evolutionary organic model had prevented emergence of a social science (1907:199).

Josiah Strong (1914:5) believed that the scientific method was superior because it was based on the absolute harmony of all truth. "Science, by discovering the laws of nature, reveals the divine methods and enables us, by adopting them, to become efficient laborers together with God unto the kingdom" (Strong, 1902:104). Strong (1914:94) agreed with Rauschenbusch in the use of Spencer's organic model of society because it emulated Paul's description of the body of Christ.

Scientific theory could thus show the validity of the biblical model of society's division of labor. Washington Gladden (1902:23) and George Herron (1893:30) also expressed their strong faith in science.

In particular, the social gospelers needed a science that would aid them in their quest to rid American society of its social problems. The social science which they argued they needed was continually referred to as sociology. Beginning in the 1880s, the social gospelers frequently called for the establishment of an appropriate sociological base for their social reform strategies. However, social gospelers did not believe that American sociology as it had been developed by their contemporaries Ward and Sumner was adequate for the task of ameliorating the society. Neither Lester Ward's nascent Comtianism nor William Graham Sumner's Spencerian pessimism would do. Although they accepted Spencer's organic analogy, his laissez-faire social reform outlook, championed by Sumner, did not serve the social gospelers' activist orientation. And although Comte and Ward advocated social reform, both had rejected Christianity, making unreserved acceptance of their sociology impossible. A new version of sociology was necessary, one that was compatible with basic Christian principles and usable for social redemption.

One of the best early statements of the type of sociology the social gospelers wanted was made by Gladden in 1886 in a chapter entitled, "Christianity and Social Science," in his *Applied Christianity*. Gladden (1886:212) defined social science as "the social relations of man to man and the duties growing out of those relations." There ought to be no schism between Christians and sociologists, but the closest sympathy and cooperation, he argued (1886:215), because in reality they have the same goal, social betterment. Gladden (1886:216) was critical of Spencer's unchristian attitude, although he frequently quoted Spencer's sociology favorably in his writings. Gladden (1886:222–243) specifically stated the ways in which sociology could aid Christianity and also showed how Christianity might assist the growth of sociology. Sociology could serve Christianity in the following ways: (1) sociological studies of vice, crime, pauperism, and ignorance could provide valuable information that Christians needed to document the scope of America's social problems; (2) Christians could gain some useful hints from the suggestions of social science as to the means necessary to rid society of its social ills; and (3) sociology could help elucidate some of the more important truths of theology and thus give the Christian gospel a scientific foundation. Christianity could assist sociology by: (1) giving moral invigoration to sociologists and insuring that sociology's methods would be Christian and (2) suffusing its theories with Christian ideas for a science of political economy, dealing with the production and distribution of wealth. Christian input would see to it that sociology did not become another physical science:

> There is a tendency to carry the methods and maxims of physical science into this realm; to make Biology not merely the analogue of Sociology, but identical with it; thus confining the attention to physical forces, and putting all the stress on physical remedies. To correct this aberration, the Christian teaching respecting the spiritual nature of man needs to be steadily held in mind (1886:243).

Thus Gladden had very specific goals in mind for American sociology and hoped to make it into a useful ally of the social gospel. How successful Gladden believed he had been in bringing his vision of sociology to fruition is revealed in his essay of 1902:

> With the work of the leading modern economists and sociologists every minister ought to be acquainted. Not that he is to preach economics or sociology, but he needs to be familiar with the constructive ideas on which these sciences are based, and with the facts by which they are supported. In the work of some of these students of society he will find much that will greatly aid him, for there are not a few of them to whom the larger aspects of these problems are fully revealed. But the Christian student must always be on his guard against a pseudo-science which ignores the spiritual realm (1902:23).

George Herron was also very specific about the spiritual orientation that sociology must take. In a chapter entitled "The Scientific Ground of a Christian Sociology" in *The Christian Society*, he observed:

> Sociology has not yet become a science. . . . The observing of existing phenomena apart from moral facts and forces, a reverence

for statistics and an aversion to principles, has been the fatuity of all
attempts to create a science of sociology. No sociological method is
so wholly unscientific, or so misses the chief facts, as that which
confines itself to observing and tabulating social conditions. . . .
Many will listen with interest to facts which are seen, quite as ready
to believe erroneous statistics as true. . . . Unless it is primarily a
science of righteousness, sociology can not be a science of society. Its
work only begins with the observing of existing phenomena. It must
give society a knowledge of how to create phenomena that shall be
just. When it attempts to be scientific through the inductive study of
social conditions and statistics, without making moral causes of
wrong conditions the main object of study and correction; it passes
into that profound ignorance that always darkens the understanding
that has no ethical vision. Sociology can become a science only by
becoming a science of redemption. Only by grounding society in
right social faiths and laying the axe of truth at the roots of social
falsehoods, by regenerating society with right social visions, will
sociology fulfill its scientific vocation, which is the education of
society in justice. . . . Sociology must become a science of justice to
be a science of society (1894:17–19).

An interest in the study of sociology had begun in the 1880s. But
the absence of a well-developed sociology acceptable to the social
gospelers kept the decade a period of discussion rather than practical
application. As the decade wore on the demand for a foundation of
social science beneath all reform became more and more insistent,
resulting in a quest for a Christian sociology. Richard T. Ely, in his
1889 text *Social Aspects of Christianity*, made a strong plea to divinity
schools to introduce courses in economics and sociology because social
science could teach men how to better fulfill the second commandment
of love toward one's fellow man. Ely proposed that half of the
theological students' time be devoted to the social sciences, and that
divinity schools become the chief intellectual centers for sociology. In
the 1890s, the attempt to lay a sociological foundation for religious
reform activities grew even stronger, and one of the major reasons for
the rapid spread of sociological study and interest during this decade
was the social gospel.

The 1890s became the decade for the first great blossoming of
sociology in America. Here, four aspects will be dealt with: (1) the

proliferation of sociology courses; (2) the increased output of social surveys and statistics; (3) the new impetus for social work and the birth of the settlement house movement; and (4) the attempt to Christianize industry and politics. The following chapters will show how the first generation of American sociologists can be seen as, each in their own way, responding to the social gospel's plea for a moralistic, scientific, reform-oriented sociology.

By 1900, a very significant number of colleges and universities had introduced courses in sociology into their curriculum. J. Graham Morgan (1969:50) documented the fact that, by 1900, 227 colleges and universities out of 683 surveyed included the teaching of sociology in their studies. Furthermore, sociology had been introduced at 136 out of 469 church-related colleges and 91 out of 214 nondenominational schools. Only seven of the church-related schools had adopted sociology prior to 1890, while 129 introduced it in the 1890s (Morgan, 1969:51). Those denominations most involved in the progressive religious ideas of the social gospel were also those most willing to support sociology in their educational institutions. The four denominations that were most favorable to sociology at their colleges were the Congregationalists (17 out of 22), the Methodists (40 out of 99), the Presbyterians (22 out of 74), and the Baptists (18 out of 62). Of the 81 Catholic colleges in America only six introduced sociology, showing that the social gospel was still primarily a Protestant-dominated theology in the 1890s. In a survey by L.L. Bernard in 1909 (p. 165), it was estimated that almost 400 colleges and universities were then teaching sociology, almost doubling the figure for 1900. In 1894, Ira Howerth (p. 113) had discovered forty professors teaching sociology. Fifteen years later, Bernard (1909:186) located fifty-five full-time sociologists and an additional 372 professors whose teaching loads included sociology courses.

Two examples of the introduction of sociology at the college level, one a large university, Harvard, and the other a small denominational school, Geneva College in Beaver Falls, Pennsylvania, document the relation between sociology and the social gospel in the 1890s. Harvard had had Francis Greenwood Peabody on its faculty since the 1880s, and his department of social ethics was a focus for social gospel reformism. However, Peabody was considered more of a theologian than a social scientist. Harvard had two social gospel sociologists in the 1890s, Edward and John Cummings, who taught in the economics department. Robert Church has written about their influence at Harvard (in Buck, 1965:1–17, 18–90). As early as 1885, a social reform orientation was beginning to appear in the social science curriculum at Harvard, as was evidenced by the growing attendance in Peabody's classes. The economics department brought Edward Cummings to the school in 1892 to introduce sociology courses with an orientation toward social reform. Both Edward and his brother John felt that statistical studies of social problems constituted the first step in the inductive study of the development of society (Buck, 1965:57). They argued that the Christian millennium could not possibly arrive anytime soon because society did not yet have enough sociological data to create a truly scientific reform movement (Buck, 1965:45). Their hope was that once enough factual and statistical evidence was assembled proper solutions would inevitably reveal themselves. Implementation of the solutions by the church and other reform-oriented groups would then be possible. Thus the Cummings brothers were early adherents to the positivist claim that science can indeed save humankind. What separated them from later positivists such as Lundberg or Ogburn was the religious framework in which they practiced their social science.

Geneva College, the only Reformed Presbyterian college in the United States, first instituted a program in sociology in 1895. The program included eight courses: among them were economics, constitutional law, American and English history—which concentrated on the development of social and political institutions from the Middle Ages to modern times—and political philosophy—which dealt with the development of the state. In the economics course Richard Ely's *Outline of Economics* text was used. The principal sociological paradigm employed in the course was the social organism model, of which Christ was to be the head. An upper division economics course dealt solely with social problems (*Geneva College Catalogue*, 1895–1896:12–14). In 1897, the program was redesigned separating political science from sociology courses. The three sociology courses listed covered (1) the development of social institutions from their origin until the formation of the national state, (2) the nature, law, and authority of the state, and (3) the application of Christian principles to present social problems. The aim of the third course was to show the necessity of making the teachings of the Bible the controlling principle in political and industrial action (*Geneva College Catalogue*, 1897–1898:26). The new course descriptions in the 1900–1901 catalogue (pp. 17–18) showed a clear social gospel orientation. The three-course sequence to be taken in the senior year had the following content:

> 30. This course treats the nature of society, the relation of society and the individual, the principles of society, the historical evolution of these principles, the ethical ideal and the ethical actuality. Text: Stuckenberg's *Introduction to the Study of Sociology*.

> 31. This course treats the different theories of the state as illustrated by history, contrasts the sociological and the biological views and points out how the prevalent sociological view demands obedience to Jesus Christ the Lord of the social as well as the individual conscience.

> 32. This course deals with the source and delegation of political authority and law, the principles governing this delegation. The view is taken that the realization of the social ideal demands the application of the teachings of Jesus Christ to the social life and the acceptance of these teachings as the law of the state.

In 1901, among the new sociology courses offered were (1) historical development of sociological thought and (2) scientific socialism (1901–1902:16).

The professor who taught all of these courses was James Melville Coleman, who was at Geneva from 1892 until 1908 (Glasgow, 1908:109, 328). A graduate of Geneva, Coleman also had a seminary degree and a degree from the University of Michigan. He served as a minister both prior to his appointment at Geneva as well as after he left the institution. In 1903 he published Social Ethics, in which he attempted to summarize the thoughts he had presented in his courses. In it he interpreted the Kingdom of God as a present social fact and quoted favorably from Herron's *Christian Society* (Coleman, 1903:308, 353). In another essay "The Psychology of Social Redemption," Coleman (no date:5) clearly stated his social gospel orientation: the purpose of Christ's mission was primarily social, to bring about the establishment of heavenly conditions on earth.

The social gospel also made a large impact on theology schools and seminaries in the 1890s, with sociology entering the curricula of a significant number of them (Hopkins, 1940:149). Among the seminaries to introduce sociology was Meadville Theological Seminary (Morgan, 1969:48, 51). In 1891, Meadville instituted a visiting lectureship of Practical Christian Sociology. Among holders of this position prior to 1900 were Washington Gladden, Francis Peabody, Jane Addams, and Jacob Riis. In 1892, Hamilton Theological Seminary, a Baptist school with which Walter Rauschenbusch was connected, instituted a visiting lectureship in sociology (Morgan, 1969:51). Albion Small was the 1896–1897 guest lecturer while his fellow University of Chicago sociologist Charles Henderson served for 1899–1900. In 1894, Chicago Theological Seminary created the first chair in Christian Sociology and Graham Taylor was appointed to the position (Hopkins, 1940:157).

However, probably the most thorough attempt to make sociology a vital part of seminary training took place in 1894 when Hartford Theological Seminary opened the Hartford School of Sociology. The program was a three-year graduate course set up to study social problems, social history, population or demography, and the family (Hopkins, 1940:165). Among its faculty and visiting lecturers were John Bascom, John Commons, Carroll D. Wright, and Lester Ward (Morgan, 1969:51–52).

More evidence of the close ties between Christianity and sociology can be seen in the large number of sociology professors and instructors with theological training. Of the 298 professors who had taught sociology courses prior to 1900, almost one-third had received some theological training and practically all of these were ordained ministers (Morgan, 1969:52). Other historians of American sociology, such as Robert E.L. Faris (1970:7) and Roscoe and Gisela Hinkle (1954:3), have noted the large number of ministers in the early years of the discipline, but have been at a loss to explain it adequately. The explanation lies in the fact that in the 1890s the social gospel was the welcome ally of both sociology and social reform. Throughout the decade, prominent social scientists lent their influence to the social gospel by writing books on social Christianity (Hopkins, 1940:257). Even the potentially dangerous secularizing tendencies of the sociology of religion were employed favorably by the social gospelers. The sociological analysis of religion gave scientific sanction to the social gospelers' critique of the traditional individualistic ethic of Protestantism (Hopkins, 1940:274). Sociologists such as E.A. Ross (1969:196–217) argued that religion was a social force, one that could be employed for the purposes of either social control or social change. Social gospelers hoped to move the church from the former to the latter. Churches and religiously sponsored organizations asked social scientists to come and lecture to them on reform topics, and professors such as Albion Small and Charles Henderson frequently participated in such endeavors (Hopkins, 1940:267).

Even the most popular textbooks used in sociology courses show a clear relationship between sociology, social reform, and social Christianity. In 1909 the five most frequently used textbooks were: (1) Small and Vincent's *Introduction to the Study of Sociology*; (2) Carroll D. Wright's *Practical Sociology*; (3) Franklin Gidding's *Elements of Sociology*; (4) Arthur Fairbanks's *Introduction to Sociology*; and (5) Charles Henderson's *Social Elements, Institutions, Character, Progress* (Ellwood, 1907:212). All were conscious attempts to relate sociology to the tenets of social Christianity.

Once sociology had discovered its calling, as it was envisioned most clearly by Washington Gladden (1886:212–243), the social gospelers could then use it in their attempts to create social reform agendas which were both religiously and scientifically plausible. William D.P. Bliss (1898) constructed a 1,500-page *Encyclopedia of Social Reform* whose list of contributors included Edward Bellamy, John R. Commons, Franklin Giddings, Graham Taylor, and the English Christian sociologist Sydney Webb. A major discussion of Christian sociology appears in the encyclopedia (p. 249).

Josiah Strong (1914:78, 1904:100), who was very impressed by the growth of sociology departments in America, made frequent references to the writings of Charles Henderson. Walter

Rauschenbusch's (1907:214, 261, 1912:185, 265, 288, 290) writings show numerous usages of works by such social scientists as Richard T. Ely, E.A. Ross, Franklin Giddings, Graham Taylor, and Jane Addams.

Two areas in which the social gospelers especially desired the assistance of academically trained sociologists were social surveys and statistical compilations. Surveys and statistics, once complied, would be very effectively employed by the social gospelers to awaken American society to the scope of its social problems. Once aroused, Americans would then see the necessity for social reform.

The primary function of the social survey for the first generation of American sociologists was the descriptive analysis of social problems, and the quantitative portrayal of deplorable social conditions. The survey served as an "ethnographic" account of the lives of those who had been most negatively affected by industrialization and urbanization. The reports were filled with accounts of factory areas, slums, and ghettoes. Frequently the groups discussed in this literature were referred to as the "dependent, defective, and delinquent classes" (Ellwood, 1907:590). Charles Ellwood (1907:594) suggested that an entire year course should be taught that dealt with these "abnormal" or "depressed" classes in American society and the present scientific methods for treating each particular group. Social surveys were to provide much of the material upon which such courses would depend.

The use of statistics to bolster statements concerning social conditions separated the social survey from popular forms of muckraking journalism. Two famous surveys that dealt with tenement life in New York City were Jacob Riis's 1890 *How the Other Half Lives* and Charles Stelzle's (1903) *The Working Man and Social Problems*. Both make frequent use of statistics to back up their descriptive accounts of the nature of New York slums. For example, in order to document the extent of the liquor problem in the ghettoes, Riis (1906:210) pointed out that in New York City below 14th Street there were 4,065 saloons, but only 111 Protestant churches. He hoped to show that the saloon and not the church was the real arbiter of morals in the slum. Riis also made very effective use of photographs in his book, helping his readers to clearly visualize the conditions he was describing.

Photography became an important instrument in the hands of social reformers. Probably the best of the sociological photographers was Lewis Hine (1974), who had studied sociology at the University of Chicago in the 1890s. Hine's (1981) photography probed the darker side of American society: poverty, deplorable factory conditions, child labor, and the plight of immigrants, women, and Blacks in the early twentieth century.

Nevertheless, statistics rather than photography, became the major criterion for validating the extent of contemporary social problems. In their works, the social gospelers frequently employed statistical accounts that were the result of sociological research. Statistics were thus to become an essential part of sociological methodology. In Bernard's (1909:191) survey, 57 out of 109 institutions reported making use of statistical methods. One of the reasons that American sociology adopted its strong advocacy of quantitative statistical methods was the initial social gospel influence on the discipline. Social gospel ministers needed empirically quantifiable statements so that their message could not be disputed or dismissed as mere moralizing.

Among the social gospelers, Josiah Strong was one of the most forceful advocates for the use of statistical data. As early as 1886, Strong's *Our Country* had made use of statistics from economists, demographers, and sociologists. In 1904, Strong was to initiate an annual volume entitled Social Progress: *A Year Book and Encyclopedia of Economic, Industrial, Social, and Religious Statistics.* The purpose of the volume was to provide an adequate source of information about social problems and included demographic statistics, surveys on industrial conditions, child labor statistics, crime statistics, poverty statistics, and measures of alcohol abuse (1904:1–2, 81–84, 99). Strong's volumes were to supplement William Bliss's *Encyclopedia of Social Reform*, considered at the time to be the standard reference work on social problems, partly because of its statistical analysis—e.g., crime statistics, pp. 399–411. Walter Rauschenbusch (1909:232–233) made use of statistical data also to back up his ideas about poverty and low wages.

Given the fact that there is no inherent reason why sociology should have been an empirical, quantitative, or statistically based discipline rather than a descriptive or qualitative one, there must be historically specific reasons why American sociology chose this method over its competitors—e.g., the verstehen method employed by Weber and other phenomenological German sociologists. The fact that the social gospelers felt they needed a strong statistical base for their claims helps to account for the emphasis on empirical calculation in American sociology, an orientation that would in the twentieth century come to dominate the American sociological perspective.

Of particular significance in the 1890s was the participation by and influence of women in the social gospel movement, social reform attempts, and in sociology. Taking part in religiously based reform movements was not entirely new for American women. In the reform attempts that accompanied the Second Great Awakening, and the antislavery crusade, women had played an active part. Reform movements permitted women to take up tasks outside of the home and to expand beyond their traditional roles of wife and mother. Women could be workers, speakers, leaders, and fund-raisers, thus gaining a new sense of identity outside the home. As Rosenberg (1971:98) has interpreted nineteenth-century reformism, some of the betterment movements of the 1830s and 1840s, much as anti-alcohol and anti-prostitution leagues, appealed to women because within them they could express a normally unspoken hostility toward the male and his dominant position and, at the same time, attempt to control the vices of the baser sex.

One of the social gospel reform organizations participated in by women in the 1880s and 1890s was the Women's Christian Temperance Union (WCTU). Frances Willard, the WCTU's president during those decades, had been converted to a social gospel outlook through reading the works of Edward Bellamy (Bordin, 1981:108). While previously the WCTU's position had been that alcohol was the cause of poverty, broken homes, divorce, and many other social problems, Willard's new stance regarded alcohol abuse as the result of deplorable social conditions. Thus the WCTU shifted its reform focus from shutting down bars and saloons to trying to solve the social problems which led people to drink. An unjust society had made alcohol into an inevitable escape from poverty, and only fundamental changes in the environment would heal that portion of the population. Alcoholism would only cease in a re-created society such as the one Bellamy envisioned in *Looking Backward*. Willard and the WCTU became involved in a wide range of reform activities that foreshadowed the settlement house movement. Among the reforms proposed by the WCTU in the early 1890s were an eight-hour work day and a five-and-a-half day work week, shelters for the care of children of working mothers, kindergarten classes, federal aid to education, vocational and technical training for men and women, free school lunches, social rooms other than saloons for the urban poor, and prison reform with separate facilities for women offenders and model juvenile facilities for dependent and neglected children (Bordin, 1981:13–14, 108). Willard also openly supported Terrence Powderly's Knights of Labor, and she advocated shifting the American economic system toward socialism through the gradual nationalization of railroads, telegraph system, public utilities, and factories (Bordin, 1981:105, 108). Many of the WCTU's positions would soon be taken up by Jane Addams and others in the settlement house movement.

Jane Addams, the founder of Hull House, became in the 1890s the major female spokesperson for the social gospel. Although she was first inspired by British social Christianity while visiting Toynbee Hall in London in 1888, Addams became an ally to American social gospelers such as Graham Taylor, George Herron, Walter Rauschenbusch, Albion Small, Charles Henderson, and Richard T. Ely (A. Davis, 1973:95, 97, 119). In fact, Addams was quite ambivalent about Christianity until she encountered the social gospel. However, her decision to establish a settlement in a poor section of Chicago was essentially a religious commitment to the kind of Christianity she had witnessed at Toynbee Hall: a religion of social action (A. Davis, 1973:51). Addams stated in 1892:

> The gospel must be put into terms of action and Christianity has to be revealed and embodied in the line of social progress. . . . Christianity is not a set of ideas which belong to the religious consciousness that

is proclaimed and instituted apart from the social life of the
community (quoted in Porterfield, 1980:165).

Addams thus received her inspiration from the social gospel, which she
discerned as a renaissance of Christianity, a movement toward the
religion's early humanitarianism when the spirit of Christ was
expressed in social service (Lasch, 1965:29, 40). Under Addams's
leadership the settlement movement flourished (from six settlement
houses in 1891, to seventy-four in 1897, to over 100 by 1900, and to
over 400 by 1910), and was especially appealing to both women and
clergymen who had been influenced by the social gospel (Davis,
1967:12). A poll taken in 1905 indicated that eighty percent of the 339
settlement workers interviewed were active church members with most
coming from denominations that were strongly influenced by the social
gospel such as the Congregationalists, the Presbyterians, the
Episcopalians, and the Unitarians (Davis, 1967:27).

The appeal of the settlement house movement to women is
exemplified in the life of Jane Addams, because her experience was
typical of that of the first generation of college-educated women in
America. Addams, like many of her college-educated female peers,
remained unmarried and was therefore an anomaly in a society in which
to be a woman meant fitting into the prescribed roles of wife and
mother. Addams's personal struggle as a young woman was to break
away from the traditional conception of the role of women based on
piety, purity, domesticity, and submissiveness. She was already groping
toward a new conception of the role of women that would make them
more active participants and special leaders in the world's affairs, while
preserving and making special use of their womanliness when she
discovered the settlement house model (A. Davis, 1973:23). Addams
asserted that social reform activity was a legitimate outlet for educated
American women, because in school women had been socialized to
help alleviate suffering. Those women who chose not to marry needed
an outlet for their ameliorative disposition, since they had no husband
or children upon whom to lavish their time and energy. Addams felt
that for women "the desire for action, the wish to right wrong and
alleviate suffering, haunts them daily" and that "from babyhood the
altruistic tendencies of daughters have been cultivated. They are taught

to be self-forgetting and self-sacrificing, to consider the good of the Whole before the good of the Ego" (quoted in Lasch, 1965:37–38). Addams's personal solution, as well as her suggestion to other unmarried women, was settlement house work and, in fact, most female settlement house workers were unmarried (Davis, 1967:34).

However, no matter how much Jane Addams wanted to escape the stereotyped models of women perpetuated by Victorian America, her settlement house philosophy was firmly rooted in the ideology of the home—domesticity. This philosophy had even been given a scientific basis by Catherine Beecher in her 1841 work *A Treatise on Domestic Economy* (Porterfield, 1980:124). Homemaking was to become a science. In the expanded domesticity envisioned by women such as Addams, the world was to become a Christian home. According to some interpreters of theology, probably the key ingredient in feminine spirituality in America has been the desire to sacralize space. Addams at first started with Hull House itself, in which she attempted to create a wholesome domestic environment, and then moved beyond to turn the local community and later the entire nation into a place ruled by Christian values that originated in the home.

When Jane Addams and her associate Ellen Starr opened Hull House in 1889 they were in a sense furnishing their first home. They thought of the settlement house as a home rather than as an institution and tried to make it as attractive as possible (A. Davis, 1973:59). Jane even put out her inherited silver, just as any newly married woman would. Knowing little about the actual nature of their community residents' plight and nothing about how to deal with the problems, Addams and Starr were at first convinced they could help by sharing their knowledge of art and literature with the immigrants and by opening their house for receptions, clubs, classes, and lectures. Showing Italians slides of Florentine art was one of their early attempts to bring high culture to the masses (A. Davis, 1973:67). However, they quickly realized their naiveté and made plans to institute a nursery and kindergarten and start classes on health, cooking, and sewing for the young women.

Addams's interest in social reform was motivated by her perception that America's urban poor had no opportunity to develop the stable family from which moral culture sprang. She became convinced that environment was much more important than heredity. If the community would provide decent housing, better parks and playgrounds, and good schools, it was possible to produce better citizens. Thus Addams moved beyond the confines of Hull House to attempt to domesticize the community. She referred to her movement into social reform as municipal housekeeping:

> Women who live in the country sweep their own dooryards and may either feed the refuse of the table to a flock of chickens or allow it innocently to decay in the open air and sunshine. . . . In a crowded city quarter, however, if the street is not cleaned by the city authorities no amount of private sweeping will keep the tenement free of grime; if the garbage is not collected and destroyed a tenement mother may see her children sicken and die of diseases from which she alone is powerless to shield them, although her tenderness and devotion are unbounded. She cannot even secure untainted meat for her household, she cannot even secure fruit. . . . In short, if woman would keep on with her old business of caring for her house and rearing her children she will have to have some conscience in regard to public affairs lying quite outside of her immediate household. The individual conscience and devotion are no longer effective (quoted in A. Davis, 1973:187).

Addams argued that women were specially qualified for modern municipal housekeeping, and because of their empathy and intuition could lead a moral reform movement, thus transferring their natural talents from the home to society.

Addams and other settlement house leaders, such as Graham Taylor in Chicago and Robert Woods in Boston, made it clear that their movement was not just another form of organized charity, but a genuine social reform movement. The differences in both their underlying social theories and their methods were profound. Charity workers emphasized the individual causes of poverty, while settlement workers stressed the social and economic conditions that made people poor. Unlike charity societies that were built on the assumption that the upper class had a responsibility to help the needy, the settlement movement was based on what Jane Addams referred to as "the theory that the dependence of classes on each other is reciprocal" (Davis,

1967:18–19). Thus the philosophy of the charity organization movement led to philanthropy, and the philosophy of the settlement movement, to reform. Francis Peabody (1900:29) agreed with the settlement workers that traditional Christian philanthropy was not the answer to the social question. It was not until the second decade of the twentieth century that the gulf between the two groups was narrowed.

As if following Peabody's (1900:124) or Rauschenbusch's (1907:189) model of society as a formation of concentric circles or spheres, the settlement reformers first became concerned with those issues that directly affected home life—children's and women's issues—and later moved on to ameliorate the masculine worlds of work and politics. One of the first issues taken up by settlement workers was children. Addams and Starr initiated nursery and kindergarten programs at Hull House early in their career. Later, settlement workers fought to abolish child labor. For example, Florence Kelly of Hull House was assigned by the governor of Illinois in 1891 as a special investigator for the Illinois State Bureau of Labor to study child labor in the sweat shops of Chicago (Davis, 1967:125). Based on pioneer American psychologist G. Stanley Hall's theory that children were still close to lower, more animalistic evolutionary stages, Addams argued for the construction of parks and playgrounds as an outlet for their animal energies (A. Davis, 1973:152). Addams became involved in the leadership of national reform organizations such as the National Playground Association and the National Child Labor Committee.

Jane Addams was not only concerned with young children, but was in the forefront of a movement to consider adolescence as a special time between childhood and adulthood (A. Davis, 1973:151). One of the results was Hull House's assistance in the establishment of the first juvenile court in the United States in Chicago in 1899, so that adolescent offenders would not be processed or punished as if they were adult criminals (A. Davis, 1973:150). In her 1909 book, *The Spirit of Youth and City Streets*, Addams argued that the combination of forcing youth to work and at the same time denying them access to organized play led them to delinquent activities in such places as "gin-palaces" and dance halls.

> This stupid experience of organizing work and failing to organize play has of course brought about a fine revenge. The love of pleasure will not be denied, and when it has turned into all sorts of malignant and vicious appetites, then we, the middle aged, grow quite distracted and resort to all sorts of restrictive measures (quoted in Lasch, 1965: 86–87).

Addams went on to describe how the modern city overstimulates the adolescent. "The newly awakened senses are appealed to by all that is gaudy and sensual, by flippant street music, the highly colored theatre posters, the trashy love stories, the feathered hats, the cheap heroics of revolvers displayed in the pawnshop windows, as well as movie theatres, dance halls and drugs" (quoted in A. Davis, 1973:154). Addams's suggestions as solutions to these diversions clearly showed her assumption that the lower-class, urban environment of saloons, dance halls, and street life needed to be changed and made more like a middle- or upper-class neighborhood. She suggested that the plays of Molière and Shakespeare replace the cheap movie, that chaperoned parties substitute for the dance halls, that recreation centers and settlements could compete with the saloons, and that parks, playgrounds, and competitive sports could replace the seeking of adventure on the streets (A. Davis, 1973:154).

The settlement movement also strongly supported reforms that would better the lives of women, such as improving the conditions under which women worked, vocational and domestic training, women's suffrage, improving tenement living conditions, and ending prostitution. Hull House's female programs had first been limited to giving classes in cooking and sewing, but gradually they expanded into areas that focused on bettering the social position of women.

Jane Addams's arguments for women's suffrage were also directly related to her domestic ideology. Addams argued that women needed to be given the vote so that they could bring their special ameliorative temperament to bear upon the social problems of the day. In concerning themselves with public problems of the day, women were only pursuing their traditional home activities in a larger context, society, which had taken over many of the functions formerly exercised by the family (Lasch, 1965:143–144). Once women had been given authority over the home by men, and the home was seen as the woman's special sphere, they then claimed the legitimate right to speak out on and vote on any issue that they believed might directly impact upon the family. For example, Addams believed that once suffrage was granted, women would put an end to prostitution, an evil that men had failed to outlaw. In her 1912 book, *A New Conscience and an Ancient Evil*, Addams argued that women, once given political power, would quickly eradicate prostitution, as well as rid the society of one of its major causes, alcohol. Addams believed that women did not enter into prostitution willingly but were tricked into a life of white slavery while under the influence of alcohol.

However, the settlement workers did not stop with aiding children and women, but attempted to take on the male worlds of work and politics as well. For example, Hull House became a center for labor reform lobbying and political rallies for workers in unions or on strike. Settlement house director Robert Woods of Boston adopted Booker T. Washington's ideas concerning vocational training for Blacks (and immigrants), arguing that it offered the downtrodden a way to success in American society (Davis, 1967:51). Settlement workers quickly realized that almost all the questions they dealt with—e.g., labor standards, housing improvements, the condition of women and children, parks and playgrounds, education, sanitation, etc.—involved public policy and were thus political issues. The settlement movement, in rather rapid fashion, changed from local community outposts to a national reform movement with a long political agenda. For Addams, this meant taking the political world as her circumference and attempting to domesticize the masculine sphere of politics. In the 1890s, Addams realized that in order to bring change to the impoverished community surrounding Hull House, she would have to defeat the machine-backed politicians that ruled Chicago (A. Davis, 1973:122). Although she failed in this attempt, Addams continued to use political means to bring about her reforms. In 1912, Addams seconded the nomination of Theodore Roosevelt for president on the Progressive Party ticket. The party's platform contained all the social reform policies that Addams had backed for almost two decades, and settlement workers were convinced that the election of 1912 could be the climax of their long struggle for social justice.

Having virtually no information or statistics upon which to base their critical statements, settlement workers either compiled their own or commissioned sociologists to complete surveys for them. Richard T. Ely had strongly urged Jane Addams and her staff at Hull House to begin systematic social investigations and to publish their findings. The result was the 1895 volume, *Hull House Maps and Papers*, completed by surveying the neighborhood, block by block, house by house, to determine nationality, family composition, and income (A. Davis, 1973:97–99). The first and most important study of the northern urban Black was the investigation carried out by W.E.B. DuBois, *The Philadelphia Negro*, published in 1897. This study was initiated by Susan Wharton, a member of the executive committee of Philadelphia College Settlement. Asking for assistance from the University of Pennsylvania to document the problems of Philadelphia Blacks, the university appointed the young DuBois, a Black sociologist, to direct the major portion of the study (Davis, 1967:96). Another example of the types of surveys and statistics compiled by or for the settlement house workers was Bliss's *Encyclopedia of Social Reform*, which included articles on such topics as parks and playgrounds, women's suffrage, and crime (1898:972–975, 1410, 399–411).

One of the results of the settlement house movement was the incorporation of its domesticized version of the social gospel into sociology in America. This led to a rather large influx of female students into sociology at both the undergraduate and graduate levels in the 1890s. Up until 1901, twenty-eight percent of graduate sociology students were female (117 majors) and seventy-two percent male (420 majors), the female percentage being considerably higher than in other academic disciplines (Morgan, 1980:4). Many of the students of the new science of sociology directed their attention to the settlements, perceived to be "sociological laboratories," in which they could observe segments of society in operation. The assumption was that, through observation and involvement, particularly of society's pathological manifestations, greater scientific understanding of how to ameliorate such conditions would emerge (Morgan, 1980:9, 11). Jane Addams came to think of herself as a scholar, referred to herself as a sociologist, and offered up Hull House as a sociological laboratory where young instructors and graduate students, especially from the University of Chicago, could come to do research. Chicago professors Albion Small, Charles Henderson, and George Herbert Mead were among Hull House's many visitors (A. Davis, 1973:97). Addams wrote articles for the early issues of the *American Journal of Sociology*, and other essays written and researched at Hull House appeared in that journal as well (A. Davis, 1973:101).

Sociology was taught at a number of prestigious women's colleges. Bryn Mawr had Franklin Giddings on its faculty from 1888 to 1894 prior to his move to Columbia University, where he simultaneously taught female students at Barnard College. Edward Cummings, who also taught later at Harvard, came first to Radcliffe College in 1891 and became professor of sociology there in 1894. Other women's colleges which introduced sociology included Elmira (1892), Vassar (1892), Smith (1892), and Wellesley (1897) (Morgan, 1980:13–15). An interesting insight into the acceptability of sociology as an appropriate subject for women is given by the description of the course, "Principles of Sociology," introduced at Randolph-Macon Women's College in Virginia in 1898—sociology was not even taught at the school's brother institution, Randolph-Macon College. The course description stated:

> This course is specifically adapted to meet the requirements of the ever-increasing demand of intelligent women in the management of the various charitable and philanthropic organizations of modern society. The object is to train the student to an intelligent grasp of the great social problems that confront us at this stage of our civilization, and to the solution of which the women of the future will be called upon in even larger measure to contribute (Morgan, 1980:15–16).

Among the topics covered in the course were charities and corrections, workingmen's insurance, factory legislation, the labor movement, college settlements, tenement house reforms, sanitation, marriage and divorce, and the church in relation to social reform.

Charles Ellwood's (1907:590) description of how sociology should be taught as a college subject shows a strong compatibility with a social reform platform acceptable to women. Ellwood proposed that a three-course sequence in sociology be given to all undergraduates. The three courses were: (1) an introduction to the scientific study of social problems; (2) a study of the abnormal class of society—the dependent, defective, and delinquent classes—and of methods of scientific philanthropy in dealing with them; (3) a critical study of sociological theory.

In L.L. Bernard's (1909:187) survey it was found that ninety-two colleges with programs in sociology offered some kind of practical work or field experience in settlement, charity, or other similar endeavors. Among the list of colleges that had their students participate in settlement work were Asbury College, Brown University, George Washington University, Iowa College, McCormick Theological Seminary, Midland College, Ohio State, Tulane University, University of Michigan, University of Minnesota, University of Wisconsin, Lake Erie College, New York University, Columbia University, Normal College (New York), University of Chicago, and Washington University (St. Louis) (Bernard, 1909:193–194).

A question that must be raised at this point is how males responded to the growing influence of women and their home-based social reform activities. Would men join in this process of further feminizing social reform or attempt to masculinize the movement so that it would be more appealing to males? Walter Rauschenbusch (1907:367) was very ambivalent about the growing feminization of the church and the social gospel. He argued that churches had become overwhelmingly feminine and preoccupied by concern for individual salvation and questions of personal and family morality. Sandra Sizer (1978) has documented the increasing feminization of the image of Christ in the gospel music of the nineteenth century. On the one hand, Rauschenbusch (1907:8) was troubled by such changes and stated that the strenuous insistence on righteousness advocated by the Old Testament prophets was not merely the private morality of the home but the public morality on which national life was founded. Halting injustice and oppression must be the goal. When these kinds of public questions got thorough discussion, men would flock to the movement. On the other hand, Rauschenbusch had praised the settlement movement for taking on the types of public issues he felt should be at the forefront of the social gospel.

A movement which originated in the 1890s to reassert the masculinity of religion became known as "muscular Christianity." Probably the most important book upon which the new theology was based was Thomas Hughes's 1890 *The Manliness of Christ,* in which Christ was presented not as meek or gentle or in any way effete, but as forceful, dynamic, and manly: the first muscular Christian (Kett, 1977:189, 203). One of the advocates of the new remasculinization of Christ was Luther Halsey Gulick who, in 1899, became director of the YMCA. Under his regime the YMCA not only came to stress extensive physical activity for boys and men but also became involved in the social gospel movement, shifting its focus from individual salvation toward programs to meet newly discovered social needs (Visser 'T Hooft, 1928:26). In 1903, Gulick was to become director of physical education activities in the New York City public schools, and later became one of the founders of Boy Scouts of America, helping to create the sports ideology which has shaped the image of masculinity in the United States ever since (Kett, 1977:204). However, probably the key figure in making social reform a fit activity for noneffeminate males was Theodore Roosevelt. Joe Dubbert (1979:136) has pointed out that in the eyes of many men, reform and social reformers were not highly regarded in the nineteenth century. They were seen as artificial, effeminate, soft compromisers who could not successfully struggle with the world as it was and, therefore, wanted to soften life. Roosevelt radically altered the perception of the reformer as a weak, unmasculine type, changing it into the image of a vigorous, forceful man. Roosevelt was perceived as the kind of virile male who could rescue America from corruption without effeminizing American institutions in the process. The chaos and confusion that the new urban industrial environment presented at the turn of the twentieth century would have to be subdued and controlled by men, just as their predecessors had conquered the wilderness. Roosevelt became the leader of the Progressive movement, one of the political movements spawned by the social gospel movement. At his nomination for President by the Progressive Party in 1912, he led the delegates in singing their battle song "Onward Christian Soldiers," thus assuring men of the masculinity of the reform movement (Dubbert, 1979:125). Muscular Christianity helped men to reclaim portions of the masculine domain that the new woman was perceived to be infringing upon.

Not only did the social gospel lead to an early growth in sociology and the settlement movement, it also directly affected the Protestant church in America. In the first twelve years of the twentieth century, most of the major denominations appointed official social service or social action commissions or agencies. However, this never resulted in the full acceptance of social gospel principles among the rank and file of American Protestants whom the national organizations represented (Hopkins, 1940:280). Examples of denominations that formed social service programs were: Episcopal—with Jacob Riis's assistance—1901; Congregational, 1901; Presbyterian—under Charles Stelzle's direction—1903; Methodists, 1907; Unitarians, 1908; and Northern Baptist Convention, 1908 (Hopkins, 1940:280–293). In 1908, thirty denominations came together to form the Federal Council of Churches in Christ in America. Its concerns were centered not on doctrinal issues but upon social interests; thus, the social gospel had succeeded in bringing the major Protestant denominations in America together. The council strongly supported the notion that courses in economics, sociology, and the social teachings of Jesus be established in all theological schools and colleges (Hopkins, 1940:302–311). The council's "social creed," published in 1912, shows just how closely it can be identified with the social gospel. According to the creed the churches must stand for:

(1) Equal rights and complete justice for all men in all stations of life.

(2) Protection of the family, by the single standard of purity, uniform divorce laws, proper regulation of marriage, and proper housing.

(3) The fullest possible development for every child, especially by the provision of proper education and recreation.

(4) Abolition of child labor.

(5) Regulation of the conditions of toil for women as shall safeguard the physical and moral health of the community.

(6) Abetment and prevention of poverty.

(7) Protection of the individual and society from the social, economic, and moral waste of the liquor traffic.

(8) Conservation of health.

(9) Protection of the worker from dangerous machinery, occupational diseases, and mortality.

(10) The right of all men to the opportunity for self-maintenance, and for the protection of workers from the hardships of enforced unemployment.

(11) Suitable provision for the old age of workers, and for those incapacitated by injury.

(12) The right of employees and employers alike to organize for adequate means of conciliation and arbitration in industrial disputes.

(13) Release from employment one day in seven.

(14) Gradual and reasonable reduction of hours of labor to the lowest practicable point, and for that degree of leisure for all which is a condition of the highest human life.

(15) A living wage as minimum in every industry, and for the highest wage that each industry can afford.

(16) A new emphasis upon the application of Christian principles to the acquisition and use of property, and for the most equitable division of the product of industry that can ultimately be devised (Hopkins, 1940:316–317).

A major area of concern of the social gospel was race and ethnic relations. However, a far from unified opinion was expressed in the writings produced by the social gospelers concerning both immigrants and Blacks. In fact, both nonracist social gospelers and racist ones can be found. In addition, some changed their attitude toward race relations over time. One example was Josiah Strong—his *Our Country* was one of the most nativistic tracts ever written—who later became a strong advocate of racial justice (White and Hopkins, 1976:113, Strong, 1914:159). What factors would cause the social gospel to have such an ambivalent attitude toward minorities, the very poor and oppressed groups they desired to help? Probably one of the major reasons was the vision that social gospelers and other white Protestants had of a homogeneous Christian civilization that would in America set the stage for the establishment of the Kingdom of God on earth. As long as the immigrants were Protestant and rather easily assimilable into American culture, they were not seen as a threat to the future religious utopia. However, once the source of immigration turned toward the Catholic nations of eastern and southern Europe, accompanied also by the immigration of nonchristian Asians and Jews, the Protestant establishment was forced to react to the perceived challenge to its hegemony.

Lawrence Davis (1973) has written an important study of changing Baptist attitudes toward immigrants, among both Baptist social gospelers and traditionalists, focusing on the period between 1880 and World War I. He argues that up until the 1880s, Baptists expressed a strong faith that Protestantism could convert all newcomers and mold the nation's culture; thus, America's open-door policy toward immigration was justified. The major exception early in the 1880s was the Baptist position toward Chinese immigration, which was one of complete restriction, because it was argued the Chinese would never assimilate (L. Davis, 1973:21). But, by the end of the 1880s, Baptists had come to regard most immigrants as undesirables whose customs and beliefs threatened the very foundations of our society. The incoming tide of new immigrants—Poles, Italians, Slavs, Russians, Jews—was regarded as a potentially debasing influence that would destroy God's intentions for a Protestant, ethnically homogeneous America. Not only were arguments put forward to the effect that the new immigrants were biologically inferior to the peoples of northern and western Europe, in addition, Catholics were labelled as religiously inferior because of their stubborn refusal to convert to Protestantism (L. Davis, 1973:40, 86–88). Failed Baptist attempts to Protestantize Catholics largely accounted for the sectarians' negative attitude toward "popish" immigrants. Conversion of Catholics to the Baptist faith was numerically a giant failure. For example, by 1921 there were only fourteen Polish Baptist churches in the United States, with 1,400 members (L. Davis, 1973:96, 112). Throughout the 1890s, liberal and conservative Baptists, social gospelers, and those who preached individual salvation alike, expressed disdain for Catholicism. Following the Haymarket riot of 1886, immigrants were accused of bringing in socialist and anarchist ideas that might subvert American democratic and free-market institutions (L. Davis, 1973:58, 66). A major voice speaking out against the predominant anti-immigration trend was Walter Rauschenbusch, who continued to believe in the possibility of a cosmopolitan interpretation of an all-inclusive American race. His was one of the few pro-immigrant voices among Baptists in the 1890s, and throughout his life Rauschenbusch fought against restrictive immigrant legislation (L. Davis, 1973:82, 95). However, another social gospeler, Charles Henderson, proved that a liberal outlook on religion did not necessarily imply a pro-immigrant attitude. In 1888, Henderson urged Baptists to make every effort to wean Polish-Americans away from the Roman Catholic church, and characterized the Poles as "ignorant, riotous, and dangerous to social peace" (L. Davis, 1973:112). Davis (p. 162) summarized the relationship between the social gospel and the new immigrants as follows:

> The social gospel created a milieu in which a new receptivity toward persons of the Old World would be possible, but this does not follow inevitably from its premises. When combined with an ardent moralism, as in the case of Samuel Zane Batten, the new theology could lead to all the anomalies of the progressive mind, one of which was a concern for the immigrant as the victim of his environment along with severe criticism of non-Protestant nationalities. Not only Batten, but Leighton Williams and Charles Henderson, allowed themselves to be swept up in this type of thinking, which demonstrates that little positive correlation in fact existed between one's involvement in the social gospel and his participation in the increasingly liberal attitude toward eastern Europeans. Only when social Christianity kept its concern for the spiritual in balance did its general outlook help to bring about a pro-immigrant disposition.

In the twentieth century, Baptist attitudes toward immigrants began to change favorably as did those of Presbyterians, Congregationalists, Methodists, and Episcopalians largely as a result of mission work among immigrants and contacts with those who did convert to Protestantism (L. Davis, 1973:136, 160). By World War I, Baptists had made such a turn-about in their opinion of immigrants that they did not join the anti-foreign sentiment of the war period and later stood up as a denomination in opposition to the National Origins Act (L. Davis, 1973:190).

Norris Magnuson (1977) has also documented that changing attitudes toward immigrants were the result of contacts between them and evangelical social workers and mission workers at the turn of the twentieth century. Missionaries' attitudes tended to be more sympathetic than those expressed by the social gospelers. Similarly, those involved in the settlement house movement were less prejudiced and more active in working for immigrants than other progressives (A. Davis, 1967:xiii). All of these studies point to the fact that the religious groups that had genuine close contacts with minority groups tended to develop more positive opinions about them. However, this affirmative result was not true for all. Although most settlement workers avoided the nativist movement, both Robert Woods and James Reynolds joined immigration restriction leagues (Davis, 1967:92–93). Jane Addams, in particular, stood up against xenophobia. She argued that the foreign born should conserve and keep "whatever of value their past life contained," rather than be forced to quickly assimilate to American culture (A. Davis, 1973:72). Addams encouraged the preservation of customs, dress, and language in order that the process of Americanization would not be so harsh as to destroy the older heritage that each group brought with them. Because of her beliefs, Addams created the Labor Museum at Hull House in 1900. Here, she tried to preserve some of the immigrant skills of weaving, pottery-making, and handicrafts that seemed to be threatened by industrialism. Her hope was also that by employing the older skilled artisans as teachers, she could restore some of their pride and confidence, and perhaps give the younger generation some respect for their parents' skills and national heritage (A. Davis, 1973:123–129). The settlement movement emphasized that each immigrant group had something positive to contribute to American culture (Davis, 1967:90).

However, almost none of the settlement workers regarded the immigrants' drinking of alcoholic beverages as a positive contribution to conviviality in America. Instead, settlement workers led by Jane Addams, other social gospelers, the WCTU, and traditional Protestants all attacked the drinking habits of the foreign born and sought to prohibit the sale and use of alcohol nationwide. Allen Davis (1967:82) summarized the attitude of settlement workers toward the saloon as follows:

> Most settlement workers were aware that the saloon provided a natural social center in their neighborhoods. Many were opposed to consumption of alcohol. Every day they observed the effects of over-indulgence on some of the men and their families. They saw the saloon as a refuge for the derelict, the street-gang, the prostitute and the pimp, and also as the source of much political corruption. Most of all, they saw the saloon as leading to the downfall of the young, who were first attracted by its gay and gregarious atmosphere, then trapped by its temptations. Many settlement workers for this reason came to support prohibition as a method of social reform even though they realized that there were social and economic circumstances that often drove a man to drink—poverty, living in an overcrowded room, working at a meaningless job. . . . At least part of the settlement workers'motivation in campaigns to make social centers out of schools, parks and libraries came from the attempt to find a social substitute for the saloon.

Joseph Gusfield (1963:3–5) has argued that the anti-drinking campaign directed at Catholic immigrants was really a "symbolic crusade" waged by native American Protestants who supported temperance or abstinence ideals, and who did not wish to see their beliefs ignored by the newly arrived followers of the pope. The larger the influx of non-Protestant peoples, the greater became the symbolic importance of the drinking issue as a means of distinguishing morally between the reputable and the disreputable. Abstinence was urged upon the immigrant by Protestants; the new arrival was to demonstrate that he was developing middle-class habits of industry, frugality, and sobriety.

Certainly these factors created a deep ambivalence in the Catholic community concerning the dominant Protestant culture and its attempts to help the immigrants adjust to life in America. By 1890, two groups had appeared within the Catholic church's leadership, one group supporting rapid assimilation, the Americanizers, and the other urging the preservation of one's home culture, the nativists (Abell, 1968:xxiv). Anton Walberg, an ultra-nativist, argued in 1889 that immigrants should cultivate, as fully and as long as possible, the language and customs of their respective homelands (Abell, 1968:37–51). Walberg felt that the influences of the Anglo-Americans on the Catholic immigrants was almost as demoralizing as the disastrous effect Whites had had on the Indians. He stated that the Anglo-Americans were preoccupied with material wealth, in the pursuit of which they trampled on every cardinal virtue and practiced every form of refined wickedness. In the decade after Walberg's writings appeared, the battle between the Americanizers and their opponents was fought to a standstill. Each side veered from its original position, finally agreeing that slow, steady Americanization was as desirable as it was inevitable (Abell, 1968:38). The result was the formation of American Catholic social liberalism, which was very closely tied to the social gospel. Its major objectives were taking part in the social gospel crusade for social justice, cooperation with non-Catholics, and rapid Americanization of immigrants (Abell, 1968:xxiv). As early as 1889, the Baltimore Catholic Congress published a document stressing the need for greater cooperation between Catholics and non-Catholics in the areas of philanthropy and social reform (Abell, 1968:182–189). William J. Kerby—professor of sociology at Catholic University for forty years beginning in 1897—in 1900 published an essay in which he attempted to document the potential value of the study of sociology for Catholic theologians and social reformers (Abell, 1968:265–267). His essay is remarkably similar to those produced by Protestant social gospelers who advocated sociological study, and Kerby favorably mentioned the writings of Bliss and Herron. Kerby's work proves that there were ties between leading Catholics and social gospelers at the turn of the century (White and Hopkins, 1976:214–229).

Also essential to an understanding of the social gospel's attitude toward race relations were the perspectives adopted concerning Blacks. In an era characterized by beliefs concerning the innate racial inferiority of Blacks many social gospelers simply went along with prevailing ideology, although a significant number rejected these ideas and advocated full equality of the races. Washington Gladden is a good example of the latter. In the 1890s a staunch supporter of Booker T. Washington and his policy of gradual betterment for Blacks through manual training, Gladden, in 1903, met W.E.B. DuBois and read his *The Souls of Black Folk* (White and Hopkins, 1976:103–107). Gladden came to the conclusion that Washington's stance represented a docile acceptance of the inferior status of Blacks, and switched his support to Dubois's policy of granting Blacks full equality immediately. However, in the 1910s Gladden became more pessimistic about the progress the "talented tenth" had made and rejected the DuBois position.

Like social gospel ministers, settlement workers tended to be ambivalent about Blacks. Although by 1910 there were ten settlements scattered across the country especially for Blacks, many did not want integrated houses because they feared the presence of Blacks would drive the White clients away (Davis, 1967:94–95). As a result, settlement houses tended to be segregated affairs. Settlement workers leaned toward Booker T. Washington rather then DuBois. However, three of the founders of the National Association for the Advancement of Colored People (NAACP), Mary White Ovington, Henry Moskowitz, and William English Walling, all had spent time working in settlement houses. These three were supported and assisted by a number of their settlement house colleagues when the NAACP was organized in 1909 (Davis, 1967:96–102). Jane Addams was elected as one of the thirty-five first members of a permanent NAACP committee "to organize a complete plan of defense for the legitimate rights of the Negro race in this country" (Davis, 1967:102). The Salvation Army, an evangelical reform organization, also tried to deal with problems experienced by Blacks within the urban environment and had Black soldiers as well (Magnuson, 1977:120).

The discussion of the attitudes of reformers toward Blacks leads to the question of whether the social gospel made any inroads into the

South, where the majority of Blacks resided prior to their mass migration to the urban centers of the North. Was the South untouched by the social gospel just as it had largely ignored the reform movements which followed the Second Great Awakening? Although it was long thought that the South did not respond to the social gospel and progressivism, recent studies have shown otherwise (White and Hopkins, 1976:80–97). The major distinction between the northern and southern social gospel was its focus. In the North, urban problems and issues were the major concern, while in the South, which had not as yet experienced the massive industrialization of the North, rural problems such as illiteracy, farm tenancy, and racial discrimination were regarded as important areas for amelioration. Probably the best example of conspicuous Christian involvement in social reform was the work of the Southern Sociological Congress. The congress was originated in 1912 by Ben Hooper, the governor of Tennessee, and an advocate of social reform. More than 700 ministers, educators, social workers, and heads of the health, penal, and welfare institutions assembled in Nashville for a four-day meeting featuring sessions on child welfare, courts and prisons, public health, organized charities, racial problems, and the social mission of the church (White and Hopkins, 1976:84). The Southern Sociological Congress met annually until 1919. Northern social gospelers such as Walter Rauschenbusch, Graham Taylor, and Samuel Zane Batten were invited to address the organization. The most striking parallel to the northern social gospel movement was the "social program" officially adopted by the congress. This statement of purpose sounded very much like the social creed of the Federal Council of Churches, but it also addressed the region's special problems such as racial injustice, the convict-lease system then dominant in southern penology, and educational backwardness. The Southern Sociological Congress expressed the common hopes of a large number of socially concerned leaders who believed that the churches were essential and natural allies in any movement for social betterment.

A leader in the fight against racial injustice in the South was Willis D. Weatherford, YMCA Student Secretary for colleges in the South and Southwest. In 1910, Weatherford published *Negro Life in the South*, the first textbook in the field, which by 1916 had been read by

50,000 college men and women (White and Hopkins, 1976:107–113). A supporter of W.E.B. DuBois, Weatherford was aware of the need to change both persons and institutions to bring about genuine equality for Blacks. He was also painfully aware of how the Bible had been used by racists to justify slavery and continued discrimination against Blacks, and called for the establishment of a Biblical theology that would pervade and transform southern society. In 1914, acting as chairman of the Southern Sociological Congress's annual meeting, Weatherford ended the practice of segregating White and Black delegates at the convention; Blacks sat on the main floor with the White delegates for the first time. This event forced the congress to move from a Memphis theater to a local church but gained Weatherford new respect in the Black community (White and Hopkins, 1976:93–94). Unfortunately, the problem of locating hotels and convention facilities that would allow integrated meetings continued to plague the Southern Sociological Congress and its successor, the Southern Sociological Society, through the 1950s (Simpson, 1988). Nevertheless, the southern social gospel movement can be credited as an early forerunner of the civil rights movement.

Two final areas of intense social gospel concern were the economic and political institutions of American society. Almost all of the social gospelers stopped short of advocating socialism as the economic or political model America should adopt. Although capitalism was perceived to be a system that was causing tremendous social suffering and dislocation, most felt that reforming the institution through making it more equitable to all was sufficient and none advocated a violent Marxist-type revolution.

Washington Gladden (1886:34) sought to Christianize capitalist economics by giving workers a fixed portion of the profits made by their particular firm. Thus, Gladden advocated an early version of profit-sharing as the solution to the low wage problem. If corporate industrialists would only see the management of their businesses as a form of stewardship, they would begin to treat workers as human beings and ultimately as brothers. Employers must provide disability pensions for those injured in factory accidents, become concerned about the physical health and safety of workers, and remake the workplace into an environment that was bright, airy, and comfortable so that workers would be more contented (Gladden, 1888:38, 175–176). Gladden (1886:87–89, 125) strongly supported labor unions but was against the establishment of a central government bureaucracy to regulate the industrial life of the nation. In his mind, supply and demand economics must continue—because it worked—although the system needed modifications to insure that workers were protected.

Similarly, Francis Greenwood Peabody sought to Christianize or spiritualize American industry rather than dismantle it. Peabody (1900:277) argued that Jesus' teachings concerning industrial life focused upon directing the forces of ambition and emulation away from economic satisfaction and toward spiritual ends, as exemplified by the passage, "Lay not up for yourselves treasures upon the earth, but lay up for yourselves treasures in heaven." The Christian administration of one's business could become the industrialists' contribution to the Kingdom of God. A modified version of capitalism could work, and the present system's injustices alleviated. Peabody (1900:287) rejected socialism, arguing that Jesus was not a socialist, although he believed that Jesus' social teachings certainly seemed compatible with socialism.

Walter Rauschenbusch, however, took a more critical stance toward American capitalism and came closer to advocating socialism than either Gladden or Peabody. Rauschenbusch (1945:113) argued that capitalism was sinful because it brought with it human misery, discontent, bitterness, and demoralization. The purpose of the capitalistic system was not to supply human needs but to make a profit for those who directed industry. Because its consideration for human life was secondary, the free market system was fundamentally unchristian (Rauschenbusch, 1912:313). Arguing that the thrust of the Christian message was in behalf of the poor and oppressed in society, Rauschenbusch (1907:361, 1910:51–52, 1912:419) urged strong support for labor unions seeking justice from management, the end of the practice of child labor, compensation in cases of disablement or death through industrial accident or occupational disease, pensions in old age, and care for working women during the period of maternity. However, even these reforms would not complete the necessary transformation of the American economy. Rauschenbusch (1945:113,

1912:311, 1910:62) looked forward to a day when a socialistic type economy would govern itself, without the necessity of employers, and the workplace would become a cooperative fraternal environment. In a statement that shows similarity to Marx's faith in the revolutionary potential of the proletariat, Rauschenbusch (1907:414) argued that "Christianity should enter into a working alliance with the rising class, and by its mediation secure the victory of these principles by a gradual equalization of social opportunity and power."

Just as the social gospel had no united opinion about how best to Christianize the economy, it also held varying attitudes on how to approach politics and whether this would require sacralizing the state. However, almost all wanted to retain the traditional Constitutional separation between church and state rather than institute a Christian theocracy or Christian socialism. Walter Rauschenbusch, James Melville Coleman (1903:59), and Shailer Mathews all agreed on retaining the traditional separation of church and state but hoped to modify political policies with social reform leanings. Mathews's stand on this issue was nearest the consensus viewpoint. He (1918:57) held that Christianity did not have a revolutionary attitude toward the state and civil authority, and that, in fact, Christians were to be model citizens. While church and state as institutions should be kept separate, politics and religion should not and are indeed fundamentally interrelated (1910:59). It is the state's function to support and enforce morality in the society, and morality's source is, of course, religion. Similarly, although the Christian gospel as a message of divine deliverance was separate from any specific political programs, that gospel was to have a bearing on politics (1910:58). Mathews (1910:59, 61) argued that what was needed was for Christians to enter politics and to go about Christianizing legislation by subjecting it to an ethical test: "Does this legislation bring about justice?" The resulting remedial legislation might not cure all of America's evils simply by enacting laws, stated Mathews (1910:132), but in his opinion there were few ills that could be cured without morally based laws. Mathews's position was a challenge to the political stance of Sumner and other laissez-faire theorists, who advocated avoiding tampering with the current system. Mathews (1910:149) concluded that although the church as a church should not enter politics, it should train its members to go into politics as Christians and seek to bring about justice.

Both Josiah Strong and Washington Gladden were in agreement with Mathews's approach. Strong (1898:105, 67) argued that American cities especially needed Christian politicians, who would combat the bosses and political machines that had taken control of municipal politics and were blocking social reform. Gladden (1886:101) believed that the role of the present state could be modified by the influence of Christians to increase its duties, e.g., passing legislation that would aid the poor, alter patterns of taxation, or repress monopolies.

However, none of these ministers wanted to replace American democracy with some other form of political system. Although the American government had not as yet fulfilled its promise of delivering justice, the social gospelers were optimistic that the state could be easily modified to carry out its Biblical mandate. As a result, there was no need to discuss alternative models of the state or propose violent political change. The social gospelers, although many had read Marx, did not believe a socialist state was necessary. Rauschenbusch, for example, proposed only a communistic factory workplace but not a socialist state.

However, the major proponent of a more radical approach to the current political situation was George Herron, the most socialistic of all the social gospelers. Herron hoped to break down the boundaries between church and state and replace American democracy with a communitarian theocracy. The state must become Christian, making Christ and His political teachings, as discussed in the Sermon on the Mount, the supreme authority in law, politics, and society (Herron, 1893:29, 30). American democracy had failed to live up to Christ's standards and must be replaced. However, Herron (1895:20) felt that the transition to a theocracy could take place peacefully, without the necessity of violent revolution. The major function of the new Christian state would be to bring about God's purposes in history; the state must be the organ for carrying out God's will on earth (Herron, 1895:54, 57). The state must direct the nation toward social justice—i.e., socialism— and collectively lead the people toward social perfection. The newly Christian state could assist in the final preparations for the Kingdom of

God on earth, establishing the very conditions that would mandate its consummation. America would then be prepared for its millennial role as the great moral voice and force for the entire world. Herron (1895:68) stated:

> A Christian national policy would compel the state, not only to refrain from doing evil to our neighbor nations, but to do them good. As a Christian nation we are bound to sacrifice ourselves in procuring justice for Japan, in giving freedom to the Russians, in helping to save united Italy from disaster, in protecting Armenian Christians, as we are to defend our shores from foreign invasion.

Herron's statement can be viewed as prophetic, in the sense that after the two world wars, America did rise to a position of world leadership, and assuming that its ways were morally superior, accepted that it had a mission to protect the world from evil.

In summary, the social gospel was a key factor in the establishment of sociology in America. In addition, American sociology's initial agenda was in large measure set by social gospel theology. Having briefly noted the attitudes expressed by the social gospelers on such issues as politics, economics, immigrants and Blacks, the poor, labor, cities, the family, feminism, and the church, we now turn to an examination of the thinkers who represented the mainstream of American sociology during the late nineteenth and early twentieth centuries to see how they responded to these social problems.

PART II

CHAPTER 4

Protestant Theology in Mainstream American Sociology

The University of Chicago

Sociology established itself as a legitimate intellectual subject, worthy of a place in American academia, early in the 1890s. During its first three decades, American sociology was profoundly influenced by social gospel thought. The goal of this section is to document the relationship between social Christianity and mainstream American sociological thought. First to be considered will be Albion Small's sociology department at the University of Chicago. Small set the early course not only for Chicago sociology, but for much of American sociology as well. Besides Small, three of his Chicago colleagues, Charles Henderson, George Vincent, and Marion Talbot will also be discussed. Charles Ellwood took Chicago's brand of "Christian sociology" to the University of Missouri.

In the next chapter, sociology at the University of Wisconsin will be covered. Richard T. Ely and E.A. Ross established another beachhead for social Christianity at the University of Wisconsin, and there were able to sacralize the state government, turning it into an experiment showing how the social gospel might be able to reform the entire nation. Charles Cooley, who taught at the University of Michigan, was to be strongly influenced by the social gospel's emphasis on Christian community and brotherhood in his writings on the family, primary groups, and childhood socialization.

Although William Graham Sumner cannot legitimately be labelled a social gospeler, his sociological theory can be shown to represent a secularized version of another form of Protestant theology. Sumner, who vehemently opposed almost every idea put forward by the social gospelers, sought to establish American sociology as a secularized version of Calvinist theology. Sumner will be discussed in chapter 6.

Albion Small (1854–1926) was asked by President William Rainey Harper in 1892 to come to the University of Chicago and found a department of sociology, the first such department in the world. Small accepted the challenge, welcoming the opportunity to bring his version of Christian sociology to full fruition. Small was the son of a Baptist minister, had gone to Colby College—a Baptist college in Maine—and then trained for the ministry at Newton Theological Seminary. Small spent the next two years (1879–1881) studying in Germany, in Berlin and Leipzig. Most American intellectuals of this era spent time studying abroad. Small's interest in German sociology was to be a lifetime devotion. After returning to the United States, Small went back to Colby, teaching history and introducing sociology, from 1881 to 1888. In 1889 he took a one-year leave and obtained a Ph.D. in history at Johns Hopkins under Richard T. Ely. He returned once again to Colby, this time to serve as its president, until Harper called him to Chicago in 1892, where he served as department chairman until his death in 1926 (Dibble, 1975:2). At Chicago, Small attempted to mold American sociology into a holistic discipline that would aid in bringing about the Kingdom of God on earth.

Probably the best way to understand Small's prophetic vision of sociology is through reading his sermons. Although Small never took a pastorate, he was a lay preacher throughout his life and frequently participated in Baptist congresses. See, for example, *American Journal of Sociology*, Vol. 1:2, p. 231, which announces Small's participation at a Baptist congress. Within his sermons Small outlined his beliefs concerning the Kingdom of God and clearly reveals their social gospel roots. Ultimately, it was his theology that led him to espouse certain sociological theories while rejecting others. Thus, any analysis of Small's sociology must begin with his view of the Kingdom.

In Small's theology the major purpose of Jesus' life was not to create a solitary path for individuals to travel in order to enter the afterlife but to revolutionize social relations within the world so that all might dwell in the Kingdom of God on earth. Jesus stressed the social side of human nature over the selfish, individualistic side. Therefore, Jesus' message could now be recognized as the vitalizer of every moral and religious growth that has benefitted humanity in the Western world. This was the social meaning of Jesus' promise to bring about a "more abundant life" and to Christ's personal demonstration of how man could fulfill his destined self. Jesus' aim was "more life and better life"; human beings should progress from their selfish lower states to higher, more cooperative ones (Small, 1915:186). "Jesus was ready to scrap former rules of life whenever he found them hindering more than they promoted the expansion of life" (Small, 1915:186).

Jesus, as the all-knowing judge, was to be the final arbiter in all disputes or conflicts involving human groups and their selfish interests. Since Jesus knew what was best in the long run for all groups involved in competition or conflict, he made all his judgments for the good of all humanity. Small stated that "Jesus' Kingdom means the largest conception that can be entertained in a given situation, of the entire community of interests which fixes the proportional rating of all contending special interests" (Small, 1913b:81). Jesus' legacy was a community of believers dedicated to this high purpose. "For nineteen centuries Christians have been preaching and trying to believe that we are members one of another, that we must work together in order to live ourselves out" (Small, 1896a:401). Christians must seek first God's Kingdom, and His righteousness, and then all things would be added unto them (Small, 1913b:78). There was no hope of putting human affairs on a satisfactory basis until human beings consider first not the individual, but the entire moral order: this was the meaning of Jesus' Kingdom (Small, 1913b:79).

Thus the final arbiter of individual worth would be a person's merits as a factor in the well-being of the whole of society. But the Kingdom would not come without a cost, and Jesus recognized that sacrifice would be required to bring about a better world (Small, 1915:188). "The world will reach the crest of its prosperity when we learn the full economy of each person's sacrifice, and when each person volunteers his kind of sacrifice for the good of the whole" (Small, 1915:189). Theologically, Small was giving additional sacred significance to one's "calling," following a long line of Protestant thought that can be traced back to Luther (Weber, 1930). Occupations must now, according to Small, sacrificially serve humanity as well as God. Unfortunately, throughout most of history, sacrifice had been involuntarily demanded of certain portions of society rather than freely offered. But human life would not be genuinely spiritualized until it had become genuinely socialized (Small, 1915:193). Socialization, as Small used the term, referred to the attempt to replace selfish individualism with social cooperation.

Although Small's source of revelation for these ideas was his Christian faith, he felt that science, logic, and reason would also lead humankind inevitably to the very same conclusion about the social meaning of life. Thus sociology and theology were complementary and not competing frames for viewing reality. Christianity, sociology, social work, and social reform would all share the same perspective and work jointly toward the goal of helping bring about the Kingdom. "Whether we arrive at this principle through the traditions of religion, or through direct perception—i.e., working in the slums in a settlement house—or through the findings of social science, it is the only secure foundation for society" (Small, 1913b:80). Small argued that all of the following were synonymous phrases: Kingdom of God, human society, natural law, the moral order, social justice, and "the welfare of all." Jesus had been anticipating modern sociology when he said "Seek ye first the Kingdom of God" (Small, 1913b:80). It is essential to recognize when reading the works of early Christian sociologists that Kingdom and society are interchangeable concepts.

Small's grand theory, with which he hoped to encompass all of social reality, can be seen as a translation of his theology into a secular social scientific language that would be acceptable to all intellectuals, whether Christian or not. In his sociological writings Small usually tried to shy away from employing theological concepts so that his theories would be evaluated on their scientific merit and not written off as religious dogmas. Small regarded social life as an organic unity or whole, and borrowed frequently from Spencer's metaphor of society as a biological organism (Small and Vincent, 1894:91). This aspect of Spencer's thought fit nicely with Small's interpretation of society as the Christian community at large, gradually bringing about social cooperation—the secular equivalent of fellowship.

However, Small could accept neither Spencer's individualism nor his laissez-faire attitude toward social reform. Small also rejected William Graham Sumner's Spencerian sociology, because in Small's mind such a social model was fundamentally unchristian. Small rejected individualism wherever it reared its head, whether it be in evangelical Christian theology, Spencerian sociology, classical economics, or laissez-faire political science.

> We are today recognizing the total fallacy of the individualistic interpretation of life. The dependence of individuals is the first law of life. . . . We are just as fatally at odds with the final law of life if we suppose the center of things is a plan for our soul's salvation, as if we assume that the moral fulcrum is a scheme of individual rights in economic competiton (Small, 1913b:78–79).

He praised the economic theories of Adam Smith because Smith had not reduced human beings to "economic men," a tendency later economists were guilty of (Small and Vincent, 1894:43).

From his Christian presuppositions, Small created a teleological theory about the direction or development of human society in history. Discovering the teleological pattern in history became Small's first step in establishing an intellectually adequate sociology. Only when he knew the end of the social process, could he estimate the value of different or current activities in relation to the ongoing social process. Once the end of history was known, Small could then bifurcate all of social reality; those activities were good which promoted social progress, and labelled as bad were those that retarded it (Small, 1904:28). Of course, he believed he had already uncovered the teleological direction of history in his reading of the Bible, and specifically in the rediscovery of Jesus' social mission. Jesus' goal of bringing a more abundant life for all was translated by Small into a theory of the gradual working out of conflicting "interests" in social life. The abundant life was to encompass all of mankind's interest:

health, wealth, sociability, knowledge, aesthetics, and righteousness. Small (1908a:433–438) argued that he had discovered the notion of interests in Ratzenhofer's sociology—which he had studied while in Germany—but actually chose to employ this model because it gave specificity to the rather vague concept of "the abundant life." Small's theory of the gradual social improvement that has characterized history can be summarized in his most famous sociological axiom: "Society, or human association, is a continuous process of realizing a larger aggregate and better proportions of the six interests" (Small, 1900:202).

Small's view of the psychologically well-adjusted individual was identical to his theory of a well-balanced society: "The life of the individual is a process of achieving the self that is potential in the six interests which prompt all human desires" (Small, 1900:202). The individual was, in effect, the society writ small. The individual was to ideally express equally all of the six interests, while at the same time being willing to sacrifice his own desires so that others could be allowed an opportunity to maximize their interests. In order to give credence to such an optimistic view of human society, Small included a positive belief concerning human nature in his theories. Small believed that human beings were fundamentally "cooperating animals" (Small and Vincent, 1894:61). As a result, history would be characterized by a gradual movement toward increased cooperation, since this was part of mankind's telos. Small's opinion concerning the modern division of labor incorporated the same faith that specialization, integration, and interdependence of parts led inevitably toward social progress (Small and Vincent, 1894:99).

The direction of history had been from more primitive expressions of the interests to modern, morally superior ones. For example, the wealth interest had moved from the selfish collection of material possessions to the trusteeship of wealth. Similarly, the aesthetic interest had changed from "delights in the hideous" to the "deification of beauty" (Small and Vincent, 1894:176). Small's own brand of ethnocentrism was incorporated into his analysis of the evolutionary change in the righteousness interest: "The Chinaman devoutly burns his stick of incense before the Joss: the earnest Christian aspires to live in harmony with the omnipotent and loving Creator and

Ruler of the universe" (Small and Vincent, 1894:177). In another essay, Small (1904:38–46) lists all the major achievements that modern society has made in its expression of the six interests. Medicine, sanitation, police, fire protection, and improvements in housing represent the health interest. The wealth interest has been modified by modern industry, machinery, skilled labor, transportation, communication, trade, and commerce. Positive changes in sociability are evidenced by political rights, labor laws, labor unions, reform movements, pension and insurance systems, and social settlements. The knowledge interest is expressed best in modern science including sociology and ethics, and the spread of knowledge through public education. Modern literature, painting, music, and the other arts demonstrate progress in the aesthetic or beauty interest. Finally, religion or righteousness has shifted from spiritual interests in the other world to an emphasis upon life in the present world, and the sphere of religious activities has enlarged to include local, national, and international concerns. Small's conclusion was that the next principal stage in the social process would be essentially ethical and intellectual. The "social movement"—i.e., the social gospel—was itself a sign of human advancement, argued Small (1897b:345).

Small's description of the improving nature of the various interests demonstrated his faith in evolutionary progress. But, like the social gospel ministers, Small also noted the terrible negative consequences that had accompanied industrialization, urbanization, and modernization and labelled these as social problems. Again, Small echoed the social gospel in his focus upon ridding American society of problems which were standing in the way of the final consummation of the Kingdom.

However, despite his similarity in outlook to the social gospel, he expressed a deep-seated ambivalence about the "Christian sociology" of his day. This can be accounted for primarily as a result of the fact that although Small remained a "believer" in Christianity throughout his life; because of his social science training he believed he had transcended his religious upbringing. This serves to explain why Small spoke so negatively about much of what had been labelled Christian sociology in the 1890s. What most Christians who were becoming involved in sociology lacked was a broad enough vision about the complex nature of social reality, the coming Kingdom, and how to best bring it about. Small felt that his brand of sociology could supply the necessary holistic view of the social process the social gospel lacked.

The following examples from Small's writings illustrate his ambivalent feelings about the social gospel and Christian sociology. In his inaugural essay in the first issue of the *American Journal of Sociology*, Small (1895a:15) says:

> To many possible readers the most important question about the conduct of the Journal will be with reference to its attitude toward "Christian Sociology." The answer, is in a word, toward Christian sociology, sincerely deferential, toward alleged "Christian sociologists" severely suspicious.

In his introductory textbook written with George Vincent, Small (1894:19, 32, 38) made these comments:

> The most dangerous social doctrinaires among us are not the theoretical anarchists who attack social order directly, but those zealous prophets of righteousness who teach that the only reason why the Kingdom of God cannot be established on earth tomorrow is that Christians will not put their knowledge of social principles into practice.... Christian purpose and aspiration cannot furnish technical skill or information. Piety without knowledge of facts would work disaster in politics and economics.... Sociology is just now passing through a stage of struggle for the application of scientific principles of investigation, in place of loose criticism and silly utopianism.... The faults of the Christian Socialists have been those of zeal without knowledge. They have been more eager to prescribe social remedies than to acquire precise understandings of social conditions. Like certain men who prefer to call themselves Christian Sociologists, they have been inclined to quarrel with economic facts rather than to discover the real meaning of the facts.

While Small cited the Christian Socialist movement in England, such as J.F.D. Maurice and Charles Kingsley, and Christian sociologists in the United States as a major force in the establishment of sociology as a discipline, he remained ambivalent about their continued input into sociological theorizing, and extremely critical of any "schemes of social salvation" they might devise without an adequate sociological basis (Small and Vincent, 1894:32, 37–38).

In what represents the major seeming paradox in Small's sociology, he then went on to argue that a theory of social reality based solely on Jesus' thought or the Bible is inadequate. However, we have already seen that Small did just that himself, in developing his theory of the social process upon the Biblical principle of "the abundant life." Small's way out of his self-created paradox was to argue that once all the facts were in, Christianity would be proven to be ethically nonethnocentric, and thus able to be applied universally. However, such a conclusion could only be drawn at the end of a long study of other perspectives, not prior to investigation. In one of his most revealing essays, "The Limits of Christian Sociology" (1896b:510), he attacked "narrow-minded" religious social scientists who fail to be as thorough as he:

> Whether Jesus taught more or less truth that must be assimilated in ultimate sociology, that truth was very small—in form at least—an incidental portion of his whole teaching. . . . The belief of Christians that everything which Jesus taught is true, seems to be changed by some zealous Christians into the form "nothing which Jesus omitted to teach is true." . . . Its platform is "Christ knew everything; therefore, by virtue of calling myself a Christian, I know everything." Consequently men who understand neither Christianity nor sociology assume the right to call themselves "Christian sociologists" and to teach their own version of both. We do not object to the use of the term "Christian Sociology," but we decidedly object to ignorant and opinionated abuse of it. The fundamental principles of human relationship which Jesus expounded must be recognized and applied in any permanent successful social program. . . . However, this does not exhaust the subject matter of sociology.

Small continually repeated that one could not use Jesus as a justification to sacralize any one program of bringing about social reform and considered such claims made by Christian sociologists to be fraudulent.

The New Testament leads us in the direction of the best social progress. The Christian revelation means that right is sovereign and will prevail, but Jesus did not profess to furnish specifications that would inform us in advance what the specific right is in all the changing complexities of life (Small, 1898b:347).

The importance of Jesus' message does not lie in a blueprint for structures, but of presenting us with the moral attitude a man ought to take up when creating structures or performing tasks. . . . If there are people who think they can go to the Bible and get ready-made solutions to our labor problems . . . they are doomed to be not only disappointed but dangerous. Yet, Jesus touched on the problem of poverty as it was known in his day. In telling people how to act about the bare necessities of life—Matthew 6:25–34—Jesus reveals the secret of all permanent social harmony (1913b:73, 76).

Small clearly demonstrated that he believed a social scientist must transcend Christianity in order to gain a total picture of reality. Sociology must be more than social principles deduced solely from the Bible.

Let us grant that the New Testament contains the nucleus of all that men need to know about the spirit of ideal human society. Let us assume human life since men have peopled the earth; the reactions between human groups and their physical environments; between groups and their units, between groups and contemporary groups; between groups and their posterity. From all these facts and from such of them as can be discovered, we have to learn the laws of cause and effect, physical and psychical, to which or by means of which approach to the Christian ideal is to be accomplished. To say that this field of knowledge does not exist or to say that it is within the scope of New Testament records is puerile perversity with which argument is impossible (1896b:511).

Small called for study in such fields as sociology, history, anthropology, political science, and ethics to augment Christian theology in establishing a holistic portrait of human society. Small (1895a:13) also advocated the introduction of European social thought so that the American vision of a just society could be broadened and universalized. Sociology, as the "queen of the sciences"—a concept borrowed from Comte—would be responsible for assimilating the data provided by the other social sciences (Small and Vincent, 1894:54). Since this task was itself tremendous, Small advocated holding back on social reform attempts until many more facts were in, so that ignorant mistakes would not be made that would throw the social process off course.

> Men are so anxious to solve social problems that they have no time to study society. The shortest way to reach the ability to solve social problems is not to try to solve them at all for a long time, but to learn how to state them (Small, 1897a:152).

Once this task was accomplished sociology would be a genuinely scientific discipline through its coordination of the knowledge gathered by all the disciplines and its discovery of the laws of society. Only then was that scientific knowledge to be made available for the amelioration of society (Small, 1903a:468; 1908b:11). Small (1898a:114) defined the "social problem" as the problem of knowing society, both actually and potentially, its current condition and its presumed future.

Small tended to follow the same division of sociological theory and reform advocated by another pioneer American sociologist, Lester Ward. Static sociology represented "the study of what is," while dynamic sociology was the attempt to improvise models of social reform that would move society to where it ought to be (Small, 1895c:195). Small chose to concentrate his talents on the former, though he never lost sight of the ultimate goal, creating a dynamic sociology that would guarantee the arrival of the properly envisioned future.

In his own personal journey to become a man of knowledge through exposing himself to the social sciences, Small reached a position regarding science and religion quite different from the one chosen by William Graham Sumner. Although both came from devout Christian backgrounds, Sumner felt he had to ignore Christianity's claim that it offered absolute truth while Small did not. Primarily through the study of anthropology, Sumner came to the conclusion that truth is a culturally produced and culture-bound phenomenon and developed the idea of ethnocentrism to explain the relativity of all social knowledge, including Christianity. Small's response to the Christian faith was to try to construct a synthesis of all knowledge, including the Bible, in order to arrive at absolute truth. Small believed that such a synthesis would thus include Christianity and transcend it at the same time.

By combining Christian truth and other "truths" Small hoped to create a nonethnocentric view of the world and ultimately a system of morality that all could live by. Sociology would then have a major significance in the field of ethics, because only through sociological study could one establish ultimate values (Small, 1903b). Small rarely backed down from his claim of being able to construct absolute morals. He believed that society was gradually moving toward conformity to universal moral values that the sociologist could discover (Small, 1913b:80). Small did not dispute the fact that there are many subgroups in a society that would hold conflicting values. In fact, such an idea was an integral part of Small's theory that interest group conflicts were a natural part of the contemporary social order. However, Small argued that there was enough agreement between conflicting groups for them to establish core values that are the basis of consensus in society. This common will or consensus was the result of the community of thought and feeling shared by all human groupings (Small and Vincent, 1894:349–350). Once again, it is quite evident that Small had returned to the Christian concepts of "community" and "fellowship" to underpin his sociology.

The closest Small came to admitting the possibility of relative values was in a discussion of his ideas on "social health" and "social disease" (Small and Vincent, 1894:267–268). He stated that current attempts to develop the concept of "social normality" led to the conclusion that it was a relative term, because a system of ethics had not yet been universally accepted. Although society was moving toward a consensus of values, it was still far from adopting absolute standards. But, even though humankind had as yet only a tentative understanding of social health, some things were clearly normal or abnormal. While phenomena such as the theater, ballrooms, and saloons were "gray areas" open to question, obvious pathological conditions included such conditions as unsanitary tenements, poverty, vice, crime, machine politics, child and female labor, dangerous occupations, and even the traditional church (Small and Vincent, 1894:271, 286, 296). Small attacked the traditional church's attitudes toward social problems as being pathological for a number of reasons: the church had been concerned with future happiness rather than this-worldly interests, regarded unjust social conditions as God's means of testing individual character—the social gospel's assumption was that social problems were God's testing of a people's or nation's character—argued that all earthly inequalities would be made right in heaven, held to the belief that the world was fundamentally evil, and had divided the activities of life into separate "secular" and "religious" spheres.

Despite his cautions to those attempting to uncover social normality, Small never wavered from his conviction that sociology was not only a historical and descriptive science but a critical and ideal one as well. Sociology must use all of the social facts at its disposal as the raw material for creating social ideals. Sociology was ultimately an ethical discipline, an account of society as it ought to be, and the only basis for social ethics (Small and Vincent, 1894:65–67).

Obviously, Small's version of social ethics must be superior to that of all others, including those of other social gospelers, because his ideals took into account the complexities of social reality; most others sought to offer limited perspectives—e.g., religious—of the world. Small presumed that his version of sociology was the correct one and proceeded to establish himself as the "gatekeeper" of the discipline, both in its social gospel form and its more secular variations. Small had at his disposal a very powerful tool, the *American Journal of Sociology*—which he founded in 1895 and served as chief editor of until his death in 1926—to accomplish this task. Small used the articles he selected, the book review section, and the short editorials he wrote himself to present his own vision of sociology. Opposing points of view certainly appeared—especially noteworthy are the articles by W.I. Thomas, a fellow Chicago sociologist, whose atheism and "liberal" attitude toward sexuality and women didn't please Small. A whole series of articles written by social gospel ministers, sociologists, and laypersons appeared in the *American Journal of Sociology* while it was under Small's tenure. Examples included essays by Jane Addams

(1896, 1899a, b, 1905, 1912a, 1914); Samual Zane Batten (1902, 1908); John R. Commons (1897, 1898, 1899a, 1899b, 1899c, 1900a, 1900b, 1900c, 1900d, 1908); Arthur Fairbanks (1903); Florence Kelly (1896, 1898a, 1898b, 1899, 1904, 1911); Shailer Mathews (1895a, 1895b, 1895c, 1896a, 1896b, 1896c, 1896d, 1896e, 1896f, 1899, 1900, 1912); Francis Greenwood Peabody (1913); Walter Rauschenbusch (1896, 1897); Josiah Strong (1895); Graham Taylor (1899); Robert Woods (1914); and Carroll D. Wright (1895). Also making frequent contributions were two of Small's allies, Charles Ellwood—who published nineteen articles in the first twenty-five volumes—and E.A. Ross—who wrote an amazing fifty-one articles in the same time period. On the other hand, those that Small opposed—such as Sumner, with only two articles, and Franklin Giddings, with seven articles in the first twenty-five volumes—had few of their ideas expressed in the journal, even though they were leading sociologists.

　　Small also used the book review section as a forum to praise those that he supported—e.g., his (1923a, 1923b) glowing reviews of Charles Ellwood's *The Reconstruction of Religion* and *Christianity and Social Science*—and make critical comments about those whose sociology or theology did not meet his standards, for example, Small's (1913a) review of Rauschenbusch's classic social gospel work *Christianizing the Social Order*—or to attack those he fully disagreed with—e.g., his (1896d) review of Franklin Giddings's *Principles of Sociology*.

　　Two other methods were used by Small to gain control over the domain of sociology and keep out "heretics." One of these methods was personal correspondence. For example, after Small changed his opinion concerning the validity of George Herron's Christian socialism, he wrote to Richard T. Ely informing him that he should no longer associate with Herron. While Small (Small and Vincent, 1894:71) had previously praised Herron's essay on the "The Scientific Ground for a Christian Sociology," Small rejected Herron's turn toward socialism. In an 1894 letter to Ely, Small condemned Herron's sociology as being unsafe, unfactual, and dogmatic. Small argued that Christian sociology was moving from the "saner" Ely to the "dangerous" Herron, and Small could not support such a change of direction. Herron did not first make sure of his "facts" before offering to preach programs (Rader, 1966:134).

The other method Small used to dispose of his enemies and those he considered inadequate sociologists was through historical revisionism. As, in quite different manners, Michel Foucault (1972) and Stanford Lyman (1978b:90–94) have shown, historical knowledge can be used as an aid in legitimating authority, and one whose history has been accepted as a socially legitimated "true" version of the past holds tremendous power. Small (1916) placed himself in such a position by becoming the first historian of American sociology. Small could then attack those he despised, such as Sumner, for attempting to place sociology on the wrong course, and largely ignore fundamental influences in American sociology, such as the excessively moralistic social gospelers, because he felt they were amateurish. Small (1916:732–733) mentioned nothing about Sumner's contributions to American sociology and instead attacked him: "Sumner referred to himself as a sociologist in a book which still seems to me to be a picture of what a sociologist should not be." Small's (1916:771) description of Christian sociologists is limited to one paragraph in which he mentions that a more comprehensive history—Small's work was 140 pages—would include people like Francis Peabody, Graham Taylor, and Jane Addams. Thus, in the first history of American sociology, its Christian roots are already being purposefully forgotten. Those who had refused to follow Small's "revelation" were being excommunicated from the discipline.

Small's (1915:196–197) attempt was to create a division of labor between genuine scientific sociologists and social reformers such as the social gospelers. Even though the two groups needed each other if the task of setting up the kngdom was to be completed successfully, ministers and sociologists must acknowledge the fact that their unique areas of expertise had definite boundaries that should not be crossed. Small was very specific about the separate roles that sociology and theology were to play in remaking the world. He (1895d) summarized his views in a short editorial entitled "Christian Sociology":

> Christianity's relation to social problems is one thing, but its relation
> to the problems of sociology as a science is quite another. . . . Social

science will bring us material, put it in its order, and help us to a
sound understanding of it, and we shall use it more than ever before.
From Christianity we shall get the highest scientific incentive,
inspiration to the love of truth . . . and to the diligent use of scientific
resources.

The assigned tasks for the sociologists and the social gospelers were
clearly demarcated by Small. Sociology's goal was to develop a
scientific "methodology" able to understand the complexities of social
reality. Small did not use the term "methodology" in its modern
sociological sense as empirical or mathematical; he meant by
methodology developing an adequately grounded social theory. Small
showed little concern with developing the type of mathematically
precise analysis and correlations that have come to dominate
positivistic American sociology. Although he did hope to give an
emphasis to the field of statistics, surprisingly he rarely used them in
his own sociology (Diner, 1975:535). But he stressed over and over
again that sociology's major emphasis should be placed on
"methodology," and not reform.

> Sociology is not, first and foremost, a set of schemes to reform the
> world. Sociological methodology has the task of arranging all the
> kinds and sources of knowledge of men to each other (Small,
> 1898a:113).

Sociology's primary task was not to reform society but to understand it
(Small and Vincent, 1894:19). Understanding society required the
employment of two methodological tools. The first was causal analysis
(Small, 1898a:120). Small believed that sociologists, because of their
holistic understanding of all the facts, had the ability to take these facts
and to uncover the laws of cause and effect that guided society and
social interaction. The second tool he (1898a:125) advocated was the
use of abstraction—very similar to Max Weber's ideal types—in order
to discover both the similarities and differences that existed between
the various social groups living in a society.

Small had a great faith that the kind of knowledge to be
produced by sociology would be universally applicable. The current
world's evils existed solely because society had not as yet applied

sociological knowledge to its institutions, which were as yet still inadequately based on defective social knowledge.

> We must recognize that if institutions are defective, it is because they are a reflection of defective social knowledge, and that much information must be gathered before safe substitutes for prevailing social conditions can be derived (Small and Vincent, 1894:19).

At some point in the future sociology would develop knowledge that could once and for all rid evil from the world. Small's faith in knowledge triumphing over evil may seem simplistic today, but during his era many believed as he did.

However, at times Small fought the conclusions to which his ideas seemed to be inevitably leading, that sociological science was to be the final arbiter of truth, the new god of humanity. He recognized that one must make certain to hold the vision of the Kingdom above science.

> We must not make science a god. We must hold about science the vision and intelligent direction of our endeavor to realize the vision (Small, 1896c:564).

Creating and reaffirming the vision, as well as endeavoring to bring that vision to fruition, were the roles Small assigned to the church. In one of his sermons, Small (1913b:82) stated: "Pure religion means taking the next steps toward realizing the Kingdom of God." On another occasion he (Small and Vincent, 1894:38) praised the social gospel for creating the vision.

> The Christian Socialists . . . have done good service in maintaining the position that ultimate sociology must be essentially Christian, because they have led religious leaders of all denominations to see the need to investigate social problems.

Sociological science could not become a god, Small believed, as long as it continued to draw its inspiration from religion, and in particular, social Christianity. Only a science cut off from God would end up deifying itself.

Throughout his career, Small emphasized both the close ties between theology and sociology, and at the same time favored a strict separation or division of labor between sociologists and social reformers. This division was maintained within Small's own department of sociology at Chicago. Charles Henderson was a social gospel minister who had a joint appointment in the sociology department and the divinity school. Small and Henderson seemed to work out their differences amicably.

> Although Henderson's center of attention was betterment, and mine was the methodology of social investigation, we never from the first to the last had the slightest difference of opinion about the division and correlation of our own work and that of our students. Each of us recognized in the other's program the correlate of his own (Small, 1916:770).

Those that were willing to abide by his division of labor Small praised. But those that did not and dared cross the boundary into sociology without displaying willingness to use the proper sociological methodology he despised.

Since true sociologists represented an intellectual, ethical, and spiritual elite in any society, Small argued that the reins of power should be turned over to them. Sociologists were to be the modern day equivalent of Plato's philosopher kings. Obviously, they had special knowledge that was not shared by the common man. While ordinary individuals understood reality from a limited ethnocentric position, sociologists were to seek to gain a "conspectus of all social activities in their interrelations, not to scrutinize separately one department of life" (Small and Vincent, 1894:99). Sociology was the attempt to understand how any particular fragment of human life had a bearing upon the rest of human life (Small, 1903a:468). Sociologists were then to take this unique perspective and apply it for the betterment of society. Small's goal was to use sociology and ultimately the entire university as a board of arbitration to settle societal conflicts of interest, such as management versus labor, manufacturers versus consumers, or the rich versus poor (Small, 1910:697; Dibble, 1975:68). If a particular group's desires or interests were unattainable, sociologists must make this known to the group and educate them to the facts. But if their goals were attainable, sociology should aid the group to achieve its ends (Small, 1897a:170). Small (1895b:100–101) praised groups that relied on facts and experts to go about social reform. The hero of his novel *Between Eras* was a sociologist who was called in to arbitrate a long strike that was caused by seemingly unresolvable conflicts between management and labor. The sociologist Randall points out the faults of both sides' entrenched positions and guides them toward friendly cooperation (Small, 1913b:315). Small's major worry was that sociologists might become prophets without honor, knowing the truth but unable to get anyone to listen to them (Small, 1913b:308). His hope was that current societal leaders would see the necessity of turning over much of their power to sociologists. Needless to say Small's vision never came to be— although the state of Wisconsin did undertake an experiment along these lines under Ely's and Ross's direction—and it appears that the huge growth of the federal and state bureaucracy from the 1930s has served only to co-opt sociology rather than allow sociologists to determine policy.

Although Small was not often specific about just what his vision of the coming Kingdom was, he sometimes spoke openly about the direction American society should take. Small felt he could not support either capitalism as it now existed or any of the more radical forms of socialism because both were not truly Christian. He accused capitalism of being founded upon unchristian principles, and, paradoxically, Small claimed that the entire capitalist structure was being supported by bastardized versions of Christian theology. Small tried to expose both. In his (1920a:693) view, "[t]he corporation is a deathless, supernatural selfishness vested by the state with super-personal powers" and the growth of the corporation had not brought about justice. In *Between Eras: From Capitalism to Democracy*, Small summarized the evils of capitalism. Its acquisitive orientation was clearly unchristian.

> Capitalism is a scheme of cumulative inequality; cynical selfishness masquerading as democracy. . . . Capitalism is an inhuman use of capital. . . . The capitalist view of success is control of the market and it is not considered immoral to concentrate on commercial success . . . but, capitalist success or progress has had to be paid for at a

tremendous cost of pain and sorrow and waste (Small, 1913b:48, 376, 29, 36).

Small (1913b:349) considered the theory that the profits of capitalism will automatically be fairly distributed as an obvious fallacy.

Small (1919b:286) accused Christianity in America—except for the social gospel—of being supportive rather than critical of the materialist ideology that undergirds capitalism. First, the Protestant work ethic had stimulated thrift, prudence, and careful calculation of material advantage but never bothered to ask if such rationalization produces justice. Second, the otherworldly views of much of Protestant theology had ignored materialism through escaping to the "spiritual realm." Small's conclusion was that religion was indirectly responsible for the "valuations of material ends that religious creeds would never directly endorse." The only solution would be to Christianize the economic structures of American society.

> Our historical Christianity has only succeeded in making the spiritual motive supreme in the case of individuals, never making the spiritual motive supreme in a civilization (Small, 1919b:286).

Small did not view socialism as being a viable alternative economic model that could replace capitalism. Small did not agree with Marx's theory—though he did share much of Marx's critique of capitalism—nor did he see eye to eye with Christian socialists like Herron. Small (1912:816) referred to Marx's theory of socialism as not being plausible, possible, desirable, or probable. However, socialism had been helpful in illuminating the plight of those at the bottom of society, which capitalism tended to ignore. Small (1912:815) agreed with Marx's theory of class conflict but argued that Marx did not take seriously the possibility of future class cooperation. Small (1912:816) made the same criticism of Marx's planned social regeneration he had made of the social gospel. "From the standpoint of social science any plan at all for correcting the evil of capitalism is premature until we have probed deeper into the evils themselves."

Small (1895e:276) was searching for an alternative economic structure that would modify capitalism without the necessity of turning to socialism and would ultimately Christianize the economic sphere.

Small made two major proposals that he felt would fundamentally alter capitalism and make it into a morally responsible institution. The first was for the state to intervene and begin to regulate those industries that could be considered "semi-public corporations"—e.g., utilities and railroads (Small, 1896a:398–410). Small believed that the state must act as the insurer of public rights, making ties between the state and business necessary. Corporations must be seen as servants of the public and not its masters. When institutions step out of line, the law should be used to bring them back into line. Small was here opposing Sumner's laissez-faire political stance and making one of the early arguments for governmental intervention to guarantee workers' and consumers' rights.

Small's second suggestion was that management and labor begin to cooperate for the good of all concerned, rather than regard each other as adversaries. If this could be accomplished, the watch-dog role Small was advocating for the state might not even be necessary. This solution becomes the major theme of Small's labor novel, *Between Eras*. Cooperation and compromise were required of both sides. Unlike the socialists, Small (1898b:350) was unwilling to criticize all rich men or successful capitalists as evil. Small felt there were many such men who had strong social consciences and wanted to aid society. Small's appeal to them was to serve as examples of how to reform their firms. Capitalists must realize the necessity to cooperate with workers rather than antagonize them (Page, 1969:139). Owners' resolutions to diminish the ill-workings of their factories and corporations would result only from a genuine outpouring of religious commitment, to take on the attitude of Christian stewardship. Capitalists must recognize that there were duties that went along with wealth. The only genuine reform of capitalism would occur when factory owners realized that they were in a partnership relationship with labor—specifically one of Christian brotherhood—and extended to them a measure of control of the workplace. Workers must be given a full share of management responsibility in affairs that affected their interests.

Workers must fundamentally alter their attitude toward the workplace as well. They should no longer see their time spent at work as just a job. They must accept responsibility for such things as product quality, factory safety, and corporate morale. The answer lay in instituting democracy in the workplace, making corporate decisions into joint resolutions of management and labor. In Small's (1913b:383) novel, the labor strike is resolved when both sides agree to cooperate. The new contract between the company and the workers stated:

> The company agrees to designate a standing committee of conference, to act with a similar committee of the employees, in taking into consideration all the affairs of the company, particularly everything affecting the interests of the employees, and from time to time propose modifications of the general policies of the company, whenever the conferees are able to unite on recommendations which in their judgement would tend better to protect all the interests concerned.

Small praised corporations that took steps along the line he had proposed. In particular, Small (1914:568) took note of Henry Ford's attempt to modify the nature of management-labor relations, including Ford's profit-sharing experiment, and felt Ford might set new standards for industrial relations.

Throughout much of his sociological career Small advocated intensive study of the facts of society prior to any attempt to ameliorate social problems. However, during World War I, Small's attitudes seemed to change. For the first time, he appeared to be advocating immediate social reform. Small also became much more open about his Christianity during the war. It appears that the event that changed his outlook—in fact frightening him into action—was the Bolshevik Revolution (Small, 1919a:482; 1920a:692). Pragmatism becomes Small's new outlook, the nation must act now to Christianize its social institutions—especially management-labor relations—or face the potential of a disastrous socialist revolution in the United States. America could no longer wait for sociology to come up with all the remedies first; action must be immediate.

Small appears to have spent the last years of his life as an embittered man because sociology was not following the course he felt he had set for it. In the 1920s, sociology had not yet devoted itself to the ultimate solution to universal problems, let alone help usher in the Kingdom. In fact, Small (1920b:25) saw sociology heading in another direction, one he opposed. Rather than representing a unified view of reality, sociology seemed to be fracturing itself into various subdisciplines. The vision might be lost.

Small's colleague for more than twenty years at Chicago was Charles Henderson (1848–1915). Although Henderson is today even more forgotten than Small, his legacy to American sociology is also quite important. Henderson (1904:318) shared Small's vision of the gradual arrival of the Kingdom of God on earth, as conflicting groups with their own interests learned to cooperate. But more importantly, Henderson represented the practical or applied side in Small's division of labor between sociological theorists and social reformers. Henderson both wrote about and was an active participant in settlement house work, other forms of charity, philanthropy, and social work, the industrial insurance movement, prison reform, and child welfare leagues. Within his writings, Henderson made a separation of the "worthy" and "unworthy" elements of society, especially in his discussions of the famous three D's—the dependent, defective, and delinquent classes—and in the process founded the subdisciplines of criminology and sociology of deviance. It seems that Henderson's "Kingdom" was to exclude many, especially those with irreparably diseased wills. Sociology was to help determine the "salvageable" from the "unsavable" and provide means for "handling" both categories. One of Henderson's positive contributions was the direct observation of social groups in their "natural settings"—a method he advocated— which was to become an important part of the tradition of the Chicago school of sociology under W.I. Thomas, Robert Park, Ernest Burgess, and others.

Charles R. Henderson was born in 1848 in Covington, Indiana. He was educated at a small Baptist college in Chicago, subsequently closed as a result of lack of funds, whose charter was acquired by the University of Chicago (Diner, 1975:519). Henderson then studied at Baptist Theological Seminary and later served as a minister in Terre Haute and Detroit. In the 1880s he was a leader in several charitable organizations and became a publicly known figure when he successfully arbitrated a strike of street railway employees in Detroit (Diner, 1975:519). In 1892, Chicago's president, William Rainey

Harper, approached Henderson, whom Harper knew through his Baptist connections, and offered him a position as university chaplain. Henderson made it clear he was interested in the post only if he could combine it with teaching and research. (Diner, 1975:519). Harper then approached Small to see if Henderson could be placed within the sociology department. Small agreed and Henderson came to Chicago in 1892. Henderson served both as professor of sociology and university chaplain until his death in 1915, during which time the sociology department and the divinity school were regarded as complementary. In the divinity school, Shailer Mathews and Graham Taylor were preaching and writing about the social gospel (Diner, 1975:520, 540–541).

Henderson held a deep commitment to the social gospel's faith in the Kingdom of God on earth. His (1915b) sermon, "The Everlasting Kingdom of Righteousness," written at the end of his life, makes this quite clear. The Kingdom of God was Jesus' central theme, and Jesus' vision was of a future time in the world's history when justice would be realized. In God's divine plan for developing humanity to perfection—Henderson (1895b:383) held an optimistic belief in human nature as essentially just and good—there were many elements undergoing amelioration. These included religion, politics, government, commerce, science, art, love, parenthood, friendship, and even public hygiene, athletic exercise, and recreation (Henderson, 1915b:26). Henderson refused to separate the world into sacred and secular spheres; God was sovereign over all of social reality. Henderson (1895a:327) believed that America was a particularly progressive country because of its earlier attempts to Christianize social institutions and quoted favorably de Tocqueville's statements concerning the uniqueness of the intellectual and moral associations that had been developed in America.

In order to complete the task of establishing the Kingdom, the intelligent minister or Christian social reformer would make use of the findings of scientifically trained sociologists. Henderson reaffirmed Small's division of labor between sociologists and social reformers. Henderson (1901:466) referred to his role as "social technology" or practical sociology—the forerunner of what is now called applied sociology. Sociology as an all-encompassing science was to deal with both "what is and what ought to be." Practical sociology was to seek to discover and present in systematic form principles that would regulate social conduct in conformity with ends, while social technology was to be the method for the realization of what ought to be (Henderson, 1901:466–468). Sociologists and other social scientists were to develop the specific knowledge necessary to ameliorate society.

> From psychology we can learn of the ethos of human beings, such as the moral sense of obligation, and the commanding ideas of benevolence, justice, and the completeness of life. However, theoretical sociology is necessary for an understanding of the institutional forms through which the moral beliefs find expression (Henderson, 1901:470).

The technical knowledge of the social sciences was then to be applied by religious leaders, reformers, and politicians who desired to better human conditions. If these ameliorists acted without the scientific knowledge only sociology could produce, they would be practicing in ignorance. Applied sociology was to be an ongoing process of applying better and better methods as sociology became continually more sophisticated (Henderson, 1912d:215). For example:

> The social policy toward dependents must be based on a scientific technique—by systematic observation of social phenomena, by induction from facts, by performing experiments with methods under varied conditions, by inventing working hypotheses and putting them to the test of reality (Henderson, 1904:323).

Positivist science was thus to be devoted to religious or moral ends. Henderson (1895b:383) considered sociology to be the most immediately useful scientific instrument for the teacher of ethics and religion, and regarded it as an intellectual necessity for pastoral work. The new science of sociology was "divinely inspired" wrote Henderson in 1899. "God has providentially wrought out for us the social sciences and placed them at our disposal" (quoted in Diner, 1975:524). Unquestioning faith in a providentially provided sociology would lead Henderson to adopt popular scientific beliefs of the era—now long discredited—such as Lombrosian criminology and eugenic sterilization of defective portions of the population.

In his book, *An Introduction to the Study of the Dependent, Defective, and Delinquent Classes*, first published in 1893, Henderson (1906) demonstrated his faith that social science could diagnose and provide cures for social problems and deviant behavior. One example is Henderson's use of Lombrosian criminology—the theory that criminal traits are biologically inherited and can actually be seen externally in the physical features of offenders. For example, Henderson (1906:226) claimed that criminals had pointed skulls, heavy jaws, and that the orbits of their eyes were too large compared to those of normal persons. They also had asymmetrical heads, receding foreheads, and zygomatic arches that are large and prominent. Physical appearances differed as well between criminals who commit varying offenses. Thieves have small heads, murderers large ones, while sexual offenders have projecting eyes, delicate features, and thick lips and eyelids (Henderson, 1906:226–227). As unsalvageables, the purpose of the penal system was to keep atavistic criminals off the streets to insure society's safety. But prison should not be regarded as punishment, Henderson (1906:277) argued, because hereditary criminals could not be held morally responsible for their behavior. Thus, biological criminology worked as a "salvation device," removing blame from the individual. Henderson (1906:219, 226; 1900:316) advocated turning the prison into a giant criminological laboratory: performing experiments on hereditary criminals, measuring their bodily or physical characteristics, and even performing dissections of criminals' brains—one hopes, only after they were deceased. Already, findings of such brain dissections had shown defects of the quality, shape, and weight of brain cells. For those found to be biological criminals, Henderson (1904:328) advocated sterilization as the ultimate societal cure, so that future generations of atavistic brutes would not be produced.

Henderson can thus be considered part of the first American movement to medicalize deviant behavior. Although Albion Small (Small and Vincent, 1894:267) used the medical terminology of pathology and disease in his sociology, his statements were primarily metaphorical. Henderson's use of the medical model was quite literal. One of the mistakes made by late nineteenth-century social science—which has continued on to the present and, in fact, grown rather than diminished—was the literal translation of social problems, such as crime, juvenile delinquency, alcohol and drug abuse, and homosexuality into medical problems—a social movement Conrad and Schneider (1980) have characterized as the gradual replacement of the moral notion of "badness" by the medical designation of "sickness." It seems paradoxical that a Christian scholar such as Henderson pioneered a movement to do away with the fundamental religious concept of sin, but such an idea could not be easily reconciled with the positivistic aspects of Henderson's perspective on social reality, and, as a result, was jettisoned.

However, Henderson could not bring himself to do away with the Christian belief in free will altogether, since the ability to choose between good and evil was so fundamental to traditional evangelical Christianity. However, positivistic social science could be employed to discover those in the society whose free will had been impaired or destroyed by biological heredity or "sickness." In order for such afflicted individuals and groups to join in the covenant community, their wills would first have to be fully restored so they could function effectively. Sociology, social work, and psychology could offer cures for the diseased wills of some. Those that were savable could be admitted into the earthly Kingdom—a purified society. But, because of his acceptance of biological determinism and Lamarckian evolutionism, Henderson was led to conclude that the wills of many in the lower classes had been irreparably damaged. Thus they would never be able to be cleansed for Kingdom life, and must be consigned to prisons, mental institutions, homes for the feeble-minded, or sterilized.

Henderson did not, however, feel that one could explain all forms of deviant behavior, and in particular crime, by resorting to biological or evolutionary explanations. External social conditions had something to do with why some individuals turned to crime. Henderson was directly involved in the late nineteenth-century conflict over biological vs. sociological explanations of deviant behavior—what is today known as the "nature-nurture debate." His own ambivalence over whether biological heredity or the social environment was the dominant force in determining behavior appeared not only in his discussion of crime, but also in his ideas about mental illness, poverty, and race (Henderson, 1906:15–16, 12–13, 29).

In Henderson's perspective, biology or heredity was the dominant factor in crime, poverty, and the respective plights of immigrants and Blacks; but external environmental conditions were seen as forces that could either reinforce or alter biologically inherited traits (Henderson, 1906:34). For example, although Blacks had inherited "race traits" including drunkenness, licentiousness, shiftlessness, criminality, and amorality, these race defects have been further compounded by prejudice of Whites and the inability of Blacks to find employment (Henderson, 1906:29). But, despite his claims that social conditions were an important factor, Henderson (1906:15–16) remained primarily an evolutionary, biological determinist and even believed in a Lamarckian theory of the inheritance of acquired or learned characteristics. He applied Lamarckianism to his theory of poverty or pauperism, which led him to the conclusion that the laziness or licentiousness of poor parents could be passed on genetically to their offspring (Henderson, 1906:27–29).

These beliefs, of course, affected Henderson's proposed solutions to America's social ills. In addition, however, Henderson's ideas were shaped by his vision of the Kingdom of God, whose realization must always be given ultimate importance. The combination of his vision of the Kingdom with a biologically based environmental sociology led Henderson to make distinctions between the "worthy" and the "unworthy" elements of society. Only the worthy should receive help or assistance from philanthropists, charities, or social workers, such as the settlement house movement. Henderson's (1906:22–23) Kingdom vision required him to be primarily concerned about the quality of the race or nation as a whole, which he regarded the "degenerate or abnormal dependent classes" to be dragging down. Adapting Darwin's idea of the survival of the fittest to society, Henderson (1906:19) reasoned that the evolutionary tendency of the unfit was toward extinction. By providing social services to the degenerate this group was being helped to survive and in the process becoming societal "parasites." Thus, in order to save society the degenerate or abnormal portions of the dependent classes must be separated from their worthy portions—e.g., those whose failings arise from defective external environmental conditions and not inferior heredity. The worthy could then be helped while the unworthy were to be either ignored with the hope they would become extinct, institutionalized to protect society from their evil influence, or prevented from procreating their own kind.

The major scientific problem for Henderson's model of deviance became developing criteria by which his bifurcation of the unfortunate branches of humanity could be made. Although statistics could aid social reformers in getting an accurate picture of what aggregate proportions of the population fell into the worthy and unworthy categories, it was up to the various social agencies dealing with the socially marginal to assign workers to investigate individual cases of pauperism to see if the family asking for assistance was indeed sufficiently worthy to receive it (Henderson, 1906:24, 63).

It appears that Henderson combined his biological theories with beliefs supplied from traditional Christian morality in order to come up with his "scientific" criterion for labelling the unworthy. Among the worthy dependents who should receive assistance were orphaned and destitute children, poor widows and deserted wives, and the aged, since all of these groups could be regarded as having done nothing to deserve their fate. Also, Henderson (1906:25) advocated public charity for the diseased and injured, including the deaf, blind, and the mentally ill— although these groups probably would fall under those categories Henderson would not permit to produce future generations of defectives. Those whose plight was the result of ignorance or "feeble-mindedness" should be aided, as well as those temporarily unemployed because of fluctuations in the capitalist economy (Henderson, 1906:30). Henderson (1907a–f; 1908a–d; 1909a; 1910; 1915a) was a strong advocate of industrial insurance to assist hardworking laborers through depression periods. Those who had supported the Protestant work ethic were to be counted among the worthy.

Henderson's (1906:26–29) list of the unworthy elements among the lower classes showed his reliance on traditional Christian morality and also the fact that he chose to ignore the situational factors that might have led to poverty among the "disreputable." In Henderson's sociology the unworthy were those whose fall was caused by their own unsocial habits, such as foolishly wasting money on alcohol or drugs. Ranking high on Henderson's list of unsocial habits was sexual licentiousness.

> The excesses, abuses, and perversions of the sexual function rank with drink among the chief causes of social parasitism. . . . Sexual excess produces feebleness, it causes people to lose the will to work, and can produce in children insanity, epilepsy, and idiocy (p. 27).

Sexual excess was clear proof of the moral bankruptcy of such individuals.

> The want of high spiritual, religious, intellectual, and aesthetic interests offers an empty soul for the incoming of unclean demons (p. 28).

The condemnation of both alcohol users and those who were producing large numbers of children was of course directed at Catholic immigrants, who not only drank but were reproducing faster than their Protestant neighbors, threatening thus to conquer the hegemony that Protestantism currently held in American society.

Henderson (1914:645–646) held a similarly low opinion of the Chinese and their culture, predicting that Chinese ways would eventually be radically transformed by superior Western practices. Henderson (1904:322) was also critical of the fact that Chinese immigrants were stealing jobs from native-born Americans by working for lower wages.

> So long as hordes of this class are permitted to come freely to America, to live herded in unfit habitations, and to compete for places with our naturalized citizens who have already won an advance, the case is hopeless for our own people.

Also on Henderson's (1906:28–29) list of unsocial traits were "shiftlessness" and "roving." The shiftless were those who lacked industrial habits or ambition—the lazy—while the roving showed contempt for the obligations of marriage and family. Wife-deserters were included in the latter category.

When we analyze Henderson's (1906:29) use of the phrase "race traits," we discover that he believed it was possible that entire races could be placed in the unworthy category. In particular, Henderson argued that Blacks occupy such a low position in American society because of their own drunkenness, licentiousness, shiftlessness, criminality, and amorality. Surely, such a debased stock of people would not be part of the future Kingdom. Henderson (1906:21) argued that "communities of such debased stock breed and continue to live due to public and private charity," and that such assistance should be discontinued and, thus, parasitism ended. The natural law of the survival of the fittest could then run its course without interference.

Henderson was of course not the only early sociologist to try to separate the worthy and unworthy portions of society. Albion Small attempted the same type of bifurcation.

> Defective, dependent, and delinquent classes are dead and poisonous matter, foreign and dangerous to the social body and not part of the capable, willing people who make up society. It is not the chief duty of society to act as guardians to these people (Small and Vincent, 1894:80).

Thus, in Small's view, the unworthy were not even to be considered part of society, but sociologically defined as "outsiders." Small's Kingdom, like Henderson's, was to be exclusionary.

> The aim of sociology is not a theory and practice of charity, but an effective policy of rational sociability which shall include the largest possible number of men in fellowship of reciprocally helpful cooperation (Small and Vincent, 1894:82).

Obviously those defined as defectives, dependents, and delinquents could not be considered reciprocally helpful elements of society. Small was uncertain how many in these groups could be saved. Their presence in society could be taken as evidence of a "symptom of diseased social conditions," and if sociology would develop cures for such conditions then perhaps some would be able to rejoin Small's society (Small and Vincent, 1894:80).

Henderson's influence reached beyond the college campus because of his many outside activities. He was director and later president of the United Charities of Chicago, president of the Chicago Society for Social Hygiene, the head of a state commission on social insurance and of a municipal commission on unemployment (see Henderson, 1915a). Henderson was also an active member of the Civic Federation, the Chicago Vice Commission, and on the board of directors of the University of Chicago Settlement—see Henderson (1899) for his history and positive evaluation of the American settlement house movement and his other works (1896b–d) for a comparison with settlement work in Germany. Henderson (1905; 1911; 1912a–c) was also involved with the Infant Welfare Society, both in the United States and Europe.

Henderson also served as president of the National Conference on Charities and Corrections, the forerunner of the National Association of Social Workers (Diner, 1975:524). While Henderson was at Chicago, sociology and social work were regarded as complementary disciplines, each reinforcing the other. Not until 1920, five years after Henderson's death, did the University of Chicago establish a separate School of Social Service Administration, formally distinguishing sociology from social work (Diner, 1975:543). Henderson was also very influential in late nineteenth-century penology. He was a close associate of Frederick Wines, the son of Enoch Wines, both of whom were the leading penologists of their respective eras. Frederick Wines had adopted Lombrosian theories regarding criminal offenders, just like Henderson.

Although Henderson's brand of biological criminology was later rejected for genuinely psychological and sociological explanations, his emphasis upon social problems and deviant behavior has remained an important concern within American sociology. While at Chicago, Henderson taught courses on the family (1909b), the labor movement, urban and rural conditions, the history of philanthropy (1898), and practical social work (Diner, 1975:537).

Another lasting contribution made by Henderson (1896a:396) was his reliance on the "laboratory method"—today known as participant observation. Henderson stressed that research must be based on first-hand observation and intimate experience of the ordinary, everyday life of the poor, the orphaned, the criminal, and the ill treated. Other Chicago sociologists, such as W.I. Thomas, Robert Park, Ernest Burgess, and, later, Herbert Blumer would adopt Henderson's laboratory method. As Diner (1975:551) has noted, it was paradoxical that a middle-class do-gooder's concentration on the lower classes led sociology to embrace direct investigation and participant observation:

> American university teachers were generally a sedate class of men. They stayed away from low life, from the poor, and noisy, drunken brawling conduct. The generation of sociologists who were horrified by these things and who felt a more or less Christian obligation to alleviate them did not enter into direct contact with them. They did the next best thing: they associated with social workers who knew first-hand and they encouraged their students to study them. In this respect W.I. Thomas was the proper disciple of Charles Henderson. He actually did what Henderson thought desirable to do.

As W.I. Thomas said of Henderson:

> He once requested me to get a bit of information from the saloons. He said that he himself had never entered a saloon or tasted beer (quoted in Rosenberg, 1982:122).

Thus, Thomas's finding of the first set of letters in a trash can, which became the basis of *The Polish Peasant in Europe and America,* and Robert Park's admonition to his students that they must "get the seat of their pants dirty" to study urban life are part of Henderson's legacy to sociology.

The third important member of the University of Chicago sociology faculty who was strongly influenced by the social gospel was George Vincent (1864–1914). Vincent has become an even more forgotten figure than Henderson—in Donald Carns's (1971:4) introduction to a reprint of the original Small and Vincent text, he admits to knowing nothing about Vincent. George Vincent was the son of John Heyl Vincent, one of the two founders of the Chautauqua movement in upstate New York in 1874. The relationship between Chautauqua and sociology at the University of Chicago was another important link in the social gospel-sociology connection at the turn of the twentieth century. Both William Rainey Harper, Chicago's president until his death in 1906, and George Vincent were leaders in the Chautauqua movement.

Chautauqua was also one of the links between the earlier nineteenth-century utopian communal movement and the social gospel. Although laymen and ministers came to spend a Chautauqua summer in a utopian rural setting, they were to take the lessons learned at Chautauqua back to the "world" when they departed (Morrison, 1974:17). In its first three decades, Chautauqua covered a wide variety of topics and programs and served as a platform for many of the leading Christian reformers of the day. The temperance movement—Frances Willard of the WCTU appeared at the camp in 1896—Christian young people's groups, physical training for boys, and a strong emphasis on cultural activities were all part of Chautauqua (Kett, 1977:193). In 1881, John Vincent, who was a bishop in the Methodist denomination, advocated establishing the study of sociology "from the Christian point of view" for the clergymen who came to Chautauqua (Morrison, 1975:49). In the 1880s, Chautauqua became committed to the "sociological movement," hoping to contribute to the Christian regeneration of American society through applying "scientific" knowledge to the solution of social problems.

William Rainey Harper helped to further this attitude during his terms—1887 to 1892—as principal of Chautauqua's College of Liberal Arts. Harper, a devout Baptist—but never an ordained minister—had come to Chautauqua in 1883 and retained his association with the organization until 1895 (Morrison, 1974:73, 76). Harper was to take Chautauqua's sociological interest with him to the University of Chicago when he became its first president in 1892. Like Chautauqua, the newly founded Baptist university was, under Harper's direction, dedicated to contributing to the improvement of society by providing both the knowledge and action needed for the Christian solution to social problems (Diner, 1975:515). Harper made himself personally responsible for the recruitment of faculty and brought Albion Small and Charles Henderson to the university. Chicago's summer school term was patterned after Chautauqua's summer programs, with the hope of bringing in students who had already received college degrees and giving them special instruction that would be useful in nonacademic, business, or reform pursuits.

George Vincent, who had grown up at Chautauqua, came to Chicago in 1892 as one of the first graduate students in the sociology department. He was quickly added to the teaching staff, received his Ph.D. in 1896, and stayed at Chicago until 1911, when he resigned to become president of the University of Minnesota. Throughout his professional life, Vincent maintained his association with Chautauqua. In 1888, he had been appointed Vice-Principal of Instruction; in 1898, Vincent succeeded his father as Chautauqua's Principal of Instruction, and from 1907 to 1915 he held the top post as president of Chautauqua Institute (Richmond, 1953:36, 54, 56). In 1917, Vincent accepted the position of president of the Rockefeller Foundation, for whom he directed projects on public health and war relief (Morrison, 1974:83).

Vincent did not publish extensively and thus left but a small written legacy. He did co-author the first sociology text with Small, but the work seems to primarily represent Small's influence. Vincent may have contributed the section on rural society (pp. 112–116), because elsewhere he supported the development of rural sociology (Vincent, 1898:1–20). Vincent advocated a Christian approach to sociology (1906:6), supported both Small's division of labor between sociologists and social reformers (1896:485; 1904c:145–160; 1906:9) and his theory of the rivalry of social groups (1911:469–484), attacked Spencer's anti-religious orientation (1904a:710), and pioneered the sociological study of ancient civilizations (1904b:737–754) and journalism (1905:297–311). Vincent (1896:490) was a severe critic of William Graham Sumner and attacked Sumner's *Folkways* when it appeared in 1907. Vincent's (1907:415) argument was that Sumner was not truly a sociologist at all.

> Among nearly 700 authors cited in the book, there is hardly one known as a sociologist. With sociologists, Professor Sumner has little in common.

In particular, Vincent argued that sociology could not accept either Sumner's anti-reform orientation or his concept of ethnocentrism. The latter was particularly objectionable because it demonstrated Sumner's rejection of the universal validity of Christian theology. Chicago's Christian sociologists sought to be moralists, boldly proclaiming that values were universal, and could not accept Sumner's presupposition that "immoral never means anything but contrary to the mores of the time and place" (Vincent, 1907:415). On Sumner's fatalism and anti-reform orientation, Vincent (1907:416–417) says:

> So vivid and dominant does his idea of a blind, remorseless power become that the futility and folly of attempting to modify or direct it are borne in upon the reader with chilling effect. Certainly the first impression is that of an almost fatalistic determinism. Philosophy, religion, and ethics are declared to be products of the folkways and "not creative or determining forces."

If Sumner's concept of cultural relativism were to become dominant in sociology—which it ultimately would—then Christian sociology was doomed. Sumner was thus an enemy to be defeated at all costs.

Another largely forgotten member of the Chicago sociology faculty was Marion Talbot, one of the original staff hired in 1892. Talbot's interests and courses show a direct link to the female-directed aspects of the settlement house movement and support for the type of "municipal housekeeping" that Jane Addams proposed. A pioneer in what was later called "home economics," Talbot taught courses in "sanitary science" in the sociology department from 1892 to 1904, when a separate department of "household administration" was created. She sought to justify the place of sanitary science within sociology, stating in 1896:

> It implies a recognition of the principle that a very close relationship exists between sanitary conditions and social progress. Sanitation and sociology must go hand in hand in their effort to improve the race (quoted in Diner, 1975:520).

Among the courses offered by Talbot were "House Sanitation," "Sanitary Aspects of Food, Water, and Clothing," "The Economy of Living," "General Hygiene," "The Citizen as Householder," and "Food, Supplies, and Dietaries." Although Talbot is the most direct link, the settlement movement's domesticized list of reforms received support from other Chicago professors and the *American Journal of Sociology*.

Child welfare, juvenile delinquency, the need for a separate juvenile court system, and the problems of women in the labor force were some of the domestic issues discussed in the journal.

Talbot's hope had been that sanitary science would be an androgynous endeavor, not limited merely to socially oriented women. But Harper's creation of a separate department for her courses indelibly identified Talbot's interests as feminine (Rosenberg, 1982:49). Feminine reformers were thus cut off from the more masculine endeavor of sociological theory. The creation of a separate social work department in the 1920s severed the last tie between the previously unified "masculine" and "feminine" versions of sociology. The unity of sociology, social work, social reform, and domestic science with social Christianity that had existed under Small, Henderson, Vincent, and Talbot would be discarded for gender-specific disciplinary orientations.

Although Talbot was not able to realize her dream of an androgynous domestic science, other women students at Chicago used the newly emerging field of sociology to help develop theories that attacked the very core of Victorian American beliefs concerning masculinity and femininity. Rosalind Rosenberg (1982) has argued that women such as Helen Thompson Wooley and Jessie Taft first put forward the ideas that would later become dominant in the social scientific study of sex roles and become the basis of mid-twentieth-century feminism. Wooley, whose work influenced W.I. Thomas's writings on sex differences, pioneered the psychological study of gender-based distinction in her 1903 work, *The Mental Traits of Sex*. In it, she argued that training and social expectations, not physiologically inherited traits, were the causes of unique male and female temperaments.

Jessie Taft—both W.I. Thomas and George Herbert Mead were her mentors—attacked both the idea of the natural suitability of females for housework and domesticized reform activities in her 1916 book, *The Women's Movement from the Point of View of Social Consciousness*. Taft also developed the concept of social marginality— prior to Park and Stonequist—and used it to explain the origin of the contemporary women's movement and its attempts to reform society. Women were refusing to remain marginal human beings in a world dominated by men. But traditional sex roles and understandings of gender distinctions had to be abolished before women could move toward genuine societal equality with men. Rationality must no longer be regarded as a hallmark of masculinity, nor "the maternal virtues" perceived as exclusively feminine. The female's domestic temperament was the result of cultural expectations and conditioning, not heredity. In particular, Taft was fascinated by the prostitute, who seemed to be openly renouncing Victorian standards of feminine propriety and symbolized the tension that existed in all women's lives between the natural wish for self-expression and the inhibiting effects of social repression.

In using sociology to transcend the cultural bonds that were limiting women's freedom, feminist sociologists like Wooley and Taft transcended and rejected social Christianity as well. They could not accept Jane Addams's domesticated version of the social gospel because they regarded all variants of domesticity as anathema. The social gospel movement itself was unable to accommodate sociological feminism because of its radical assault on gender determined temperament, an idea that theologians associated with the Biblical creation story of mankind as male and female. Many Christians believed that Eve's creation from Adam's rib and St. Paul's writings on marital relations foreordained women to be subordinate to men, a belief the feminist sociologists rejected. Feminism and the social gospel's version of Christianity could not be reconciled.

The writings of Talbot, Taft, and Wooley were quickly forgotten primarily because there proved to be no constituency for their work. Social gospelers found their anti-religious opinions unacceptable, female social reform leaders did not agree that women had no "natural predisposition" for municipal housekeeping, while male sociologists preempted the primarily "masculine" realm of sociological theory from them. The more "feminine" worlds of social reform, social work, and home economics suffered from a subtle form of sexist discrimination. Thus the critique the feminists were making—that much of sociology, in both its theoretical and applied areas was based on the institutionalization of the ideology of domesticity—was to have no audience until its revival by feminist social historians in the 1980s.

Charles A. Ellwood (1873–1946) took Small's, Henderson's, Vincent's, and Talbot's vision of Christian sociology to the University of Missouri in 1900—where he was to teach for the next thirty years. Ellwood had been born in Odgensburg, New York, and in 1892 entered Cornell University, where he met E.A. Ross and came to share Ross's vision of social science as a method to improve society. In 1896, Ellwood came to Chicago to study under Albion Small, W.I. Thomas, and George Herbert Mead, producing a dissertation on social psychology in 1899. Ellwood became one of the leading American sociologists of his era, writing more than a dozen books, and many articles and book reviews for the *American Journal of Sociology*. His 1910 social problems textbook alone sold 300,000 copies in its various editions (Barnes, 1968:32). His theory that American society was being remade into the Kingdom of God on earth and his attempt to reconstruct the religion of Christianity by using sociological insights will be analyzed here. In this regard, Ellwood's sociological theories concerning race, the family, and politics are important in understanding his Kingdom vision. However, in the 1920s, Ellwood rejected his earlier faith in cultural evolution and the biological inheritance of race traits. As was the case with a number of other social gospelers, Ellwood's optimism was not disillusioned by World War I. He spent a considerable amount of his time in the 1920s and 1930s traveling extensively in Europe and Latin America preaching pacifism, which he regarded as necessary for any successful social amelioration. In 1930, Ellwood moved to Duke University, to found its sociology department, and in 1935–1936 served as president of the International Institute of Sociology.

Ellwood's perspective on society and social reform was based upon his theological interpretation of Jesus' vision of the Kingdom of God. Jesus' mission was not to preach a religion of individual salvation but instead to establish a social order in which God's will would be done (Ellwood, 1929:12). Jesus' goal was an earthly Kingdom of God in which a redeemed humanity was to be realized. Ellwood (1923:213) stated:

> We believe that according to the life and teaching of Jesus, the supreme task of mankind is the creation of a social order, the

Kingdom of God on earth, wherein the maximum opportunity shall
be afforded for the development and enrichment of every human
personality.

Ellwood was a leader in universalizing the social gospel; his goal
was not only to ameliorate American society but to change the world.
This was at the core of Jesus' message, Ellwood (1925:77) argued, for:

Christianity's goal was to transcend predatory, individual, class,
tribal, and national ethics to replace these with a universalized, social,
international, humanitarian ethics.

Thus Jesus established for all mankind the patterns of true civilization.

Ellwood coupled his belief in an earthy Kingdom with a faith in
progress. He (1929:49) referred to himself as a follower of Condorcet
and felt there was good reason to believe that even the most perplexing
problems of modern civilization would soon be on the way to solution.
While Jesus had envisioned Christianity playing a major role in helping
to insure progress, a number of historical obstacles had diverted the
church from its true task for nearly 2,000 years (Ellwood, 1925:85–88).
Ellwood's list of obstacles included the early church's concentration on
salvation of the soul in a life beyond rather than on practical ethical and
social attitudes, the pagan religions and morals of the ancient world
with which the Catholic church combined Christianity, the failure to
appreciate the importance of material and economic factors in the life
of man, the extreme individualism of most forms of Protestant
Christianity, the unintelligent use Christians had made of the Bible—
assuming that all of its parts were equally inspired and equally relevant
to today's society—and the failure of the church to ally itself with
humane science. With most of these obstacles now out of the way, he
reasoned, the church could return to its original mission of establishing
Christ's Kingdom here and now.

Religion was to be adapted to the requirements of continuous
progress, then lead mankind toward an ideal society embracing all
humanity, while ceasing to be a conservative force (Ellwood, 1925:64).
Social Christianity must stress service or sacrifice for one's fellow man
as the ascetic requirement for true followers (Ellwood, 1929:211).

Religion could only be placed in service of the progress of mankind by spiritually enlightening humans to the sacrificial role required of them.

In Ellwood's theology, social science and religion were to work together to bring about the Kingdom of God. Science and religion must become allies and put an end to any disputes between them. There were two major components of Ellwood's Christian sociology. First, Christianity would need to be "reconstructed" so that findings of the sociology of religion might be incorporated into the faith. Second, sociology was to develop methods of applied social science that would speed social reform to prepare the world for the Kingdom's arrival.

The task Ellwood attempted—the reconstruction of Christianity—was monumental. He sought to make it into a social religion whose beliefs could be proven scientifically by sociologists. Traditional or conservative Christianity had to be transcended and replaced by an empirical faith. The following are typical examples of Ellwood's statements about religion and science:

> One of the greatest needs of the present is a religion adapted to the requirements of modern life and in harmony with modern science (1925:vii).

> The religion needed by the modern world is a more rational, revitalized, socialized Christianity. Only a Christianity of this sort is capable of saving modern civilization from its warring interests, classes, nations and races (1925:vii).

> True religion must be a faith consistent with the established knowledge (1923:4).

> If there is truth in religious values it will be corroborated by the independent, dispassionate investigations of science (1923:7).

Although it certainly appears that Ellwood had made science into the final arbiter of what constitutes religious truth, he cited congruencies between the Bible and social science more often than cases in which science and religion were in conflict. For example, Ellwood (1925:119–120) claimed to be a follower of Comte, yet argued that Comte erred in rejecting Christianity. With Comte, Ellwood agreed that religion must pass out of its theological and speculative stages, purge itself of all mythological elements, and move into a positivistic social stage. However, Comte's fallacy, according to Ellwood, was his failure to realize that his proposed alternative, the Religion of Humanity, was in accord with—and not in opposition to—the true Christianity of the Gospels. Ellwood sought to develop what he called Positive Christianity. His positive religion was to be like Small's sociology—i.e., to include all the facts in a comprehensive religious perspective (Ellwood, 1925:119). Although such a claim might have forced Ellwood to repudiate his Christian faith, his theologically based sociology in practice remained within the religious frame established by the Protestant social gospel.

Ellwood's sociology of religion presented the social functions of religion within the frame of an evolutionary model. These functions were divided into two categories, those that aided the progress of civilization and those that retarded the process. In Ellwood's (1929:187; 1925:49–58) perspective, religion would never disappear. Modern religion was not a survival of primitive magical practices; on the contrary, religion had evolved to its current pinnacle, Christianity, because of its cultural utility and ability to adapt itself to changing societal conditions. Ellwood (1925:49, 58) used the findings of cultural anthropologists to prove that the Christian religion had emerged in a process of evolutionary development. The truths of Christianity could thus complement the findings of sociology, and Christianity could be justifiably used as the basis for sociology.

Among Ellwood's (1925:42–47) list of the positive functions of religion, those which ought to be encouraged, were "socialization"— defined as developing among individuals the recognition of their social obligations—provision of universal values, and the establishment of the spiritual realm in the affairs of men. Progress could be greatly aided by religion, for as Ellwood (1929:188) argued:

> Societal achievements will be made not only by the cultivation of intelligence but also by the cultivation of the nobler emotions which religion encourages.

Among the negative functions of religion—those to be discouraged—Ellwood (1925:65) noted its exploitation by the dominant classes for their own interests. Religion, he urged, must no longer serve as an impediment to progress and an instrument of class oppression. Moreover, Ellwood (1925:152) argued that the world had had enough of emotional religion, and needed a rational basis for faith. He (1925:42) was ambivalent about religion's function as an agency of social control, realizing that it was now a bitter necessity, but hoping that in the near future a more perfect mankind may have no need of it.

In addition to describing the universal functions of religion, Ellwood also attempted to come up with a set of universal values or morals. Like Small, Ellwood wanted to make sure his list of ultimate values would not be labelled ethnocentric. The study of sociology was held out as the solution to this problem; sociology was to serve as the intermediary between religion and science. Religious values could claim to be scientific truth once they had been subjected to sociological analysis. Like Small, Ellwood (1923:12) believed that because of sociology's holistic framework—by attempting to incorporate all knowledge—it was the most accurate form of truth available and could be employed to test specific indigenous religious values for their universality. Among the moral principles that sociology had verified as universal, Ellwood (1923:28–29) placed the Christian virtues of love, mutual service, and socialization. Sociology had, to Ellwood's satisfaction, established itself as the basis for ethics.

The next step for Ellwood was to use his sociologically validated ethics to create programs of social reform. Humanitarian religion and humanistic science were to work side by side to bring about social amelioration (Ellwood, 1929:110). Both science and religion would find their ultimate expression in the service of bettering mankind. As Ellwood (1923:1) put it:

> A new hope has come into the world—that science may unite with religion in the work of redeeming mankind.

Although science and religion were to work together, Ellwood made sure their tasks in the process were clearly separated. The ultimate goal, the establishment of the Kingdom, had first emerged within Christianity but now had been validated by sociology as a universal goal. While religion was to furnish the motives, science must draw up the plans and furnish the means for this ideal social end (Ellwood, 1923:11). Religion must seek the aid of social science if it was to create a better human world, while, at the same time, science needed religion to motivate men to believe in the truths that science had validated (Ellwood, 1923:9–10). Religion was to inspire humanity to move on toward the final utopia, while science would clear and construct the pathway.

Sociology as a university subject was to be dedicated to social amelioration. "Sociology will be a useless and 'dead' science if it can not contribute to the solution of the political, moral, and religious problems of human society," argued Ellwood (1929:104). On the undergraduate level, Ellwood (1907:590) had proposed a three-course sequence of sociology courses. The first was to be an introduction to the scientific study of social problems, the second a study of the abnormal groupings within society—the dependent, defective, and delinquent classes—and of methods of scientific philanthropy in dealing with them, and the third, a critical examination of sociological theory. Education of college students to the nature of America's social problems and how applied sociology could solve them would produce a whole generation committed to religiously motivated scientific reform.

Although Ellwood discussed and suggested cures for most of the major social problems of his day, only three will be considered in depth here: race and ethnicity, the family, and politics. In all of these areas Ellwood applied his Christian sociological eye and then proposed scientific solutions. His early writings on these subjects reflect his uncritical acceptance of turn of the twentieth-century nativism and biological evolutionism. However, during the 1920s he struggled to clear his mind of these prejudices, although he never was entirely successful in this endeavor.

Ellwood's attitude toward each of the various ethnic groups immigrating to America depended on their assimilability—how quickly the groups were willing to be Americanized. Ellwood (1913:219) felt that in particular the illiterate immigrants from southern and eastern Europe posed a major problem, because their "consciousness of kind" made them clannish. The crowding of immigrants into enclaves in large cities would only slow down their assimilation (Ellwood, 1913:208).

The fact that many immigrants did not understand America's free institutions and were therefore not prepared to vote intelligently meant they could become lackeys for machine politicians (Ellwood, 1913:220). Ellwood (1913:217) favored what he called "reasonable restrictions" upon immigration, to slow the influx of such groups.

One of the arguments Ellwood (1913:220–221) used in favor of immigrant restriction was what he called the racial or biological argument. His sociobiologically based prejudices can be clearly seen.

> Undoubtedly the strongest arguments in favor of further restriction upon immigration into the United States are of a biological nature. The peoples that are coming to us at present belong to a different race than ours. They belong to the Slavic and Mediterranean subraces of the white race. Now, the Slavic and Mediterranean races have not shown the capacity for self-government and free institutions which the peoples of Northern and Western Europe have shown. . . . Of course, if heredity counts for nothing the descendants of these people will be as good Americans as any. But this is the question, Does heredity count for nothing? Or does blood tell? Are habits of acting and, therefore, social and institutional life, dependent, more or less on the biological heredity of peoples, or are they entirely independent of such biological influence? . . . It is scarcely probable that a people of so different racial heredity from ourselves as the Southern Italians, for example, will maintain our institutions and social life exactly as those of our blood would do. . . . Certainly the coming to us of the vast numbers of people from Southern and Eastern Europe is destined to change our physical type, and it seems also probable that if permitted to go on, it will change our mental and social type also.
>
> Another phase of this biological argument is the necessity of selection, if we are to avoid introducing into our national blood the degenerate strains in the oppressed peoples of Southern and Eastern Europe. . . . While it is undesirable, perhaps, to discriminate among immigrants on the ground of race, it would certainly be desirable to select from all peoples those elements that we could most advantageously incorporate into our own life.

Ellwood's suggestions for selectively limiting the number of immigrants of each "subrace" who could enter the country were within a decade made into law with the passage of the National Origins Act. The number of eastern and southern Europeans who were permitted entry was greatly reduced.

Although Ellwood was ambivalent about the southern and eastern Europeans because of their negative race traits and slow assimilability, his opinions about Asian immigration were very clear. Total exclusion of Chinese and Japanese immigrants was necessary because Asians were found to be, in Ellwood's (1913:225) opinion, unassimilable.

> The statement that there is no good social or political argument for the prohibition of immigration does not apply to Asiatic immigration. Here the importance of the racial factor becomes so pronounced that it may well be doubted that a policy of total exclusion toward Asiatic immigration would not be the wisest in the long run for the people of this country.

Ellwood (1913:227–228) goes on to list the racial traits possessed by the Chinese that justify a policy of absolute exclusion.

> (1) The Chinese work for wages below the minimum necessary to maintain life for the white man, and so reduce the standard of living and crowd out the white workingman.

> (2) The Chinese make no contribution to the welfare of our country; they came here to remain several years, to attain a competence, and then return to China.

> (3) The Chinese are grossly immoral, they are addicted to the opium habit and other vices, and so few women come among the Chinese immigrants that Chinese men menace the virtue of white women.

> (4) The Chinese do not readily assimilate. They keep their language, religion, and customs. They live largely by themselves, and are even more completely isolated from American social life than the Negro. In comparison with them, indeed, one is struck with the fact that the Negro has our customs, our religion, our language, and in so far as he has been able to attain them, our moral standards, but this is not the case with the Chinese.

> (5) The last and strongest argument in favor of the general exclusion of Chinese laborers from this country, however, is the racial argument. The Chinese are just as different in race from us as the Negro, and if racial heredity counts for anything, it is fatuous to hope to assimilate them to the social type of the whites. Moreover, if we

should open our doors to the mass of Chinese laborers, China would be able to swamp us with Chinese immigrants. If we wish to keep the western third of our country, it would be well not to open the doors to the Chinese immigrants.

Ellwood was particularly troubled as to how to best solve the Black problem in America. Since they were already here, a policy of exclusion was too late. Nor did Ellwood (1913:251) feel that returning Blacks to Africa was feasible, although he considered it a possibility. Blacks presented America with a major problem because their primitive tropical racial heredity made them unfit for life in a White civilization located in a temperate climate. Ellwood (1913:233–234) discussed these race traits in detail.

> The Negro race is that part of mankind which was developed in the tropics. In all the Negro's physical and mental makeup he shows complete adaptation to a tropical environment. The dark color of his skin, for example, was developed by natural selection to exclude the injurious actinic rays of the sun. . . . [T]he tropical environment is generally unfavorable to severe bodily labor. Persons who work hard in the tropics are, in other words, apt to be eliminated by natural selection. . . . Hence, the tropical environment of the Negro failed to develop in him any instinct to work, but favored the survival of those naturally shiftless and lazy. Again, the extremely high death rate in Africa necessitated a correspondingly high birth rate in order that any race living there might survive; hence, nature fixed in the Negro strong sexual propensities in order to secure such a high birth rate.

What was to be done with a race of people who were shiftless, lazy, and sexually promiscuous because of inherited biological traits? Despite being a part of American society for nearly 200 years, Ellwood (1913:252) argued that "the Negro masses of this country were still essentially an uncultivated or 'nature' people living in the midst of civilization." Although Blacks had been taught Christian morals, and many had accepted Christianity as their new faith, Ellwood still believed that their biology remained fundamentally unaltered, thus making it highly unlikely the race would as a whole ultimately be saved and become part of the Kingdom. Ellwood (1913:246) cited the high death rate among Blacks as an indication that a rapid process of natural selection among them was going on; perhaps the unfit would just eventually become extinct.

If pure Black blood was obviously inferior, Ellwood was perplexed by what he perceived to be the result of the mixing of Black and White blood that had taken place during the slavery period. Ellwood (1913:240–241) believed that the infusion of White blood into a portion of the Black population was significant sociologically, that mulattoes were socially ambitious, since their blood was now fused with that of the carriers of the Protestant work ethic. However, the result of this mixture might either be socially advantageous or it might create a new societal menace. Ellwood claimed that many mulattoes turned to crime and vice as an outlet for their new revitalized blood. He (1913:246) argued that the intermixture of the White and Black races would continue and in the future our country would no longer have pure Blacks. But this process would take time and not be completed until the end of the twentieth century. Therefore, a more immediate solution was required.

Ellwood (1913:250–251) immediately disposed of a number of solutions as impossible: (1) admission at once of Blacks to full social equality with Whites; (2) deportation to Africa or South America; (3) colonization in some state or in a territory adjacent to the United States; (4) extinction by means of natural selection; (5) popular education along the old lines. Ellwood (1913:251) was ambivalent about many of the claims of Booker T. Washington, but he did support Washington's industrial education program as a possible solution.

> Mr. Booker T. Washington has said that the Negro is bound to become adjusted to our civilization because he is surrounded by the white man's civilization on every side. This optimistic view, which seems to dismiss the Negro problem as requiring no solution, is however, not well supported by many facts. Everywhere we have evidence that the Negro when left to himself reverts to a condition approximating his African barbarism, and the statistics of increasing vice and crime which we have just given show quite conclusively the Negro is not becoming adjusted to the white man's civilization in many cases in spite of considerable efforts which are being put forth on his behalf. While we are far from taking a pessimistic view toward this social problem, we believe that most of the solutions that have

been tried or urged are failures, and that more radical methods need
to be adopted if the Negro is to become a useful social and industrial
element in our society.

Ellwood believed Washington's program of industrial education was
the best immediate solution and argued that Whites should support
schools like Tuskegee and Hampton. The economic problems of Blacks
must be solved first, Ellwood (1913:252) concluded.

Undoubtedly the primary adjustment to be made by the American
Negro is the adjustment on the economic side. Only when the Negro
becomes adjusted to the economic side of his life will there be a solid
foundation for the development of something higher.

In the 1920s Ellwood came to reject most of the biologically
based cultural evolutionism that appeared in his writings on race prior
to World War I. He had never believed that all problems of the modern
society could be explained biologically. For example, Ellwood
(1913:214) did not hold to the popular idea that immigrants brought
criminal tendencies with them; high rates of crime among immigrant
children arose from situational factors of urban living—although he did
seem to believe that southern Italians were strongly predisposed to
crime. Ellwood (1913:232) had also stated that racial heredity could be
easily exaggerated as a factor in social life and that it should not be
evoked as an explanatory device until all other factors had been
exhausted.

In the 1920s, Ellwood came to believe that for the most part it
was cultural forces and processes that shaped both society and human
nature. As a result of his adoption of a more genuinely sociological
interpretation of society, Ellwood became more optimistic about the
potential that social science might have in reforming society and
bringing about the Kingdom of God. Ellwood (1929:60) now labelled
as pessimists those social theorists who remained wedded to biology.

Whenever anything goes wrong in human society, certain pessimistic
writers find the reason for it, not in the conditions of our culture, but
in "human nature." It is a convenient scapegoat for all social evils.

Ellwood (1923:13) no longer regarded human nature as unalterable; he now described it as plastic and modifiable. Ellwood (1923:17) concluded that socialization is fundamental to personality and that the criminal and the saint are made from the same human material. Human nature and human institutions are each equally malleable, each might be perfected. A properly controlled education could be employed to rid society of its social problems, argued Ellwood (1923:19):

> If it were possible to control the learning of all individuals, it would be possible to modify the whole complex of social life within one or two generations.

In addition to rejecting biological determinism, Ellwood (1923:52) turned from his faith in cultural evolution and concluded that history reveals that there is no necessary benevolence in natural, uncontrolled social progress. If progress was to be assured, directed social change would be required.

One of the areas in which Ellwood believed directed social progress could be achieved was within the family unit. Ellwood regarded the family as the basic institution of American society. Social progress could be guaranteed if only the family were reestablished upon Christian principles. Searching for a Christian basis for the family, Ellwood (1925:188–190) turned to the writings of another sociological pioneer, Charles Horton Cooley (1864–1929). At first glance it might appear unusual that Ellwood chose to rely on Cooley's theory of the nature of family interaction, since Cooley himself did not openly profess to being a Christian sociologist. However, a more thorough examination of Cooley's theory of the importance of the family as a "primary group"—still considered to be one of the basic concepts in contemporary sociology—reveals that his idea is but a secularization of the Christian conception of fellowship among believers. Cooley's writings about the family's importance for the socialization of children were also remarkably similar to Horace Bushnell's conception of "Christian nurture," although Cooley has dropped all of the religious rhetoric in his description.

Ellwood (1925:190) agrees with Cooley's theory that family life was the fount of all altruistic instincts; it is within the family that the child learns what love means. In Cooley's (1964:36) interpretation the infant is born an animal and only gradually through proper socialization becomes truly human.

> In their crudest form such passions as lust, greed, revenge, the pride of power and the like are not, distinctly, human nature at all, but animal nature, and so far as we rise into the spirit of family or neighborhood association we control and subordinate them. They are rendered human only so far as they are brought under the discipline of sympathy, and refined into sentiments, such as love, resentment, and ambition.

In Cooley's (1964:29–30) model, it is the quintessential primary group, the family, that brings human nature into existence and thus makes the child fit for civilization.

> Human nature is not something existing separately in the individual, but a group-nature or primary phase of society, a relatively simple and general condition of the social mind. . . . It is the nature which is developed and expressed in those simple, face-to-face groups that are somewhat alike in all societies; groups of the family, the playground, and the neighborhood. . . . In these, everywhere, human nature comes into existence. Man does have it at birth; he can not acquire it except in fellowship, and it decays in isolation.

Ultimately, it is within the family that the child will learn the highest moral imperative of life, self-sacrifice for the good of the group. Cooley (1964:38) here relies upon the social gospel doctrine that self-sacrifice is the hallmark of a truly religious lifestyle. In order to truly find oneself—create a distinct self-identity—one must collectively merge his individual personality with the community's.

> In so far as one identifies himself with the whole, loyalty to the whole is loyalty to himself; it is self-realization, something in which one can not fail without losing self-respect. . . . One is never more human, and as a rule never happier, than when he is sacrificing his narrow and merely private interest to the higher call of the congenial group. And without doubt the natural genesis of this sentiment is in the intimacy of face-to-face cooperation.

Cooley's ultimate hope was to counter the forces of individualism emerging as a result of the destruction of small-town and rural lifestyles by the encroachment of urban social dislocation. He sought to reassert the primacy of the family's role in producing society's most necessary positive traits. Into Cooley's theory of society was built the goal of community, which he felt the new industrialized, urbanized nation could retain if only the family would continue to produce self-sacrificing individuals.

Ellwood (1925:204) borrowed from Cooley the idea that the modern family's major purpose was the proper socialization of children. Parents were to form a sacrificial pair, dedicating themselves to their children. Through their display of love and affection within the home, the creation of a "haven in a heartless world," parents would help develop altruistic instincts in their children. The American family was in Ellwood's (1913:156) perspective in a transitional period, moving from the "old patriarchal family system to a new democratic ethical type of family in which the rights of every one are respected, and all members are bound together, not through fear or through force of authority, but through love and affection."

Since the purpose of the family was the sacrificial socialization of children, Ellwood expressed a negative attitude toward any trends that might divert the family from its Christian mission. Included on Ellwood's list of counterproductive family trends were the rising divorce rate, the women's rights movement, birth control—except for the unfit—and sex for pleasure. It was Ellwood's (1925:206) conviction that divorce should be prevented if at all possible, because of its assumed negative effect upon the child. Sociologists should oppose divorce, he argued, and advocate life-long marital commitments, except when dissolving the family would be in the child's best interests.

Ellwood had ambivalent feelings about the women's rights movement because he believed it was largely responsible for the rising divorce rate. The Victorian family had been founded upon the sacrifice women were asked to make of their own interests and career aspirations to the home, in order to serve the needs of their husbands and children. From Ellwood's (1913:148) perspective, the women's rights movement was damaging the family through fostering attitudes of individualism among women, and leading many wives toward divorce. Both Susan B. Anthony and Elizabeth Cady Stanton had been wrong in advocating free divorce, argued Ellwood (1913:149). Ellwood's (1913:148–149) ambivalence on this issue was clearly expressed in the following statement:

> No one would claim that the emancipation of woman, in the sense of freeing her from those things which have prevented the highest and best development of her personality, is not desirable. But this emancipation of women has brought with it certain opportunities for going down as well as going up. Woman's emancipation has not, in other words, meant to all classes of women, woman's elevation. On the contrary, it has been to some, if not an opportunity for license, at least an opportunity for self-assertion and selfishness not consistent with the welfare of society and particularly the stability of the family.

Ellwood (1913:196) did not condone women entering careers, because he felt that the labor of women outside the home might become subversive to the higher values of the family. He even cautioned against permitting young single women to work, because it might make them "unfit" for home and family; they might even choose careers over marriage, thus further weakening the stability of the American family system.

Ellwood also opposed both birth control and sex for other than procreative purposes. He (1925:193) accused the movement favoring sex for personal gratification as one more example of the growing selfishness of the current age. New attitudes toward sexuality, such as those expressed in the new marriage manuals of the era, were upsetting to Ellwood (Gordon, 1978). From Ellwood's (1925:198) perspective, the main function of marriage was not the gratification of sex impulses; rather, sex was for procreation only, and sex impulses must be controlled. Birth control devices were also anathema to Ellwood (1925:202) because they would only lead further toward the immorality of pleasureful sex. Control over sexual impulses could be achieved by combining social religion and social scientific sexual education in order to raise the sexual standards of youth.

Although Ellwood did not favor birth control, he was a strong supporter of the eugenics movement, to insure the future proper development of the American people. He (1925:200–201) felt that a eugenics movement could be instituted without coercion or through birth control; he believed that the consciences of the "unfit" could be raised so that they would voluntarily agree not to produce children. Those with superior traits were to be encouraged to produce more than their normal proportion of children, while those not normal in hereditary endowments were to refrain from marriage and remain celibate. Although he never states directly who are the prime candidates for controlled breeding are, the list of those who should refrain from procreation would probably have included criminals, the insane, and the "lower races." Those whom Ellwood believed were so deviant or abnormal that they could not be controlled by the moral standards of society should be incarcerated in institutions and supported at public expense, where they could be controlled. Ellwood's (1925:205) goal was that human society be so organized as to maximize the number of "normal" homes in which children could be properly nurtured. He felt that sociological knowledge made it possible to determine who should breed and be allowed to raise children.

In his support of the eugenics movement, Ellwood clearly demonstrated that his vision for sociology went far beyond the mere description of social reality. Sociology had a role to play in the social control of elements within society. As he (1923:3) stated:

> Both religion and social science seek to understand ultimately so that they can also control.

In this regard, his hope was that American society would democratically hand over the reins of power to the religious/scientific intelligentsia that sociology would produce. Ellwood (1929:80) looked forward to an America ruled by a techno-moral elite.

> The solution is the securing of scientifically trained social, political, moral, and religious leaders who can direct the people along the right lines and raise the general level of the culture of the masses, so that they can appreciate such leadership.

Politics must be modified: the new leaders would recognize that the service of humanity was their end, and not the gaining and maintaining of power. A true democracy would only then result (Ellwood, 1925:246). The new elite would ward off class strife and prevent violent revolutions and direct itself against all the forces that oppress and degrade men (Ellwood, 1925:130, 248). True democracy and social Christianity were to be closely intertwined, absolutely necessary for the future amelioration of the world and to insure that America would not become socialist or fascist. Although the new elite were agents of social control, they would rule benevolently and not establish a totalitarian regime. Ellwood (1925:157) stressed that tolerance was to be a key trait of social leaders; it was foolish to try to use coercion to bring about social reforms. Even the existence of non-Christian religions must be tolerated, he argued. With proper socialization and education the masses would elect benevolent social-scientifically trained legislators to power and follow their lead willingly.

There were a considerable number of points of agreement between the University of Chicago sociologists discussed here. All shared a Kingdom vision, perceived its arrival to be immanent, and hoped to use sociology to hasten its appearance. In addition, none concluded that the final American utopia would be either an all-inclusive assimilated amalgamation or a diverse pluralistic society. Instead each theorist presumed the Kingdom would be bounded with some being denied access. Chicago sociology, in its discussions of social problems, criminology, and deviance, set about delineating the categories of degenerate or defective peoples, who either had to be first saved before they could enter the Kingdom, or, if found unsalvageable, barred from entry forever.

The University of Wisconsin

Although neither Small nor Ellwood ever were given the opportunity to personally bring their political and social visions to fruition by being handed the reins of political power, two other social gospel intellectuals, Richard T. Ely and E.A. Ross, were able to become "philosopher kings," if only briefly. Ely, an economist, and Ross, a sociologist, were able to have their version of the social gospel put into practice in the state of Wisconsin between 1905 and 1914. Their "Wisconsin idea" was considered to be so successful that it was hailed as the model of what ought to be accomplished on a national level by the Progressive movement. Ross and Ely brought to the University of Wisconsin a version of the social gospel that was strongly rooted in their own rural agrarian backgrounds, which seemed to blend perfectly with the democratic egalitarianism of the farming and dairy communities of the Scandinavian and German immigrants that populated the rural Midwest and made up a large portion of the constituency of the University of Wisconsin. Thus, while the University of Chicago's brand of the social gospel strongly reflected an urban outlook and concern for city problems, Wisconsin's sociology was more rural in its social philosophy (Vidich and Lyman, 1982:1048). Both Ross and Ely concluded that the state was the perfect instrument for solving social problems and ultimately bringing about the Kingdom of God on earth, once the state was reestablished as a true reflection of the will of the morally superior rurally oriented electorate. Why Ely and Ross turned to attempting to establish a Christian theocracy is an important question that can be answered only through an analysis of their lives and thought.

Richard T. Ely (1854–1943) and Edward Alsworth Ross (1866–1951) had remarkably similar biographies, both living to be nearly ninety years of age. Both grew up on farms, Ely in upstate New York and Ross in Iowa. Both were raised in homes that believed in strict Calvinism, which each later rejected for the social gospel, a theology they found more to their liking. Ely joined the Episcopal church, while Ross rejected organized churches—which he often spoke of disparagingly—favoring a more secularized version of social religion than Ely. After graduating from Dartmouth and spending time in Germany studying the thought of Rosher and Knies, Ely began his teaching career at Johns Hopkins University in Baltimore in 1881, where Ross was to become his student in 1889. Albion Small and the social gospel economist John R. Commons were also Ely's students at Hopkins. In 1892, Ely left Hopkins to take a position at the University of Wisconsin where he was to stay for the remainder of his long teaching career.

Ross attended tiny Coe College in Iowa, where he dropped his fundamentalist Presbyterianism after grappling with Darwinian evolutionism (Dibble, 1975:59). He then spent a year studying in Berlin (1888–1889), and returned to enter Hopkins. In Ely, Ross found the model for the kind of person he wanted to become, someone who could combine the roles of academician and reformer. Ross was also strongly influenced by the anti-laissez-faire writings of Lester Ward, whose niece Ross would eventually marry. After Hopkins, Ross moved quickly through several colleges teaching at Indiana University in 1891, Cornell University in 1892—where he convinced Charles Ellwood to enter sociology—arriving at Stanford University in 1893. He remained there until 1900, when he was fired by the school's benefactor, Mrs. Leland Stanford, for his racist remarks about Chinese and Japanese immigrants. In 1901, he moved to the University of Nebraska where he stayed until 1906, from there he moved to the University of Wisconsin where he was reunited with Ely. Ross was hired to chair Wisconsin's sociology department. The next thirty-one years were spent by Ross at Wisconsin. He retired in 1937, but spent 1940–1950 chairing the American Civil Liberties Union (Bierstedt, 1981:131–138).

Ross (1969) expressed a positive attitude toward the social gospel in his 1901 book, *Social Control*. He (1969:138) referred to the social gospel as social religion and contrasted it to legalistic religion— i.e., Calvinism—which he rejected for both intellectual and personal reasons. Ross (1969:197, 199) defined social religion as "the means of orienting the feelings to the advantage of the social order" and the "conviction that there is a bond of ideal relationship between members of a society and the feelings that arise as a consequence of those convictions." Ross's perspective on religion was remarkably similar to

Durkheim's functional explanation of the value of religious belief as a glue which holds society together. Ross (1969:205) contrasted social religion and legal religion as follows:

> Righteousness is not an outward conformity to command, but an inward disposition. Not obedience, but love—to God and to neighbor—is the fulfilling of the Divine Will. Wrong is a disowning of the brother relationship. . . . The struggle between "justice" and "mercy," between hell-fire and love, marks the interference of these two great orders of socializing ideas.

The goal of social religion in Ross's (1969:204, 206) opinion was bringing Jesus' envisioned Kingdom of God on earth.

> It is the mission of the religion of Jesus to proclaim the union of all men in the bonds of an ideal brotherhood. To seek the Kingdom of God and His righteousness, to realize perfect harmony with one's brethren is the first concern of the disciple.
>
> The aspiration toward the "Kingdom of God" testified to the yearning to realize here on earth the perfect community of life.

At other places in his writing Ross secularized the notion of the Kingdom by replacing it with terms such as the "growth of social consciousness" and "social control" (Page 1969:215, 232). By social control, Ross meant "a kind of collective mind" that results from social interaction and that through its conventions, ideals, and institutions has the "task of safeguarding the collective welfare from the ravages of egotism." Ross believed that social control was to be directed primarily toward group, not individual, welfare. The "growth of social consciousness" would lead to a society where values expressed by the group would make possible a world in which individuals could live contentedly. Such was Ross's optimism for creating a truly democratic society.

Ely shared many of Ross's convictions about the potential for reforming American society and expressed even more openly than Ross his faith in the social gospel. Ely was from the start one of the key academicians in the social gospel movement, and his works were widely used as texts in colleges and seminaries across the country from the 1890s through the early decades of the twentieth century (Everett,

1946:75). From Ely's perspective, the Christian religion contained within it all that was necessary for the solution of social problems. Ely stated that theology and sociology originated from the great commandment and the second commandment, respectively. While theology was the working out of man's required love of God, sociology was the response to God's command to love one's neighbor (Everett 1946:81). Ely accused the traditional church of having been negligent by spending far too much of its time on theology and ignoring sociology. Sociology was the key to bringing about the Kingdom, through developing means of rationalizing the "law of love."

It is important not to give a romantic or sentimental interpretation to Ely's and other social gospelers' use of the word "love." For late nineteenth-century Protestants, the expression of love could be strict, stern, or even authoritarian. This explains how social gospelers like Henderson or Ellwood could "lovingly" prescribe eugenics or racial exclusion as policies to be instituted for the good of the nation. Ely concluded that the law of love could best be interpreted as the "social law of service" or Christian self-sacrifice (Everett, 1946:83). Sacrificial love was necessary to bring in the Kingdom; all social conduct must therefore contribute to social welfare. Sacrifice would be required from all elements of society in order to assure improvement, although some groups may have to give up more than others; however, those unwilling to make "contributions" were to be excluded from the covenant.

Ely moved from an early optimism that God was inevitably directing social evolution toward the attainment of ideal ends, into a period in which he believed that voluntary associations might be all that were necessary to speed up the Kingdom's arrival, to a final position in which he advocated the establishment of a theocracy to insure the Christianization of American society. These changes in attitude are clearly demonstrated in Ely's writings about labor, capitalism, socialism, and economic problems in America.

Ely was critical of the way that labor was being treated under the newly emerging capitalist system in America. He was convinced that the profit motive of America's capitalist economy was based on selfishness and greed. From Ely's perspective the law of society, including business, must be based on service to one's fellows, not self-interest. The Biblical concept of the brotherhood of man was not compatible with the profit motive (Everett, 1946:85). Ely argued that monopolies and trust were disruptive forces in social life, and not positive contributors to societal betterment. Ely (1884:35) stated that the selfishness of the capitalist system was leading to the segregation of individuals, separation of classes, distrust, mutual hatred, and corruption, and if allowed to go on unabated might lead to the demise of the nation itself. The intimacy typical of rural farming communities was disappearing as a result of capitalism. In Ely's analysis, the major problem in contemporary America was class warfare, the struggle between labor and capital, and he argued that the church should side with labor in its struggle (Rader, 1966:56).

However, Ely's faith in the possibility of solving the class problem through unionization shifted dramatically in the 1880s. In the early part of the decade, Ely had predicted a violent revolutionary labor movement led by anarchists, which milder socialists such as the Knights of Labor, and the fourteen percent of the work force who were unemployed at that time would join (Rader, 1966:60). After 1884, Ely focused his attention on the Knights of Labor, whom he felt were superior to other unions in America, because they were peaceful, industrywide, and wished to cooperate with management in reforming industry (Rader, 1966:66). Ely praised the Knights for their genuine displays of brotherhood. But he remained ambivalent about labor in general and often would express his reservations. For example, even in his attempt to give religious justification to the labor movement, Ely's elitist attitude toward workers showed through.

> Christ forever elevated labor and the laborer. He worked himself among workingmen, men rude and ignorant and certainly no better than the workingmen of today (quoted in Everett, 1946:80).

In addition, Ely encouraged laborers to work hard so they could prove themselves deserving of better rewards.

> Let every workingman try to make himself more indispensable in his place, a better workman and a better man. If every member of society is ever to receive a sufficient quantity of economic goods to satisfy all

> rational wants, products must be increased in quantity and improved
> in quality. If we ever expect to use our opportunities to the best
> advantage, we must improve our characters. Banding together will be
> of little avail to worthless men or a worthless cause (quoted in Vidich
> and Lyman, 1982:771).

However, Ely was not altogether opposed to the capitalist class. He
admired wealthy men who assumed wide social responsibilities and
suggested that conscientious capitalists assume positions of leadership
in the labor movement. Workers would welcome them because such
capitalists would naturally provide superior leadership to the movement
(Rader, 1966:10, 69). In the mid-1880s, Ely believed that the labor
movement would truly unite labor and capital into a cooperative
enterprise that would lead to the moral regeneration of the industrial
system (Rader, 1966:83). However, Ely gave up on this approach when
the Knights of Labor collapsed (Rader, 1966:84).

   One of the alternatives considered seriously by Ely was
socialism. Ely was greatly interested in socialism, and in many ways it
appealed to him as a good method for gaining the much sought-after
Kingdom of God. However, Ely was much more positive about the
socialist critiques of capitalism than its proposed solution, or socialist
methods for bringing these changes to fruition. With socialism's
exposure of the failings of capitalism, Ely (1894:253) wholeheartedly
agreed.

> Socialism has undoubted strength, especially strength of a negative
> sort. It points out real defects in our present social order; its
> indictment of existing institutions is a powerful one. The wastes of
> the competitive system are so enormous as to be awful; its operations
> are as cruel as the laws of nature. In its onward march it crushes and
> grinds to powder human existences by the millions: its rubbish has
> magnitude of tremendous proportions, and this rubbish consists of
> human beings with minds, hearts, and souls—men, good men often;
> women—women with precious gifts which ought to be developed for
> themselves and others, and little children with all their possibilities.

   The problems and contradictions within socialism began to
emerge when most socialist reformers talked about their plans for
implementing a utopia. Also, Ely (1885:32) could not agree with

socialism's criticisms of religion or the family. Ely (1885:35–37) did not feel that the violence and revolution advocated by many socialists as the primary means to bring about the new regime were necessary, or in any way Christian:

> For socialists to succeed they must first sow the seeds of discontent, bitterness, and hate in the minds of laborers as a preparation for that violence and revolution which are to inaugurate a new era of peace and goodwill among men.

Advocating assassinating members of the ruling class was anathema to Ely. In Ely's vision for social reform, the end did not justify any means. Also, socialism's all-out attack on the capitalist class overlooked the capacity in all men, including the businessman, for self-sacrifice and devotion to others (Ely, 1894:180). Ely proposed his own interpretation of socialism which he referred to as "distributive justice" and defined as "that general social amelioration which proposes to sacrifice no class, but to improve and elevate all classes" (Everett, 1946:88).

However, the problem remained of how to bring about his ideal of distributive justice. The seeming failure of the labor movement had shown Ely that workers and management would never be able to bring about the Kingdom era voluntarily without assistance. Neither was Ely willing to turn to revolutionary socialism because that would have meant the end of democracy. Ely's new solution was to reconstruct the state making it into the major instrument of societal redemption. An enlightened populace would democratically elect into office a morally and scientifically superior elite, who would then rule benevolently in the best interests of all social classes.

But, before this could take place, the dominant political and economic philosophy of the day, laissez-faire individualism, would have to be defeated and replaced by the social gospel. The leading exponent of laissez-faire individualism in the country, and Ely's main target for attack, was William Graham Sumner. In 1885, Ely founded an organization whose major purpose was taking the reins of political and economic theory out of the hands of Sumner. That organization was the American Economic Association. Its constitution represented a direct assault on Sumnerian economics, stating that to assume as

Sumner did that economic problems would solve themselves was the height of folly (Everett, 1946:85). The only way to solve the problems created by the capitalist system was to first bring together all like-minded leaders into an association to study the current economic structure. Among the original members of the American Economic Association were twenty-three ministers, including Lyman Abbott and Washington Gladden, the latter a charter platform committee member (Everett, 1946:86; Rader, 1966:38).

The conclusion that the American Economic Association reached was that to solve our economic ills would require an alliance encompassing church, state, and science (Everett, 1946:86). This policy position came from Ely himself, the founder and driving force behind the American Economic Association. Ely's belief was that church, state, and science working together could also solve our social problems. Of science, he (1885:72) said: "Our principal remedy against the evils of socialism, nihilism, and anarchism is better education in political, social, and economic science." In addition, the church must stop neglecting its duty toward temporal concerns and start following the social teachings of Christ (Ely, 1885:74). Finally, Ely sought to sacralize the state, arguing that we must acknowledge that the state is indeed a divine institution, one of God's chief agencies for good in our society. The American state must become professedly Christian, since Christian morality was the only stable basis for the state (Ely, 1885:71, 73). Government administrators must act as God-appointed stewards of property, and not rule on the basis of self-interest. Ely (1885:74) concluded:

> In the harmonious action of state, church, and individual, moving in the light of true science, will be found an escape from present and future social dangers. Herein is pointed out the path of safe progress; other there is none.

Ely's constant fear was that America would remain ripe for socialist revolution if it did not solve its economic problems. He held this attitude throughout his life, and was involved in the "red scare" the followed World War I. E.A. Ross, on the other hand, approved of the

Russian revolution, seeing it as the realization of many of the ideas expressed by Progressives such as himself (Bierstedt, 1981:137).

The Christian economic policy that the newly sacralized state was to put into effect Ely (1894:253) referred to as "fraternalism" or "the golden mean." It was to be a middle position, located between individualistic entrepreneurial capitalism and socialism. Ely advocated the state take-over of certain industries, particularly utilities, which should be run on the basis of the public good rather than for profit. Public utilities such as water companies, gas companies, the telegraph, and railroads were "natural monopolies" and as such should be placed under government stewardship (Rader, 1966:89). Under this system parallel railroads, for example, could be eliminated since they were wasteful. For the other industries that remained in capitalist hands, Ely proposed the creation of regulatory commissions to insure the conduct of business in a moral manner. Ely regarded regulatory laws and commissions not as restraints on economic freedom but as compulsions to social altruism. If these changes were made they could help to stop a potential socialist revolution, through taking the steps necessary to insure the slow evolution to a Christian egalitarian society (Everett, 1946:92). It was this plan that Ely tried to put into effect in the state government of Wisconsin when he and Ross were given their opportunity to do so in the first two decades of the twentieth century.

E.A. Ross was even more adamant than Ely in his criticisms of the capitalist class in America. Ross's writings are probably best understood as a reaction of those oriented to a farmers' democracy against the growth of big business (Mills, 1943:175). It seems that Ross came away from his Iowa youth with a pronounced hostility toward those elements of society that currently enjoyed the luxury of wealth and privilege (Ross, 1973:xi). Distressed by the destruction of the agrarian-commercial economy through the capitalist appropriation of private property, Ross (1969:53) wrote:

> Private property is, in fact, a great transforming force which acts almost independently of the human will. It has an evolution of its own, and the time comes at last when it violently thrusts men apart, in spite of all their vows to draw closer together. As it warps society farther and farther from the pristine equality that brings out the best in

human nature, there is need for artificial frames and webs that may hold the social mass together in spite of the rifts and seams that appear in it. Property is, therefore, the thing that calls into being rigid structures. It is the reagent that precipitates hard crystals, the lime that changes gristle into bone.

Ross (1969:78–79) was extremely critical of the power and prestige that the upper class enjoyed simply as a result of their money. In comparison to Henderson who labelled certain portions of the lower classes as parasitic, Ross referred to the capitalist class as parasitic; it was an unworthy ruling group (Page, 1969:234). Ross argued that the success of the capitalist enterprise had convinced the businessman of his "God-given right to run this country," leading to the gouging of the consumer, the laborer, and the farmer (Page, 1969:241).

Ross's (1973) most famous statement of the evils committed by the capitalist class appeared in his 1907 treatise, *Sin and Society*—a book highly praised by President Theodore Roosevelt, whose letter appears in the preface. In the book, Ross graphically described the results of the emergence of a capitalist class who ran their businesses immorally. Ross (1973:48) referred to many of the capitalist class as "criminaloids" whom he defined as "those who prosper from flagitious practices which have not yet come under the effective ban of public opinion or law." In the 1930s and 1940s, criminologist Edwin Sutherland would develop concepts quite similar to Ross's to discuss his theory of white-collar crime. Making frequent use of Biblical rhetoric, Ross (1973:63) castigated the business class for its religious hypocrisy.

The criminaloid puts on the whole armor of the good. He stands having his loins girt about with religiosity and having on the breastplate of respectability. His feet are shod with ostentatious philanthropy, his head is encased in the helmet of spread-eagle patriotism. Holding in his left hand the buckler of worldly success and in his right the sword of "influence," he is "able to withstand in the evil day, and having done all, to stand."

From Ross's (1973:15) perspective, modern capitalists were criminaloids because they refused to recognize that the factory labor of children was slavery, that stock speculation was gambling, or that tax-dodging was a form of larceny. However, Ross (1973:51) did not regard the criminaloid as unredeemably amoral or unsavable. They wanted what most people want—money, power, and status—but were in a hurry to get it and not particular as to the means they used to achieve it. If the criminaloids proved unrepentant, Ross (1973:126) advocated holding the directors of a company personally and criminally responsible for their company's misconduct. Laws must be passed making business violations into crimes. The state must supervise business so that it would act morally. Without state intervention, business would never adopt a policy of acting on behalf of the public good.

Two other aspects of Ross's sociology that are essential to an understanding of his Kingdom vision are his attitudes toward minority groups and the family. Of all the social gospel sociologists, Ross made some of the strongest arguments for keeping America racially pure. Throughout most of his life Ross expressed a strong antipathy toward all non-Aryan ethnic groups. Ross backed his ethnocentric beliefs in Nordic superiority by a reliance on Darwinian theory, and especially the survival of the fittest doctrine. Ross (1969:3) believed that Aryans were successful because they were an ambitious race, while the Slav was docile and the Hindu quiescent. Ross (1969:21) quoted from Edmond Demolin's 1898 book, *Anglo-Saxon Superiority*, to support his own beliefs.

In particular, Ross (1914:18–23, 282) created a mythical theory about American Aryan superiority by combining the survival of the fittest theory with the American frontier thesis—taught by Ross's colleague at Wisconsin, Frederick Jackson Turner. Ross believed that the hardships of the frontier had produced in America a new superior race, the "pioneering breed." America had been peopled by Aryans, who had survived such hardships as the perilous ocean crossing, the first winters spent in the new land that decimated their weaker members, and Indian attacks. Those who had chosen to forsake the eastern cities once they were established and traveled west to settle the frontier were the more venturesome and possessed greater energy, Ross argued. Thus, the result of the frontier experience was the creation of a superior American breed. It is interesting to note that Ross did not use the same argument to discuss American Blacks, who similarly had made perilous journeys across the ocean, survived hardships and diseases in a new land, and moved west with their masters to help civilize the southern frontier.

Ross's (1914:282) major worry was that America's pioneering breed would be swamped by the hordes of inferior racial stocks that were entering America now and flooding its cities. However, not all immigrants were unwanted; those that could quickly be assimilated should be permitted to enter. They were obviously of superior—i.e., Aryan—stock. For example, Ross (1914:76) praised Scandinavian immigrants, who founded farming communities in the northern Midwest:

> No immigrants of foreign speech assimilate so quickly as the Scandinavians. They never pollute in slums or stagnate in solid rural settlements.

Ross's fervent commitment to racial purity led him to regard with disdain any ethnic group whose racial stock he believed would pollute the superior Aryans. Of Italians, Ross (1914:113) stated:

> Steerage passengers from Naples show a distressing frequency of low foreheads, open mouths, weak chins, poor features, skewed faces, small or knobby crania, and backless heads.

And of eastern and southern Europeans, among whom Ross (1914:286) included Italians, Poles, Slavs, Jews, and Russians, he said:

> To the practiced eye, the physiognomy of certain groups unmistakably proclaims inferiority of type. I have seen gatherings of the foreign-born in which narrow and sloping foreheads are the rule. The shortness and smallness of the crania were very noticeable. There was much racial asymmetry. Among the women, beauty, aside from the fleeting, epidermal bloom of girlhood, was quite lacking. In every face there was something wrong—lips thick, mouth coarse, upper lip too long, cheek-bones too high. . . . There were so many sugar-loaf heads, moon-faces, slit mouths, lantern jaws, and goose-bill noses that one might imagine a malicious jinn had amused himself by casting human beings in a set of skew-molds discarded by the Creator.

Ross (1914:237) even went so far as to predict the decline of "good looks" in America if intermarriage with such immigrants became widespread. Late in his life, Ross was to publicly repudiate much of the Aryanism that he had attempted to justify scientifically (Vidich and Lyman, 1982:1060). However, Richard T. Ely was, at the time, in agreement with Ross's early Teutonism, believing that certain races were inherently inferior. Ely rejected such ideas only late in his life as well (Rader, 1966:235).

Ross's sociology of marriage and family incorporated his nativist fears. Ross's belief in racial purity resulted in an ambivalent attitude toward birth control. On the one hand, Ross was against contraception because it might doom a population to extinction—in particular the Aryan groups—while, on the other hand, he favored birth control among the lower classes—the blatantly racially inferior groups (Bierstedt, 1981:172; Vidich and Lyman, 1982:1062). Of course, Ross was horrified that just the opposite seemed to be taking place as immigrants continued to produce large families, while Aryan groups were limiting their progeny.

However, on a more positive note, Ross was also one of the first sociologists to recognize the positive benefits of changes in the American family system. Ross's position on the modern family unit was the outcome of his more general democratic outlook toward society; if the family became more democratic that was an advance over older more authoritarian models. In comparison to Ellwood who was disturbed by the decline of the traditional patriarchal family, the rising divorce rate, and the newly emancipated woman, Ross interpreted all of these as positive signs of the emergence of a new form of family, namely, egalitarian marriage. Unlike most of his contemporary family sociologists, Ross did not write negatively about the divorce rate. He predicted that the divorce rate would drop and the American family would once again be stabilized when egalitarian marriage became widespread (Vidich and Lyman, 1982:1067).

Despite the egalitarianism and discussions of democracy in the thought of Ross and Ely, one of the seeming paradoxes of their social theory is that they were both elitists. From their perspective, in a true democracy social differentiation was not to be based on money or the power or status that money could buy, but upon education. Under their egalitarian ideal only differences in education and knowledge could justify social differentiation. Thus, sociologists, economists, and other members of the professoriat were the only group that could make a legitimate claim to becoming the technocratic elite of American society (Vidich and Lyman, 1982:1071–1072). The democratic state must be run by an educated class.

Both Ely and Ross considered themselves to be such intellectually superior individuals and therefore felt they should create social policy. Ely regarded himself as an intellectual aristocrat who could lead and direct from above the social order in the best interest of all classes (Rader, 1966:2, 10). Ross' (1969:329) elitism was also clear:

It is not society that kindles strange longings or invents new pleasures, but superior individuals. Society can only await these Prometheans and spread broadcast the fire they have stolen from the gods. If a people can provide no elite to discover the ideal goods, the higher tastes do not develop.

In Ross's opinion, the worthy elite in contemporary American society were wise sociologists and we must place them at the steering wheels (Page, 1969:236; Bierstedt, 1981:179).

By placing sociologically trained leaders into positions of political power, Ross's and Ely's goal of turning the state into an instrument of spiritual and social regeneration could be accomplished. Ross argued that the state must reverse its current role of being an agent of exploitation in league with the rich, and become a powerful force for the consumer, the poor, and labor (Page, 1969:243). For example, Ross advocated the establishment of extensive government social services to replace private "philanthropy with strings" (Page, 1969:244). Ross was certain that all right-thinking people, members, like himself, of a superior race, would come to the very same conclusions about the future of society. They would then turn to sociologists, who would offer viable political solutions to benefit the welfare of humanity (Bierstedt, 1981:183). Similarly, Ely envisioned the state as the agency that should be given the task of promoting the social conditions indispensable for human progress (Rader, 1966:38). Ely's belief was that we must reconceptualize our image of the state, regarding it as an instrument for achieving Christian brotherhood based on altruism and cooperation (Vidich and Lyman, 1982:1051).

Ely felt that the traditional constitutional separation of church and state in America had been disastrous and this practice must be brought to an end. Since both the church and the state are divine institutions, Ely argued that they should collaborate so that the gospel could be fulfilled (Everett, 1946:96). A Christian theocracy would be required to bring America to its final destiny of Kingdom life.

Under the governorship of Robert LaFollette, first elected in 1900, Ely and Ross—after the latter's arrival in 1906—were given the opportunity to put their plan for reconstituting the role of the state into action in Madison (Hofstadter, 1963:9). Faculty members proposed legislation and the state government simply passed much of it. Ely, Ross, and their colleagues were so effective at instituting their social agenda within Wisconsin's state government that in 1913 an article was written about their experiment praising it as "A University that Runs a State" (Vidich and Lyman, 1982:1068). By 1911, some forty-six members of the Wisconsin faculty were serving both the university and the state (Rader, 1966:174). Among Ely's and Ross's colleagues and students who served in this dual capacity were John R. Commons, who created Wisconsin's civil service laws, considered the most comprehensive in the United States and guaranteed to stop the spread of urban boss politics, Balthasar H. Meyer, who was appointed to both the Interstate Commerce Commission and a new railroad commission that passed legislation to regulate the rates, services, and construction of railways, and Thomas S. Adams, who as chairman of the state tax commission developed the first progressive income tax in the United States (Rader, 1966:173–174).

A very important figure was Charles McCarthy, who headed the Legislative Reference Library that Ely had founded on the campus. The library became a virtual "bill factory" for the Progressive cause, although it was supposedly a nonpartisan organization (Rader, 1966:174). Thus, social scientists became in Wisconsin the architects of social policy, and with legislative support were able to have many of their policies made into law. McCarthy coined the term the "Wisconsin idea" to describe this great social experiment, and Progressives throughout the nation looked to Wisconsin as the model state for social reform activity. The university as a whole took on the ameliorative task by supplying training to their students so that they could become future experts in politics, administration, the professions, the arts, and culture (Vidich and Lyman, 1982:1069). In this process, the social gospel was being changed into a more secularized form, undergoing rationalization so that it could serve as part of the rationale for bureaucratic administration of social problems.

The Wisconsin experiment came to an end around 1915, partially because of disputes between Ely and LaFollette (Rader, 1966:190). In Ely's mind, LaFollette was placing too much reliance on the intelligence and knowledge of the ordinary citizen, whereas Ely felt increasingly that the state needed more leadership by its educational elite.

However, many of the ideas experimented with in Wisconsin would return in the 1930s as part of Franklin D. Roosevelt's New Deal. The hope of the welfare state was that it would ameliorate some of the inequities created by capitalism. After World War II, millions of dollars in federal and state monies would be placed into the hands of social scientists with the hope they might discover more equitable social policies. The legacy of Ross and Ely, that big government could solve many of our social problems, would remain the dominant ideology until the Reagan era, when William Graham Sumner's brand of laissez-faire individualism would return in the guise of downsizing government. It is to Sumner's Calvinist vision of American society to which we now turn.

William Graham Sumner's Calvinist Sociology

The one sociologist of his generation who openly attacked what he saw to be the fallacies of the Chicago and Wisconsin approaches to sociology and social reform was William Graham Sumner (1840–1910). Sumner was the arch enemy of Small, Henderson, Ross, and Ely because he seemed to oppose everything they advocated: Christian sociology, social amelioration, and government interventionism. Small (1916:732–733) and Vincent (1907:415) tried to discredit Sumner by denying that Sumner was a sociologist at all. Similarly, Sumner (1959:ix) rejected the social gospelers, calling his discipline the science of society rather than sociology, because he so detested the work done under the latter. Sumner's laissez-faire model of political economy, as well as his anti-religious stance, raised the fury of sociologists like Small and economists of Ely's school. Although some may argue that Sumner's sole importance in the history of Christian sociology is that he served as the foil or gadfly of social gospel reformism, Sumner's sociology itself can be shown to be the outcome of his own religious beliefs. Sumner was a Protestant minister prior to becoming professor of political and social science at Yale. His sociology was, in effect, a secularized version of Calvinism. While having moved from theology to sociology, Sumner did not give up the religious belief that one could find meaning in life. Like the sixteenth- and seventeenth-century Calvinists, he sought meaning in hard work and worldly success. But, from Sumner's perspective, such success could offer at best temporary solace, because he believed that attempts at knowing ultimate truth were futile. Because he defined meaning solely through this-worldly success, Sumner fought fiercely against any forces that might impede the chance that all should have to succeed. Social reforms and government interventions were regarded by Sumner as impediments to the ordinary man's chances for worldly success. Sumner coupled this secularized Calvinist work ethic with his own version of Social Darwinism and his belief in the inevitable operation of the social process. All that the state could do, given the nature of social reality, was to guarantee that all had an equal chance to success. Sumner therefore became an advocate of civil and economic libertarianism.

Born in New Jersey in 1840, Sumner graduated from Yale in 1863, then went to Europe to finish his education, studying theology at Oxford while preparing for the ministry. In 1866, he returned to Yale, tutoring mathematics and Greek, before going into the ministry in 1869, serving at Calvary Church in New York City. Sumner spent two additional years as pastor of the Church of the Redeemer in Morristown, New Jersey. In his sermons he stressed the Puritan virtues of hard work, self-reliance, and self-denial (Bierstedt, 1981:3). Sumner claimed that the work of preparing sermons led him to investigate topics of social science and political economy (Davie, 1963:2). In 1872, he returned to Yale to become professor of political and social science, where his students complained he simply continued to preach sermons. He remained at Yale for thirty-eight years until his death in 1910. Sumner stated that he never consciously rejected his religious faith; he says he had simply put it into a drawer and discovered when he later opened it that it was gone (Bierstedt, 1981:3). Sumner continued to attend Trinity Church in New Haven regularly until the last ten years of his life.

Sumner's rejection of religion in the 1870s was part of his Comtean search to find natural laws that would replace metaphysical speculations concerning the operations of society. Sumner found the types of explanations he was searching for in the social evolutionary writings of Herbert Spencer. Sumner borrowed many of Spencer's ideas, although he was more enamored with the general theory that society is operating under the direction of natural social forces than Spencer's specific model of unilinear social evolutionism. Using Spencer as a text, Sumner taught one of the first sociology courses in America in 1875.

One of Spencer's ideas that Sumner wholeheartedly adopted was the concept of the survival of the fittest—this was also part of the Christian sociology of theorists like Henderson and Ross. Sumner argued that by tampering with the law of the survival of the fittest the disastrous result might be the survival of the unfittest (Bierstedt, 1981:11). Faith in survival of the fittest became part of Sumner's justification for his support of laissez-faire and his opposition to most social welfare programs. However, it is important to point out that

Sumner's Social Darwinism did not lead him to become a nativist like Ross or Henderson, who used Darwinism to bolster Anglo-Saxon superiority. Sumner may have been an elitist, but he attempted to remove all vestiges of ethnocentrism from his own work.

In rereading Sumner's writings, it becomes apparent that he cannot be categorized as an evolutionary sociologist, as a number of commentators have labelled him. Despite Sumner's belief in the survival of the fittest, he had little faith in systems of complex theory (Page, 1969:76). Also, Sumner was fascinated by the embeddedness of cultural habits and traditions and their resistance to change; the "cake of custom" seemed to be in conflict with gradual, irresistible evolutionary development. Sumner developed his theory of social change, or the lack of it, in his discussion of mores and folkways in his 1906 classic, *Folkways*. Sumner believed that the folkways and mores of each culture had been established gradually but once created became encrusted or habitual and thereafter difficult to change. However, Sumner also argued that it was possible that the mores of a society could disintegrate, leading to periods of cultural confusion until new mores emerged. America was going through just such a period, felt Sumner, as a result of the decline of Puritan values and the emergence of industrialization. Sumner found these changes very disturbing. To understand why Sumner was so ambivalent about modernization, we must turn to a discussion of the importance of mores. Sumner (1959:59, 231) defined the mores as:

> . . . ways of doing things which are current in a society to satisfy human needs and desires, together with the faiths, notions, codes, and standards of well living which inhere in those ways.
>
> All notions of propriety, decency, chastity, politeness, order, duty, right, discipline, respect, reverence, cooperation, and fellowship . . . are in the mores.

Mores thus make up society's underlying belief system of the way things ought to be. The folkways and mores strain toward consistency, Sumner (1959:5–6) argued, so that ideas about what is proper in regard to specific social spheres such as the family, economics, and religion tend to coalesce into a unified world view. The Orient and the Occident represented examples of how diverse world views could be. The mores of each culture took on the force of habit and became so deeply embedded that only the topmost layer of tradition was susceptible to modification through philosophy, ethics, legislation, or religion (Bierstedt, 1981:16). For example, Sumner (1959:77) showed that even social cataclysms as great as the Civil War and Reconstruction had not yet produced new mores to govern the relations between Blacks and Whites in the American South.

> In our southern states, before the Civil War, Whites and Blacks had formed habits of action and feeling towards each other. They lived in peace and concord, and each one grew up in the ways which were traditional and customary. The Civil War abolished legal rights and left the two races to learn how to live together under other relations than before. The whites have never been converted from the old mores. Those who still survive look back with regret and affection to the old usages and customary sentiments and feelings. The two races have not yet made new mores. Vain attempts have been made to control the new order through legislation. The only result is the proof that legislation can not make mores.

Sumner's discussion of mores clearly indicates that he was not an evolutionist. Progress was not inevitable. Sumner also attacked those evolutionary theorists who argued that God was directing the evolutionary process. From Sumner's perspective, world events could not be explained solely with reference to supernatural forces. Sumner rejected as well the teleology that appears in almost all evolutionary thought (Everett, 1946:18–20). He repeatedly admitted he had no vision of the final stage to be brought about by the play of natural forces. He therefore had no vision of the Kingdom and lacked the ultimate motivation shared by social gospeler sociologists that we must try to change society.

Sumner (1959:85) felt that industrial civilization could not and should not be directed by social do-gooders, because society was making its own inevitable changes and destroying the old Puritan mores in the process. Industrial civilization would, according to Sumner, create the conditions for our existence, set the limits on our social activity, regulate the bonds on our social relations, determine our conceptions of good and evil, suggest our life philosophy, remold our inherited political institutions, and reform the oldest customs such as marriage and property (Everett, 1946:16). Therefore, he (1959:77–78) concluded that we were living through a period of normlessness—what Durkheim called "anomie"—and must await the arrival of a new coherent set of mores.

> We see that mores do not form under social convulsion and discord. It is only just now that the new society seems to be taking shape. . . . Some are anxious to interfere and try to control. They take their stand on ethical views of what is going on. It is evidently impossible for anyone to interfere. We are like spectators at a great natural convulsion. The results will be such as the facts and forces call for. We can not foresee them . . . The mores which once were are a memory. Those which anyone thinks ought to be are a dream.

With the old Puritan mores being abandoned, new mores emerging but not yet decipherable, and having forgotten about his own faith, Sumner faced both a personal and intellectual future that he could have easily interpreted as absurd. His cross-cultural studies offered him no solace, because comparative analysis of mores led him to recognize cultural relativism while rejecting belief in the possibility of universal ethical principles. It seems that the Puritan work ethic offered the only ultimate meaning that Sumner could find in life. *Folkways* was based on extensive anthropological material, because Sumner had hoped that through cross-cultural comparisons one could escape the limitations of one's own culture. However, after studying anthropology, Sumner (1959:231) concluded that the mores might condone anything and that there were no universal norms.

> The mores can make things seem right and good to one group or one age which to another seems antagonistic to every instinct of human nature.

Noting that people in everyday life did not share his conclusion, and that in fact all peoples consider their own mores to be superior and absolute, Sumner (1959:13) developed the concept of ethnocentrism. He defined enthnocentrism as "a view of things in which one's group is the center of everything, and all others are scaled and rated with reference to it." Thus every culture held that their own values were right, and Sumner (1959:58) seemed to agree with them, up to a point.

> For the people of a time and place their own mores are always good, for them there can be no question of the goodness or badness of their mores.

Social observers, such as the nativist social gospelers, should not then be critical of another culture's mores, because for that people they were right.

However, Sumner (1959:26, 27, 99) did not always uphold his own relativist stand and on occasion argued that there were harmful folkways and bad mores. Among his list of harmful folkways were such Indian practices as child marriages, widow sacrifice, and wasteful food habits, such as refusing to eat cattle and allowing them to roam the streets freely. Bad mores were defined as those that are not well fitted to the conditions and needs of the society at the time.

Sumner's cross-cultural studies led him to regard as spurious the claims made by various religions that they each have universal validity. Sumner (1959:111) also pioneered the anthropological critique of Christian missionary endeavor.

> We think that our "ways" are the best, and that their superiority is so obvious that all heathen, Mohammedans, Buddhists, etc., will as soon as they learn what our ways are, eagerly embrace them. Nothing could be further from the truth. . . . It is really the great tragedy of civilization that the contact of lower and higher is disastrous to the former, no matter what may be the point of contact.

Sumner's ambivalence about religion is also shown clearly in the following statement.

> It has favored both war and peace, wealth and poverty, diligence and idleness, virginity and prostitution, humility and ostentation, indulgence and austerity. It has prescribed game-laws, cannibalism, human sacrifice, the killing of the old, suicide, incest, polyandry, polygyny, slavery, and the levirate, has guaranteed all forms of property-holding, of inheritance, and of government; has both favored and proscribed commerce and the taking of interest; it has been forced to bend to new vices. It has therefore offered no absolute

standard of morality for there is none, but has sanctioned what lay in
the mores of the time and place—or, often, what lay in the mores of
the place at some previous time (quoted in Bierstedt, 1981:4).

It is not surprising that the social gospel sociologists attacked his work.
However, it can be argued that Sumner's cultural relativist position
ultimately became the dominant one in the field of sociology; the
discipline no longer claims the ability to uncover universal truths. In
addition, Sumner's cross-cultural methodology survived—just as
Henderson's ethnographic fieldwork continued at Chicago. At Yale,
George Murdock, would adopt Sumner's approach and begin the
collection of anthropological data that would form the Human
Relations Area File (Davis, 1963:11).

In a world in which he could find no absolutes—except perhaps
relativity—Sumner substituted his own ultimate criteria of moral living,
hard work, and success. Of course, these ideals represented secularized
vestiges of the Puritan work ethic, which Sumner (1959:86) rightly
recognized as the emerging entrepreneurial ethos in industrialized
America.

> The extravagances in doctrine and behavior of the seventeenth
> century Puritans have been thrown off and their code of morals has
> been shorn of its angularity, but their life policy and standards have
> become to a very large extent those of the civilized world.

America, like any other culture, was developing its own set of
mores. American mores would naturally be based upon the Puritan
work ethic, part of the nation's original heritage. Similarly, since the
mores of each culture fit that society, Americans should live by their
norms just as Moslems should follow Islam. Sumner's own logic led
him to support laissez-faire capitalism as right for America because it
seemingly offered to all a chance at success through hard work. While
in his discussion of comparative religion Sumner employed an
objectivism social gospelers found annoying, Sumner's relativistic
tendencies were altogether lacking in his treatment of capitalist political
economy; in this area he offered the "absolute truth." Sumner identified
the "good" and the moral with individualist economic enterprise. Thus,
Sumner's advocacy of laissez-faire individualism was the result

primarily of his religious orientation, his faith in a secularized version of Calvinist election, which he bolstered with Social Darwinism.

Sumner's commitment to laissez-faire was almost complete. Society should oppose legislation that would tie the hands of business—the kinds of controls reformers like Ely and Ross tried to institute. Sumner also opposed laws that would give businesses "unfair" advantages, such as protective tariffs. The latter policy certainly did not endear him to the businessmen of his day (Bierstedt, 1981:12). Sumner (1963:122) even spoke out against using public expenditures to prevent vice, stating:

> Vice is its own curse. If we let nature alone, she cures vice by the most frightful penalties.

A drunkard in the gutter was just where he ought to be, and time and money should not be wasted on his behalf. Sumner was against the growing Prohibition movement as well, which was simply part of a wrong-headed attempt to legislate morality by attacking vice. As he (1963:123) put it: "A and B determine to be teetotallers and they get a law passed that makes C a teetotaller for the sake of D who is likely to drink too much."

As an advocate of laissez-faire government, Sumner pointed out continuously the fallacies of social reform. Sumner (1963:107) regarded all social reformers, including social gospel sociologists, as among the uninformed, seeking to alter the state improperly:

> While the state is reaching out on one side to fields of socialistic enterprise, interfering in the interests of parties in the industrial organism, assuming knowledge of economic laws which nobody possesses, taking ground as to dogmatic notions of justice which are absurd, and acting because it does not know what to do, it is losing its power to give peace, order, and security.

Sumner's (1963:179–180) most famous statement on the fallacy of social reform appears in his essay, "The Absurd Effort to Make the World Over."

> If this poor old world is as bad as they say, one more reflection may check the zeal of the headlong reformer. It is at any rate a tough old

world. It has taken its trend and its curvature and all its twists and
tangles from a long course of formation. All its wry and crooked
gnarls and knobs are therefore stiff and stubborn. If we puny men by
our arts can do anything at all to straighten them, it will only be by
modifying the tendencies of some of the forces at work, so that, after
a sufficient time, their action may be changed a little and slowly the
lines of movement may be modified. This effort, however, can at
most be only slight, and it will take a long time. In the meantime
spontaneous forces will be at work, compared with which our forces
are like those of a man trying to deflect a river, and these forces will
have changed the whole problem before our interferences have time
to make themselves felt. The great stream of time and earthly things
will sweep on just the same in spite of us. It bears with it now all the
errors and follies of the past, the wreckage of all the philosophies,
doomed ethical systems, the debris of all the institutions, and the
penalties of all the mistakes. It is only in imagination that we stand by
and look at and criticize it and plan to change it. Everyone of us is a
child of his age and cannot get out of it. He is in the stream and is
swept along with it. All his sciences and philosophies come to him
out of it. Therefore the tide will not be changed by us. It will swallow
up both us and our experiments. It will absorb the efforts at change
and take them into itself as new but trivial components, and the great
movement of tradition and work will go on unchanged by our fads
and schemes. The things that will change it are the great discoveries
and inventions, the new reactions inside the social organism, and the
changes in the earth itself on account of changes in the cosmical
forces. . . . The men will be carried along with it and be made by it.
The utmost they can do by their cleverness will be to note and record
their course as they are carried along, which is what we do now, and
is that which leads us to the vain fancy that we can make or guide the
movement. That is why it is the greatest folly of which a man can be
capable, to sit down with a slate and pencil to plan out a new social
world.

Not knowing how the new mores would appear in their final
form, but certain that industrial civilization was remolding them in its
own image, Sumner assured his upper-class students at Yale that they
were right to seek the fruits of free enterprise, demonstrating that their
actions were in line with the mores. Thus, in Sumner's sociology, a
class-stratified society was perfectly natural, the outcome of the
differing results individuals make of their chances in life. Socialism or

any system that promised to redistribute wealth was considered anathema. In fact, Sumner (1883:168) argued that socialism was sinful, stating that the yearning after equality was always the offspring of envy and covetousness. Rather, Sumner (1883:43) believed that there was no sin in being rich.

> That it is not wicked to be rich; nay, even that it is not wicked to be richer than one's neighbor.

His reliance on success as a sign led Sumner to feel disdain for the losers in the battle of life. Of the attempts by many of the social gospelers to improve the lot of the poor or lessen the stigma attached to poverty, Sumner (1963:120) would have no part.

> In these last years I have read hundreds of articles and heard scores of sermons and speeches which are really glorifications of the good-for-nothing, as if they were the charges of society. . . . We are addressed all the time as if those who are respectable are to blame . . . and as if there were an obligation on the part of those who have done their duty toward those who have not done their duty.

The "duty" Sumner is speaking of here was of course hard work. The values he stressed were work, temperance, thrift, and savings. As Sumner stated: "Industry, self-denial, and temperance are the laws of prosperity for men and state; without them advance in the arts and in wealth means only corruption and decay through luxury and vice" (quoted in Everett, 1946:20). Thus, in Sumner's mind, obtaining enormous amounts of wealth was not the ultimate goal; those in the middle class who were successful in their endeavors were to be counted among the elect as well. Sumner showed a strong interest in the hard-working individual, to whom he applied the term "the Forgotten Man." The Forgotten Man was the simple, honest laborer, ready to earn his living by productive labor. It was he whom Sumner (1963:111) argued was hurt most by the schemes of social reformers, because the Forgotten Man had no say in instituting welfare policies and always ended up paying for these programs with money from his own pocket.

> As soon as A observes something which seems to him to be wrong, from which X is suffering, A talks it over with B, and A and B then

> propose to get a law passed to remedy the evil and help X. Their law
> always proposes to determine what C shall do for X, or in the better
> case, what A, B, and C shall do for X.

In Sumner's forgotten man model A and B are sociologists or social
reformers, X is the lower class, while C is the Forgotten Man, who
becomes the victim of the reformer's or philanthropist's expensive
plans.

What value did Sumner see in sociology as a scientific
discipline? He had rejected the stance toward the discipline taken by the
social gospelers—that sociology could uncover the objective truth
about the nature and causes of our social problems, and then offer cures
that would insure a utopian future. Sociology, argued Sumner, could
not change the world, it could only reflect upon it, and even that
reflection must not be assumed to be the discovery of absolute truth. In
Sumner's perspective, sociology was a valuable tool when applied as a
method of critical thinking toward social reality. However, he cautioned
that any sociological analysis would still be subject to the fact that man
yet perceives the world "through a glass darkly." Thus, even Sumner's
sociological methodology was the outcome of his Puritan Christian
perspective. Calvinist thought holds that all truth or knowledge is the
result of divine revelation and, in Sumner's world, where God was no
longer in touch with man there could be no absolute knowledge.
Sumner's sociology was an expression of the world view of the Puritan
who is cut off from God. But Sumner does not throw up his hands in
despair. Although absolute truth is beyond his grasp, he is willing to
settle for the struggle to discover truth.

> I do not know if it is possible for us ever to arrive at a knowledge of
> the "truth" in regard to any important matters. I doubt if it is possible.
> It is not important. It is the pursuit of truth which gives us life, and it
> is to that pursuit that our loyalty is due (quoted in Davie, 1963:10).

The method of social science was to be based upon critical thinking.
This would separate science from religion. Religion was not open to
such critical thinking because its tenets were to be accepted
unquestioningly, while scientists must always be willing to put their
propositions to the test. While Sumner was conservative politically, his

sociological methodology was much more open minded in the sense that he constantly raised fundamental questions about society and had the courage to pursue such investigations no matter how many cherished and traditional beliefs might be trampled underfoot (Davie, 1963:viii). In Sumner's sociology, all theories were to be taken as tentative conclusions; only religion assumes it can offer final solutions, not so science. Although sociology could borrow the cause and effect methodology of the natural sciences, it could never be exact (Everett, 1946:14–15). Sumner almost never used statistics, feeling that sociology could make lucid statements without the aid of mathematics.

Sumner's sociology of knowledge was not similar to that of most social scientists, neither that of his own day's social gospelers, or of the later positivists or Mannheimians. All of these sociologists argued that the social scientist has a unique insight into the world that separated his thought from that of ordinary humans. Sumner was ambivalent about whether this was true. The mind of the sociologist was just as conditioned by the mores of his time as any other human being. As Sumner (1959:76) put it: "Each individual is born into the mores, and formed by them before he is capable of reasoning about them." In another discussion of the mores, he (1959:477) stated:

> People inherited them without knowing it; they are molding them unconsciously; they will transmit them involuntarily. The people can not make the mores. They are made by them. Yet the group is at once makers and made.

Sumner's claim was that not even a scientist can escape the mores of his time. But the social scientist can reflect upon them, something people in everyday life rarely seem to do. However, Sumner is doubtful whether the sociologist's reflections can be employed to change the mores. That we must accept the inevitable was Sumner's conclusion, one quite compatible with Calvinist predestination. In an uncharacteristic moment, discussed by Bierstedt (1981:8), Sumner made a claim that sociology had some potential to understand and reform the world.

> The practical utility of sociology consists in deriving the rules of right social living from the facts and laws which prevail by nature in the

constitution and functions of society. It must without doubt, come into collision with all other theories of right living which are founded on authority, tradition, arbitrary invention, or poetic imagination.

But usually Sumner (1959:68) expressed the opinion that reflection could not change the mores.

If traditional mores are subjected to rational and ethical examination they are no longer naive and unconscious. It may then be found that they are gross, absurd or inexpedient.

However, even discovery of the truth did not mean that humans would reject their traditions. Sumner's (1963:171) own conclusion was that we must be willing to accept the inevitable rather than fight against it.

A thing which is inevitable, however is one which we can not control. We have to make up our minds to it, adjust ourselves to it, and sit down and live with it. Its inevitableness may be disputed, in which case we may re-examine it; but if our analysis is correct, when we reach what is inevitable we reach the end, our regulations must apply to ourselves, not to the social facts.

Nevertheless, Sumner did not mean that acceptance of the inevitable should be interpreted as adopting a policy of doing absolutely nothing. In the last chapter of *What Social Classes Owe to Each Other* entitled "Wherefore We Should Love One Another," Sumner advocates civil libertarianism and private charity as the best methods of demonstrating Christian love in the modern world. On the one hand, Sumner (1883:157) was opposed to all forms of public or government charity: ". . . I fully believe that today the next most pernicious thing to vice is charity in its broad and popular sense." In his nineteenth-century version of "trickle down" economics, Sumner (1963:120) demonstrated how public philanthropy harmed the Forgotten Man.

The next time you are tempted to subscribe a dollar to charity, I do not tell you not to do it . . . but I do ask you to stop and remember the Forgotten Man and understand that if you put your dollar in a savings bank it will go to swell the capital of the country which is available for division amongst those who, while they earn it, will reproduce it with increase.

On the other hand, Sumner (1883:160) approved of individual acts of charity because they were based on the law of sympathy, the belief that men should share each other's burdens, and do as they would have others do to them. However, relations of sympathy or sentiment were limited to two persons only—A doing something for B—and not to be generalized to include entire social classes—A telling B what he must do for C—as the social gospelers envisioned the Biblical commandment. Sumner's (1883:158–159) example was to describe a story of a man who had a tree fall upon him.

> What now is the reason why we should help each other? . . . A man struck by a falling tree has, perhaps, been careless. We are all careless. Environed as we are by risks and perils, which befall us as misfortunes, no man of us is in a position to say "I know all the laws and am sure to obey them all; therefore, I shall never need aid and sympathy". At his very best, one of us fails in one way and another in another. Therefore the man under the tree is the one of us who for the moment is smitten. It may be you tomorrow and me the next day. It is the common peril which gives us a kind of solidarity of interest to rescue the one for whom the chances of life have turned out badly just now. Probably the victim is to blame. He almost always is so. A lecture to that effect in the crisis of his peril would be out of place. . . . Men, therefore, owe to men, in the chances and perils of this life, aid and sympathy, on account of the common participation in human frailty and folly. This observation, however, puts aid and sympathy in the field of private and personal relations, under the regulation of reason and conscience, and gives no ground for mechanical and impersonal schemes.

Beside private charity, Sumner advocated civil libertarianism as the policy that the state should adopt to guarantee that all would be given an equal chance to become successful. Such a government, Sumner (1963:103) argued, would represent the highest stage of political development. Sumner (1883:163) held that it was the duty of the state to establish justice for all, from the least to the greatest. Sumner interpreted rights as chances; the state could guarantee the chance to the pursuit of happiness but not the possession of happiness.

Although rights must be equal, this would never produce an egalitarian society because the results that people make of equal chances will be proportioned to their individual merits. Class distinctions were legitimate because they were simply the result of the differing degrees of success men have made out of their chances (Sumner, 1883:164–167). For this reason, Sumner (1883:167) opposed socialism.

> Instead of endeavoring to redistribute the acquisitions that have been made . . . our aim should be to increase, multiply, and extend the chances.

However, the state should also act to protect those who could not protect themselves. For example, Sumner (1963:123–124) favored factory legislation for women and children because they were not on an equal footing with men and could be easily abused. It was up to the state to guarantee equality for those who did not yet have it.

Paradoxically, Sumner, although the greatest critic of the social gospel, promoted the establishment of a state that would guarantee the rights of individuals rather than one that would act as an agent of social control over unworthy elements of the population. His secularized Calvinism led him to support a sociopolitical platform quite different from the one advocated by the social gospelers.

PART **III**

CHAPTER 5

The Demise of the Social Gospel

If the influence of social gospel theology upon early American sociology was as important as argued here, the question arises as to why contemporary sociology seems to have completely forgotten its religious foundations. What led to the demise of Christian sociology? This question can only be addressed by analyzing the changes that took place within both sociology and theology during the 1920s and beyond. While the American social gospel expanded its scope in the 1910s to include international concerns, the 1920s were a period of decline for the social gospel. Its theology came under attack from a variety of sources and went through a series of transformations that undermined its implications for sociology. With the decline of the social gospel, Christian sociology was cut off from its theological base. Social gospel sociology also lost one of its key allies, social work, during the 1920s as settlement house and other community workers responded to growing pressures to professionalize and, in the process of seeking legitimation, turned toward psychology.

In the final chapter, we will discuss how sociology itself rejected its initial links to social gospel theology and missions. Led by William F. Ogburn and other positivists, sociology was exhorted to divorce itself from social reform, become objective and value-free, and base its findings on mathematical research. Such a discipline would have no place for the moralistic claims of Christian sociologists. Positivists focused upon the development of an adequate mathematical technique, which they were willing to place at the disposal of business, industry, military, and government—the very same institutions frequently criticized by social gospel sociologists. The positivists were willing to be the servants of power, but in the process American sociology lost its uniquely developed critical theory. As hirelings of reigning societal elites, positivist researchers had to prove to their new potential employers that they were no longer making grandiose claims about sociology's commitment to save society and, furthermore, that sociologists did not desire the reins of power for themselves. While positivism claimed it had no preplanned agenda for social reform, positivist sociologists certainly hoped to become social managers within America's increasingly bureaucratic society. In this regard it can be argued that positivism did not really reject the social gospel, but rather that the discipline of sociology transvalued and secularized its original theological presuppositions, transforming the Kingdom into a utopian state of societal well-being, best captured by the phrase "the good life." It can be argued that much of American sociology has remained a fundamentally religious endeavor up to the present day.

In the second decade of the twentieth century the social gospel went through a period of modification and expansion, led initially by two of its major original proponents, Walter Rauschenbusch and Josiah Strong. Rauschenbusch, in his 1917 work, *A Theology for the Social Gospel*, concluded that the Kingdom of God on earth might not appear in the near future. In fact, the final utopian stage might never appear, because each consummation of the Kingdom becomes a basis for even further development. As Rauschenbusch (1945:223) put it: "The Kingdom of God is always coming, but we can never say 'Lo here.'" Rauschenbusch had thus translated the idea of the Kingdom into faith in inevitable unilinear progress. Such optimism would in the 1920s come under attack by the progenitors of modern Fundamentalism, whose perspective on the future was much more bleak.

Josiah Strong, who had expressed strong nativist prejudices in *Our Country* and *The New Era*, led a major movement to internationalize the social gospel in the 1910s. In *Our World* and *The New World-Religion*, written during World War I, Strong (1914, 1915) argued that the social gospel must take up world problems in order to become truly relevant. Of course, other social gospelers had previously recognized that their movement had implications beyond the United States. Washington Gladden (1886:214) had long believed that the social gospel and missionary activity were fundamentally interrelated. Gladden defined social science as a home mission and foreign missionary activity as universalized social science. Similarly, University of Chicago Divinity School professor Shailer Mathews (1910:156) declared that the social gospel had worldwide applications:

> The social gospel was not only intended for America and Europe. It is applicable wherever there are men and women. The work of the missionary is an illustration of its message as truly as are improved tenements and municipal reform in our great cities.

Although Mathews's (1910:154–156) version of social gospel missions tended to be ethnocentric—he justified the missionary movement as the bringer of higher civilization to the unenlightened—Strong realized that universalizing the social gospel could easily lead to American imperialism, a tendency he opposed. Strong apparently became interested in the worldwide potential of the social gospel through his acquaintance with William Bliss (1898), whose *Encyclopedia of Social Reform* listed ameliorative activities in a number of foreign countries. Between 1904 and 1906, Strong (1904; 1905; 1906) published yearbooks that contained information on social reform activities in countries around the world. In *Our World* Strong focused on the imperialist tendencies of modern industrialized nations like the United States and argued that the social gospel must oppose them. Strong (1914:114, 141, 159) criticized capitalist nations for seizing undeveloped areas, using them as outlets for their products, exploiting them for their natural resources, and engendering global racial hatred.

In 1925 Daniel Fleming attempted to create a nonethnocentric missionary theology based upon the social scientific methodology espoused by social gospelers like Strong. According to Fleming (1925:1), the missionary movement must eradicate its sense of Western or Anglo–Saxon superiority. Also, missions should no longer be concerned solely with saving souls, but should also demonstrate concern for such major world problems as the hardships created by industrialization (Fleming, 1925:119–121). Missionaries, like religiously inspired social reformers at home, would have to turn to social science for solutions to world problems.

> We have learned that it is only through steady, close, continuous, constructive study that Christian solutions can be worked out for the kinds of problems we are facing. Loyal to the scientific enterprise of the age, the facts would have first to be assembled and made known. This must be done on a scale rarely attempted by missionary societies of the present denominational type. This has been recognized in the establishment of the Institute of Social and Religious Research with its large annual budget. . . . Something no less is needed when Christians take up in earnest the task of studying, locating, and eradicating the social, national, and international sins of our day (Fleming, 1925:136).

Another aspect of the internationalization of the social gospel was its incorporation into the philosophy of ecumenical Christian organizations like the Interchurch World Movement and the World Council of Churches. The Interchurch World Movement, which was strongly social service oriented, was founded in 1919 and sought to bring together all Protestant denominations, both in the United States and in foreign countries (Visser 'T Hooft, 1928:28). In the 1930s it was hoped that the World Council of Churches would act as the major vehicle through which the American social gospel would be communicated to the world (Carter, 1971:221). Thus, the social gospel was to rid itself of its narrow nativist orientation and take on an international outlook.

Despite the globalization of the social gospel during the second decade of the century, the social gospel was soon to experience a major period of decline in popularity and influence at home. One of the reasons for the decline was the death of its three principal spokesmen between 1916 and 1922, Rauschenbusch, Gladden, and Strong. The First World War and its aftermath also negatively affected the social gospel. Some, like social gospel evangelist B. Fay Mills, rejected the social gospel during the war itself, admitting that its optimism was unfounded (McLoughlin, 1959). Walter Rauschenbusch (1945:226) had tempered his faith in progress with the onset of the war, stating that: "The Great War is a catastrophic stage in the coming of the Kingdom of

God." He no longer believed that the path to the Kingdom would be a "smooth road." However, others, such as Shailer Mathews and Francis Greenwood Peabody, saw the war in a more favorable light and embraced President Wilson's belief that this could be "the war to end all wars." Mathews and Peabody remained optimistic concerning international relations after the war, and they backed Wilson's proposal for a League of Nations. But, when the United States Senate failed to consent to the President's peace-keeping plan, the international optimism of the social gospelers suffered a major setback (Carter, 1971:24).

The social gospel experienced a decline in popularity during the 1920s for a number of other reasons as well. The twenties brought an end to the Progressive era as the nation struggled to return to "normalcy."

> By 1920 the momentum of both the progressive movement and the social gospel was on the wane. From without, the climate of the country was changing. The political triumph of the progressive movement under Roosevelt and Wilson now seemed in disarray only to be replaced by the politics of normalcy of Harding and Coolidge. The tide of nationalism which boiled up in World War I spewed out to engulf the country in negative crusades—the Red Scare, the Ku Klux Klan, and anti–immigration legislation—all of which meant a widespread attack on civil liberties. After the post-war civil turbulence the twenties seemed to many observers to be marked by a rejection of progressive idealism and an upsurge of crass materialism (White and Hopkins, 1976:243).

The social gospel was not in harmony with the mood of the nation during the roaring twenties.

Still another factor was the overall decline in the importance of ministers to public life. The descriptions of America's problems which the remaining social gospelers discussed were less likely to be taken as prophetic criticisms, but were now more easily ignored or relegated to Sunday sermons. Ministers in the twentieth century were not granted the same respect they had received in the nineteenth, and the church gradually lost its preeminent position in secular affairs.

Two elements in American society worked together in the 1920s to foster a direct assault on the social gospel's brand of theology. These groups were the business community, who had never appreciated the criticisms that had been directed at them by the social gospelers, and the conservative clergy, who were waiting for an opportunity to rid the nation of religious liberalism and bring back "old time religion." The twenties was the decade of Fundamentalist challenge to the social gospel, the former being a movement that was approved of and funded by big business. Businessmen argued that the church should return to its primary task of winning souls and let business return to handling its own problems without religious interference. Money for the mass propagation of Fundamentalism came largely from the business community. The Moody Bible Institute in Chicago, for example, directed its appeal for funds directly at big business, featuring in its ad campaign in 1920 the slogan, "The Answer to Labor Unrest" (Carter, 1971:49). Judson Rosebush (1923:168–169), an ex-student of Richard T. Ely who had become a major industrialist, attacked the social gospel as being in error in its socialist leaning positions on wages, profits, and unionism.

> The agencies of the church should be exceedingly cautious in approving specific codes, definite programs, and concrete legislative proposals; first, because of the inherent pitfalls connected with such a program; second, because there has been, as yet, no real solidification of Christian thought on many of these matters; and third, because these programs are apt to divert the church from its great spiritual task of regenerating the hearts of men.

In the 1920s, business made a concerted effort to silence the social gospel. Paul Carter (1971:65) gives examples of how this actually took place:

> One could fill out the remainder of this chapter with examples of the conservative squeeze upon the Social Gospel: letters, mostly anonymous from columns of the denominational papers, written by men who had been forced out of their pulpits for preaching social liberalism; accounts of such suppressions of the free pulpit as occurred during the A.F. of L. convention of 1926, when the Detroit Board of Commerce succeeded in inducing the YMCA and most of

the churches of the city to withdraw invitations to labor leaders to speak under their auspices; or descriptions of the "company churches" which Southern textile mill operators built and supported as adjuncts to their company towns in order to protect "their" people from college-trained ministers with "crazy socialistic ideas."

Fundamentalism not only rejected the concept of social salvation for individual soul-winning but represented an overall criticism of the liberal theology upon which the social gospel had been based. The social gospel had never, of course, become the dominant form of Protestantism in America; it had always had a stronger hold on the clergy than the laity, the more liberal denominations like the Congregationalists rather than conservative ones such as the Baptists, and upon urban rather than rural congregations. Conservative Christianity had never disappeared, although the preachers and writers of the social gospel had received most of the attention in denominational publications for well over two decades. Nevertheless, conservative Christianity had remained dominant at such places as the Presbyterian-run Princeton Seminary, led by Charles Hodge and B.B. Warfield.

The name "Fundamentalism" first emerged around 1910 when two wealthy Los Angeles laymen, Lyman and Milton Stewart, convinced leading conservative theologians to put together twelve booklets describing the basic tenets of conservative Christianity. These booklets took the title, *The Fundamentals* (Torrey and Dixon, 1970), and the Stewarts put up $250,000 to insure that they would be distributed on a mass basis to every minister in America (Ahlstrom, 1975, Vol. II:286). Among the ideas put forward as basic to genuine Christianity were concentration on individual salvation, a belief that the Bible was inerrant—which attacked the liberals' reliance upon historical Biblical criticism—and a rejection of the evolutionary philosophy of history, which was to be replaced by "dispensational premillennialism" (Ahlstrom, 1975, Vol. II:278).

Fundamentalist thought was dispensational because it adopted the idea that God's interactions with human beings consisted of a series of successive covenants. Particularly important was God's covenant with the ancient Israelites, prophets who predicted Jesus' birth, etc.

Some Fundamentalists argued that God had made a covenant with the Anglo-American Puritans who had founded the United States—a basic tenet of American civil religion. However, unlike the social gospelers, Fundamentalists believed America had broken its promises to the covenant.

Fundamentalism also rejected the basic social gospel belief that the final kingdom would be established on earth as an inevitable outcome of the historical process. The Fundamentalists were premillennialists, believing that there was a radical separation of the present "age of the church" from the coming "kingdom." They denied that the kingdom was part of the historical process and argued that even a world gradually undergoing technological improvement was doomed to be overcome by the forces of evil. The idea was that all social conditions would inevitably and irreversibly grow increasingly worse until the Second Coming of Jesus (Moberg, 1977:37). Society was, therefore, to be denounced as evil and as fundamentally unredeemable, subject to modification only by the conversion of individual souls.

Adoption of premillennialism left Fundamentalists with a major paradox concerning what their attitude should be toward the world and its troubles. If the world must be at a point of near absolute degeneration just prior to Christ's arrival, His appearance could only be hastened by adding to the world's degeneration; attempting to solve social problems would only serve to delay Christ's Second Coming. The social gospel was preventing Christ's reappearance rather than hastening it.

Fundamentalism represented the orthodox Protestant response to the challenges to the faith presented by modern science, scholarship, and changing social conditions. Those troubled by the advance of theological liberalism and the decline of Puritan morality sought to reestablish their once dominant position by a reapplication of traditional beliefs. The so-called "Fundamentalist Controversy" took place after World War I and reached a peak during the mid-1920s as conservatives fought to regain control of their denominations, sometimes successfully.

In 1922 J. Graham Machen of Princeton Seminary supplied additional ammunition for Fundamentalism with his publication of

Christianity and Liberalism. Machen argued that modern liberalism was not only a different religion from orthodox Christianity but belonged to an entirely different class of religions. The famous "Scopes monkey trial" also brought national attention to the dispute between liberalism and Fundamentalism. While journalist H.L. Mencken made a mockery of Fundamentalist beliefs in his accounts of the trial, the teacher was convicted for teaching Darwinism, a Fundamentalist victory.

The result of the Fundamentalist attack on the social gospel in the 1920s has been labelled by David Moberg (1977) as "the great reversal." This was truly a double reversal: not only did the Fundamentalist debate succeed in lessening the influence of liberal theology, it also spelled the end for most Protestant involvement in social concerns for the next forty years. Theological conservatives shunned social involvement as "the poison of the social gospelers" (Moberg, 1977:37).

Another factor that led to the demise of the social gospel in the 1920s was its close ties to Prohibitionism. Many turned to Prohibition as a surrogate for the social gospel, regarding alcohol control as the panacea for America's social ills. When Prohibition failed, many who had identified with it were disillusioned. The passage of the Prohibition amendment and the Volstead Act had been supported by the social gospelers, but they did not share the Congress's approach—criminalization of the act of drinking alcohol. Instead the social gospelers, including such spokespersons for the Women's Christian Temperance Union as Frances Willard, favored only federal control over the liquor industry and general reform of drinking habits in society. The Prohibitionists, however, favored stigmatizing the manufacturer, seller, and consumer of alcoholic beverages. The social gospelers conceived of the drinker as a victim but not as a criminal. The failure of Prohibition to curb America's love for alcohol was perceived as a loss for all those who believed morality could be legislated.

By the end of the 1920s, the social gospel was on the decline. In the 1930s, the Great Depression had an ambiguous effect on the movement. On the one hand, the depression served as a terrible lesson, showing the remaining social gospel adherents that their optimistic belief in inevitable progress had been mistaken. The social gospel had been dealt a crushing blow with the realization that the Kingdom's arrival was not near. On the other hand, some still did not reject their belief that society could be ameliorated.

The revival of the social gospel which took place in the 1930s produced a more mature version of the theology, one that was no longer naively optimistic. Led by the Niebuhr brothers, Reinhold—who spent most of his life teaching at Union Theological Seminary in New York City—and H. Richard—who taught at Yale, the revival did not seek to destroy the social gospel, as some have claimed but to refine it, making it into a theology that would take the nature of evil in society seriously. One outcome of 1930s' social gospelism was support for Roosevelt's New Deal policies.

The Niebuhrs also served as mediators between the American theological community and its European counterparts. European theologians had been critical of the American social gospel and its belief that the Kingdom of God was to be an earthly utopia. Also, Europeans were distressed by the fact that the social gospel seemed to conceive of human salvation achieved through social work, political reform, or trade unionism, instead of by the grace of God (Carter, 1971:110). The Niebuhrs brought these criticisms to the attention of the American religious community, and their writings can be seen as American responses to the social gospel's European critics. In 1932 Reinhold Niebuhr published *Moral Man and Immoral Society*, his main statement on social ethics. Niebuhr argued that the major problem from which the social gospel suffered was its naive faith in the ethical possibilities of collective groups. Niebuhr drew a sharp distinction between the moral behavior of individuals and that of social groups: national, racial, and economic. Unlike individuals, Niebuhr held that labor unions, corporations, and sovereign states are by their nature all but incapable of altruistic conduct. The social gospel had been naive in its strategy of trying to transfer the "spirit of love" from the individual to the social sphere. Niebuhr felt that social collectivities were so group centered that a tolerable justice could be achieved only by guaranteeing enough power to each to counterbalance the power of the other

(Patterson, 1977:33). Collectivities would only stop "sinning" when forced to do so.

H. Richard Niebuhr wrote "The Attack upon the Social Gospel" in 1936 (reprinted in White and Hopkins, 1976:263–269). Despite the title, it presented a balanced account of the merits of the social gospel as well as the arguments of its detractors. H. Richard, more so than his brother Reinhold, praised the social gospel for its concentration on social salvation.

> The Social Gospel is characterized by the conviction that social units of every sort are the primary human realities to which the Church ought to address itself, or that, in dealing with individuals, not the isolated soul but the social individual—the citizen, class-member, race-member—should be regarded as the being who is in need of redemption. In this regard, it is the heir of sociological science rather than of liberal philosophy. . . . Society appears to precede the individual, to mold his character, to determine his interests, to bestow rights upon him. The individual is what he is by virtue of the place in society which he occupies. . . . The Social Gospel has seen sin and righteousness as characteristics of group life . . . it has seen the problem of salvation as a social problem and it has worked for the conversion or "change" of societies rather than of individuals who, no matter how much they may be changed, yet remain bound by common social evils and participants in common social sin (quoted in White and Hopkins, 1976:264).

However, H. Richard Niebuhr could not go along with the social gospel's belief that society could be remade with little or no assistance from God.

> The strategy of the Social Gospel has largely been a strategy of self–salvation, or of salvation by works. It has tended to speak of social salvation as something which men could accomplish for themselves if only they adopted the right social ideal, found adequate motivation for achieving it and accepted the correct technical means. The social ideal has been regarded as the product of men's independent ethical insight, the knowledge of correct means as the product of social science, and religion has been looked to for the motivation. God, in this theory, becomes a means to an end; he is there for the sake of achieving a human ideal and he does not do even this directly but

only through the inspiration which he offers to those who worship
him (in White and Hopkins, 1976:267).

From Niebuhr's perspective, the social gospel had forgotten the fact
that God is the moving force in history, and that God alone could bring
in His Kingdom. Despite the revisionary work done by the Niebuhrs,
they were never able to re-create the type of mass movement that the
social gospel had generated in the 1890s.

However, the legacy of 1890s' social Christianity can be directly
seen in Roosevelt's New Deal, which incorporated many of the ideas
about social welfare that the social gospelers had been preaching for
more than forty years. The philosophy that Ely and Ross had
propounded as a part of their "Wisconsin idea" was transferred to
Washington, D.C., by Roosevelt. The only way out of the depression
seemed to be to institute policies that would promote the general
welfare of society. In 1931, the now elderly Ely had suggested that the
establishment of a "peacetime army" might help cure the depression.
Roosevelt used Ely's idea to create the Civilian Conservation Corps
(Rader, 1966:231). During his famous "100 days" Roosevelt, with the
aid of Congress, instituted a whole series of programs that would place
America on the road to becoming a welfare state. Among these
programs were the National Industrial Recovery Act, the Works
Progress Administration, and Social Security. Roosevelt attempted to
directly improve the lot of workers by making government into a
partner in collective agreements between business and labor, with
government appointed mediators acting as referees to settle disputes.
Small's vision of sociologists as Platonic problem solvers seemed to be
becoming a reality. Thus, with the coming of the New Deal, a
secularized version of the social gospel's plan for creating a divine state
that would bring about social justice was taken over by the federal
government. Once established, the welfare state no longer needed the
social gospel, so social gospelers could now relax, knowing that a
major portion of what they had hoped to accomplish was now a reality.

The impact of the simultaneous decline and secularization of the
social gospel upon Christian sociology was that the latter had now lost
a significant part of its power base. Pleas made by ministers and
theologians that young people who were socially conscious ought to

study sociology became much less frequent. Beside losing much of its support from the church, American sociology also experienced a growing separation from its major ameliorative ally, social work. Professionalization, bureaucratization, and psychologization served both to secularize the field of social work, limiting the influence of religiously minded reformers, and to lessen the impact of sociological theories upon it.

The settlement movement's brand of inner-city social work had close ties to both the social gospel and sociology. The movement's momentum had reached its peak with the Progressive crusades of the first two decades of the twentieth century. However, optimism within the movement waned considerably during World War I, which Davis (1967:218) marks as the end of the settlement era.

Two important changes in social work took place in the early decades of the twentieth century: (1) the professionalization of the helping services, making social work into a career-oriented field, and (2) the emergence of large-scale, privately supported welfare foundations and trusts that led to the bureaucratization of the discipline. Sydnor Walker of the Rockefeller Foundation, in his 1933 discussion of the changes brought to social work by organizations sponsored by wealthy philanthropies, gave his approval to the replacement of the old reformers by new trained practitioners (Ogburn, 1933:1168–1223). Walker characterized the period between 1900 and 1920 as one that witnessed the emergence of organized private charities—e.g., foundations, community chests, etc.—which replaced the church as the major source of charity in American society. It seems that men such as John D. Rockefeller and Andrew Carnegie were strongly affected by the social gospel's claim that they were not owners of, but merely God's stewards over, their own wealth. The emergence of the charitable foundation can then be interpreted as an attempt by wealthy industrialists and businessmen to be good Christians and thus display their stewardship. The work of the charitable foundation became so large that staffs had to be hired to help in the "proper" distribution of its sizable funds. Within the charitable foundation, stewardship underwent secularization and rationalization—the case of the Rockefeller Foundation is a good example (Collier and Horowitz, 1976). Social work adapted to the new requirements placed on it by the foundations. Walker stated that under foundation sponsorship social work was moving toward rationality, which he regarded as a superior form of charity work when compared to the "emotions" and "enthusiasms" characteristic of the era of settlement houses and reformers (Ogburn, 1933:1168). Social work was to develop methods for rationally testing the efficiency of social work programs, dramatically improve its organizing ability, and move toward expert training as a requirement for a career in the field, all of which would replace the need for "inspired leadership" or "strong sentiment" that had characterized social work in the Progressive era (Ogburn, 1933:1168–1169).

Beside the mandate to rationalize its methods placed upon social work by the newly emerging philanthropic trusts, social workers reacted to other pressures as well, both internal and external, to turn "helping others" into a profession based upon expert knowledge. For example, one of the first groups of social workers to turn toward professionalization were those practicing medical social work. Doctors required that social workers convince them that their services were both necessary and based upon skills clearly separate from nursing (Lubove, 1965:24).

A leading force in professionalizing social work was Mary Richmond, who in 1917 published one of the classic works on individual casework, *Social Diagnosis*. Richmond advocated casework as the major method of social work, attempting to take leadership in the field away from such advocates of social reform as the settlement workers (Lubove, 1965:11, 20). Richmond also sought to replace the patronizing moralism then dominant in helping relationships with social work service based upon expert knowledge that could be used on individual cases. Of course, this still implicitly resulted in treating clients as inferiors; moral superiority was simply replaced by intellectual or therapeutic expertise. The casework method espoused by Richmond was individualistic but neither psychological nor psychoanalytic. In the late 1920s and early 1930s the psychoanalytic revolution would come to affect social work; however, Richmond's pre–Freudian methodology recognized the importance of the larger social environment upon the individual personality. Richmond regarded the individual as rooted in his or her social environment; the latter helped to explain both the individual's personal limitations and untapped potentialities (Lubove, 1965:81). Social work services must focus upon the environment, she argued; but, rather than attempt to change it, the practitioner should seek to help the client adjust to the environment's pressures and disciplines. Ameliorating the social environment was beyond the newly reduced scope of social work.

Another important leader in revising the mission of social work was Ida Cannon, one of Mary Richmond's contemporaries. Cannon argued for a *verstehen*-type approach in dealing with clients (Lubove, 1965:35). According to Cannon, the capacity for putting oneself in the client's place and at the same time comprehending their situation objectively should be the basis of casework. Of course, such a method was also being employed by sociologists of the same period, such as W.I. Thomas and Robert Park, who had adopted Charles Henderson's qualitative form of methodology, the case study method.

In the late 1920s, Richmond's and Cannon's casework method came into conflict with the emerging psychoanalytic approach. Freudianism would influence all of the social sciences in the twenties and thirties, scoring one of its major victories in the field of social work and turning it further into an applied subdiscipline of psychology rather than sociology. Psychiatry proved very popular to social workers, partly because of its role in strengthening practitioners' convictions that the services they offered were distinct, valuable, and based upon specialized skill and training. Psychiatric social workers were to become the virtual elite of their discipline. For the psychiatric social worker, the client's personal problems or anti-social behavior were perceived as a symptomatic expression of unresolved mental conflicts or unsatisfied inner needs rather than an indication of unsolved social problems within society. As a result of the turn from Richmond's environmentally sensitive casework approach toward psychiatry, social work became part of the twentieth-century movement to medicalize personal problems and deviant behavior. Social work historian Lubove (1965:113) located the turning point of this movement from "casework to psychiatry" in the publication of Virginia Robinson's 1930 *A Changing Psychology in Social Case Work*, which advocated the

Freudian approach. From 1990 through 1930, social work had moved from a first stage of reform, through a phase of introspective counseling, to the adoption of psychoanalytic counseling. This scientification of social work did not, however, eliminate all vestiges of moralism. The openly espoused social Christian ethics of the 1890s reformers were replaced by a more subtle moral philosophy, the ideology of "health"—which continues to undergird all contemporary forms of medicalized social thought regarding deviant behavior.

With neither social gospel theology nor reformist social work any longer supplying American sociology with allies, the discipline, in the 1920s and 1930s, was free to re-create itself and seek new directions. But would sociology be able to jettison its early religiosity for a genuinely agnostic or atheistic perspective on social reality, or would it adopt another "faith"? It is to these questions we now turn.

CHAPTER 6

The Transvaluation of Christian Sociology

As we have seen, in the 1920s the gradual decline of the social gospel within the Protestant denominations that had first sponsored it served to weaken the connections between the church and academic sociology. Young Christian sociologists were left without the vigorous support from the church that their first-generation predecessors had enjoyed. Similarly, the separation of social work from sociology cut off many of sociology's direct ties to social reformism. The loss of these supports for Christian sociology left the discipline free to secularize its perspective on reality.

American sociology did undergo a major transformation and transvaluation during the 1920s. Probably the man most responsible for this change was William Fielding Ogburn (1886–1959). It is significant that Ogburn is today considered one of the true founders of modern sociology, while the religiously inspired sociologists who have been discussed thus far tend to be forgotten or relegated to sociology's premodern prehistory. Ogburn brought the era of Christian sociology to an end by attacking its moral approach as subjective and impugning its meliorism as misguided. Instead Ogburn argued for refocusing sociology on a statistical base and reformulating the character and aims of the discipline. Ogburn and his students are credited in large measure with shifting the emphasis in American sociology toward quantitative methodology (Jaffe, 1968:277–278). However, the victory for Ogburn's school of sociology did not mean the end of "religion" in American social science. Despite his claim to be creating an objective, value-free sociology, a closer analysis of Ogburn's own theories and his career reveals a deeply moralistic man, committed to the use of secular means for achieving his own vision of "post-millennialist" promise.

Ogburn was born in Butler, Georgia, in 1886; in 1908 he came to Columbia University to do graduate work in sociology under Franklin Henry Giddings (1855–1931). Ogburn's own sociological outlook can be seen as both a continuation of and reaction against Giddings's theories, making an understanding of Giddings's sociology a necessary prerequisite for the analysis of Ogburn's. Giddings was one of the other founding fathers of American sociology; in his own era Giddings's influence rivaled those of Sumner, Ward, Small, and Ross. Although Giddings's work is today read about as often as Small's or Ellwood's, it was Giddings's approach to sociology that would become dominant in America through the influence of his student Ogburn.

Franklin Henry Giddings was born in Sherman, Connecticut, in 1855 and was raised in a strict Puritan home. His father was a Congregationalist minister. After college, Giddings pursued a career as a journalist for six years. In 1887 he met Lester Ward at a scholarly meeting and was persuaded to become a sociologist. In 1888, Giddings began lecturing on political science at Bryn Mawr College. From 1891 until 1894, Giddings taught sociology at Columbia University, in addition to his full-time post at Bryn Mawr. Then, in 1894, Columbia created a chair in sociology that Giddings was asked to fill. He held his chair at Columbia for the remainder of his life.

Giddings's brand of sociology is impossible to categorize simply. On the one hand, he praised Sumner as the country's foremost sociologist, while rejecting the latter's laissez-faire political philosophy (Page, 1969:146). On the other hand, Giddings did not consider himself a social gospeler; he almost never referred to his own work in religious terms, only in scientific. Although his sociology had many similarities to social gospel thought, his version was far more conservative. Albion Small (1896d) did not believe that Giddings's sociology was adequate and frequently criticized him, although Small's theory of interest groups and Giddings's conception of "consciousness of kind"were indeed similar. Giddings's grand theory combined Comtean social evolutionary positivism with a secularized version of conservative Protestant thought.

Giddings (1898:1280) agreed with Comte that society was undergoing continual progress, moving through stages toward a final positivist millennium. In Giddings's mind, evolution moved always in the direction of societal equilibrium—an idea later borrowed by Talcott Parsons (Page, 1969:152). In the modern industrialized world such equilibrium tended to take three possible forms, which in turn became stages of development: (1) the subjugation of the weak by the strong; (2) economic exploitation; or (3) "the uplifting of the weak by the strong through education, justice, and economic aid" (Page, 1969:152). In a progressive evolutionary manner, Western society had been moving through the first two stages of equilibrium toward the third. As the major motivating factor in the process of development Giddings secularized the Christian concept of brotherhood, calling it "consciousness of kind." By "consciousness of kind" Giddings meant a feeling of togetherness or social responsibility. Small envisioned progress resulting from increased sociability among competing interest groups; Giddings held that as groups progressed they would expand their consciousness of kind to embrace larger communities, thus improving society.

> Through "consciousness of kind," humanity was being led to an ever greater commitment to universal brotherhood; and Giddings believed that Christian philanthropic enterprises, under the guidance of greater sociological knowledge, were "rapidly outgrowing the esoteric sentimentalism of their youth and devoting themselves to the diffusion of knowledge, to the improvement of conditions, and to the upbuilding of character," and as a consequence, were "uniting the classes and races of men in a spiritual humanity"(Rosenberg, 1982:153).

However, Giddings felt that consciousness of kind was practically nonexistent in groups that he labelled "anti-social," such as criminals. Such noncontributing groups would not be permitted to enter Giddings's "kingdom" the "anti-social" were to be eliminated (Page, 1969:179). Giddings's vision of an earthly "kingdom" pinned its hopes on technological advancement and material prosperity combined with expanding social control over those that might "interfere" with progress:

> The goal of telic activity is amelioration of human society through security and material abundance . . . and the socialization of entire populations with elimination of the anti-social (quoted in Odum, 1951:90).

From Giddings's perspective, philanthropy was not a form of benevolent activity as the social gospelers envisioned it but a means of social control. He made this point in an essay on philanthropy entitled "The Ethics of Social Progress."

> One portion of every community is inherently progressive, resourceful, creative, capable of self-mastery . . . while another portion, capable of none of these things can be made useful and comfortable only by being brought under bondage to society and kept under discipline until they have acquired power to help and govern themselves (Giddings, 1893:244).

Giddings (1893:256–257) went so far as to suggest that tramps should be arrested and forced to labor, and that other nations must stop shipping their burdens of "pauperism, ignorance, and degeneracy" to the United States.

Giddings (1893:226) included labor in his list of largely worthless social elements. He believed Marx's labor theory of value to be fallacious; capitalists were largely responsible for capitalism, not workers. The large classes of unskilled workers barely produce their own subsistence, Giddings argued. Soon America would not even need their labor power because machines would be able to produce everything themselves. Giddings opposed socialism and did not encourage trade unionism (Page, 1969:147).

While Giddings disparaged the lower and working classes, he praised business leaders, industrialists, and "wise philanthropists," whom he considered the appropriate societal elite for the current epoch. Laborers must learn that only business leaders are competent to control and organize industry and that the success of democracy depended upon the authority of a preeminent social class and respect for its leadership (Page, 1969:159). Thus, in Giddings's sociology there was offered an ideology supporting the current business establishment in America, rather than one accusing it of "sin." Giddings did not regard the business elite as parasitic, feeding off the misery of the working class. On the contrary, it was the continued existence of the underproductive lower classes that was the problem, and technological advancements and machine production were creating a larger and larger mass of useless individuals. Giddings's social amelioration was directed at controlling the lower classes, not improving their condition.

Sociology could, of course, be used as an aid for social amelioration, which Giddings believed was one of sociology's major goals. As Giddings stated: "It will be discovered one day that the chief value of social science, so far from being academic, is moral" (quoted in Page, 1969:150). The "moral" goals of sociology would be to assure that those in power remained there, that American democracy would be guaranteed a future, and that the society would be protected against class revolution. Giddings's belief was that through "societal engineering"—a term he used to replace "philanthropy" in his own writings—social scientists could, if given authority and power to do so, guarantee such a future for America. Giddings's vision of American democracy was therefore one of continued rule by the current elite, who would be supported by a technocratic bureaucracy of social scientists. This was Giddings's utopian "kingdom."

Giddings's use of the terms "philanthropy" and "societal engineering" was virtually synonymous. For example, compare the following two statements:

> The demand becomes daily more imperative for a public and private philanthropy that shall be governed by the results of scientific inquiry (Giddings, 1893:242).

> Sociology can be characterized as the scientific study of human society, constantly seeking more rigorous scientific methods and more effective applications to the end that society may attain a better selection, preservation, and development of a superior mankind (quoted in Odum, 1951:89).

Giddings believed that only societal engineering provided the true solution for social problems. Such amelioration must be both rationally planned and executed systematically. In order that the blueprints for directed change drawn up by sociological experts would be indisputable, they were to be based on irrefutable statistical data. Sociology, which Giddings (1898:1281) defined as a natural science, must employ the method of the natural sciences and therefore become positivistic if it was going to be successful. As a result of his vision for sociology, Giddings became the major early pioneer of the statistical method. As he put it, sociology must replace "careless looking into things" with precise observations that could be repeatable (Odum, 1951:92). Although social gospel sociologists had certainly advocated and made use of statistics, Giddings was the one early sociologist who attempted to turn statistics into the ultimate language of social research. For Giddings, only the employment of statistical methodology would guarantee scientifically valid sociological findings that could be employed for "societal engineering." A positivistic technocratic elite could improve society by helping to bring about the good life for the deserving while controlling the unworthy.

Ogburn adopted Giddings's goal of transforming sociology into a quantifiable science as his own mission in sociology. Ogburn received his Ph.D. under Giddings's direction in 1912. During World War I, Ogburn served as head of the cost of living department of the National War Labor Board and as special agent for the United States Bureau of Labor Statistics (Odum, 1951:147). Applying sociology to such practical tasks as service to the war effort would become Ogburn's metier.

In 1919 Ogburn returned to Columbia as a professor, where he stayed until his move to the University of Chicago in 1927. One of Ogburn's career goals was to build respect for social science among statesmen, responsible educators, and business and social leaders. In order to achieve this end he believed he had to advocate statistical study as the only legitimate approach in sociology. However, in order for Ogburn to turn sociology into a useful science that could benefit business, the military, or the government, the discipline would have to be rid of all theories that did not conform to his vision of the discipline. In pursuing his mission Ogburn helped bring the era of openly espoused Christian sociology to a close.

Ogburn's plan of attack was fourfold: (1) sociology must give up its claim that it alone could reform society; (2) the social sciences must become objective and value free; (3) mathematical and statistical methodology must replace all other forms of research methodology; and (4) the era of grand theory must be brought to an end. Paradoxically, Ogburn himself appeared to be guilty of many of the same shortcomings he imputed to his fellow sociologists. It seems that Ogburn believed that once he had given "scientific legitimation" to his own moralistic beliefs, they no longer rested on doubtful grounding and could be propagated as "truth." Ogburn implicitly adopted the same position as Albion Small, yet the former, unlike Small, never acknowledged his own subjective presuppositions.

If sociology were to become a discipline to be employed by government or business it would first have to repudiate its religious redemptionism. Sociology could not save the world. Ogburn asserted he had personally given up on reform after World War I. As Jaffe (1968:277) noted: "Ogburn had come to doubt that idealism per se could accomplish very much, and he grudged the time that reformist activities took away from social ones." The social gospel's critical attitude toward business and ruling societal elites along with its pro-labor leanings would need to be jettisoned, so that sociology would be interpreted by elites as a nonthreatening endeavor, and one that could be helpful to the powerful in managing society.

However, it is clear that Ogburn did not reject social reform altogether. He continued to advocate Giddings's belief that a technologically trained social scientific elite should be employed to help administer national policies efficiently. This technocratic elite would assist the government in solving what Ogburn regarded as major social problems, all of which he believed were caused by "cultural lag." Cultural lag resulted because material culture—techniques—tended to change at a more rapid pace than nonmaterial culture—customs and beliefs. To insure adaptation between material and nonmaterial culture required a high degree of planning, prediction, and control, Ogburn (1922:202, 211) argued. One of the most important functions of government would be engineering the adjustment of people's beliefs and values to the material conditions of life.

In his introduction to *Recent Social Trends*, Ogburn (1933) argued that American democracy was coming to realize more and more that it must rely on the trained experts because of their utility and indispensability to the practical operations of the government. In fact, Ogburn (1933:xxiv) stated that if the government did not respond to his plea for the social-technocratic expansion of the federal bureaucracy, America might fall prey to socialism or fascism.

> Unless there can be a more impressive integration of social skills and fusing of social purposes than is revealed by recent trends, there can be no assurance that these alternatives with their accompaniments of violent revolution, dark periods of serious repression of libertarian and democratic forms, and the proscription and loss of many useful elements in the productive system can be averted.

Thus, while Ogburn cut himself off from the social gospel's list of social reforms, he replaced them with his own agenda for amelioration.

Ogburn also called upon sociologists to rid their work of the distorting effects of bias and emotion (Odum, 1951:152). Social science must become objective and value free if it were to be truly scientific. The kind of sociology being done by the social gospel sociologists was to be considered invalid, because its religious framework made it moralistic, subjective, and unscientific. Religiously supported beliefs would not be permitted within Ogburn's vision of social science. Following Ogburn, the word "objective" took on its modern sociological meaning, while Small's use of the term was discarded. For Small, objective science could include religious knowledge as part of a holistic perspective on social reality. With Ogburn, religious beliefs were to be ignored or explained naturalistically, since only scientifically verifiable "facts" could be incorporated into a sociologist understanding of the world. Objective sociology must sever its direct relation to religious truths.

However, the question which must be raised about Ogburn's own work is whether his sociology indeed met the standard set by his own criteria. Were his writings objective and value free, or was his sociology just as subjective and moralistic as that produced by the social gospelers? With Ogburn's arrival did sociology transcend religion, or did religious beliefs make their way back into social science, this time disguised in secular and positivistic garb? Ogburn's thought, when closely analyzed, turns out to contain both moralism and religious precepts. The inability of Ogburn to create a truly secular sociology would become an ongoing problem within the discipline, one that positivistic American sociology has never resolved adequately.

Ogburn's (1922:200) inability to eliminate "faith" from sociology can be seen in his major theoretical contribution to the discipline, the concept of cultural lag. As a theory of social change it was deceptively simple: not all parts of culture are undergoing change at the same rate. In Ogburn's perspective, the material culture, made up of such elements as machines, factories, technologies, and techniques, had changed at a faster rate than the nonmaterial culture, composed of customs, beliefs, philosophies, laws, and government. The negative result of the varying speeds of change was cultural lag in the non-material culture. However, not all aspects of the nonmaterial culture were suffering from lag; Ogburn (1922:203) labelled as "adaptive culture" those portions of the nonmaterial culture that had become adjusted or adapted to the changes in the material conditions. Ogburn believed that he, and like-minded sociologists, could solve the problem of cultural lag by being permitted to make adjustments to counteract it. Some aspects of the nonmaterial culture such as religion and the family were only partially "adapted" and needed major ameliorative assistance (Ogburn, 1922:203; 1933:xix). The church was a problem because it was still clinging to supernatural religious beliefs in an age in which it should be taking on a scientific outlook. To label traditional religion as suffering from cultural lag is an example of how Ogburn incorporated his subjective opinions into his sociology. Just how ideological Ogburn's theory of cultural lag was is suggested by C. Wright Mills (1943:176–177):

> The imputation of lag is complicated by the historical judgement in whose guise it is advanced and by the programmatic content being shoved into pseudo-objective phrases, as, for example, "called for."

Ogburn's theory of cultural lag also embraced an uncritically sanguine orientation toward machines and technology, an attitude he had adopted from Giddings. Ogburn was fascinated with machines, their present uses, and their future possibilities. He wrote pamphlets on such subjects as *Living with Machines*—1933, *You and Machines*—1934, and *Machines and Tomorrow's World*—1938 (Odum, 1951:149). If the American government would only allow a technologically trained—i.e., "machine-minded"—elite to help make decisions and determine policy, then society might begin to operate like a well-oiled machine. Society must adjust its outdated customs and institutions to a materialist machine-based economy. Ogburn argued that sociology was willing to assist the nation in making the necessary adjustments. Thus, Ogburn's sociology had its concept of a "kingdom," just as all of the social gospel sociologists had theirs; only Ogburn's was to be a managerial technocracy with no need for a higher power, rather than a sociologically directed theocracy.

The famous example of how forestry had adapted to changing material conditions was an excellent choice by Ogburn (1922:204–206) because it allowed the type of societal engineering he proposed to appear in a favorable light. Forestry had become adaptive by moving from a policy of exploitation of natural resources to one of wise foresting based on conservation and replanting. Sociology could help other aspects of society to make such positive adjustments.

However, what were social scientists to do if, upon investigation, certain portions of the population were found to be "laggards" because they possessed inherently unadaptable traits? How should sociologists advise the state to respond then? Ogburn felt that America had just such a problem, and his proposed scientific solution is very revealing of his moral stance. Ogburn (1933:xxiii) held that some Americans possessed undesired inheritable traits and advocated a policy based upon preventing such individuals from procreating, a program of selective breeding to improve the qualities of the population. Thus Ogburn proposed the same solution for the problem of "deviance" that Henderson, a social gospeler, had proposed for "sin." On this matter Ogburn was a moral eugenicist who employed the rhetoric of positivism to obscure the value-laden policy he proposed. Although Ogburn considered sociology a natural science, he was willing to dispense with the rigors of natural science technique in cases in which his goals could better be served otherwise:

> The lack of knowledge concerning heredity and composition of the chromosomes of prospective parents is undoubtedly an obstacle, but breeders of livestock have accomplished results without this information.

Another example of Ogburn's moralistic sociology can be seen in his writings about recreation and leisure activities. By comparing Ogburn's thoughts on leisure to those of Charles Ellwood, it becomes readily apparent that both were equally moralistic in their outlook on this topic. The difference between the two was that Ellwood clearly stated that his theory was religiously grounded, while Ogburn claimed his was objective and scientific. Ellwood (1925:264, 269) argued that social Christianity must oppose all forms of leisure that are degrading, and included on his list drinking, gambling, and sexual immorality. Ellwood (1925:273) listed as legitimate amusements outdoor athletic sports and the supervised play of children in parks and playgrounds; the latter he believed had caused a marked decrease in juvenile delinquency. The problem with recreation was that "unsocialized forms of pleasure and amusement had not been religiously guided."

Ogburn's theory of leisure, although somewhat more complex, was equally moralistic. Ogburn's scientific perspective on leisure was based upon instinct theory. According to Ogburn (1922:356–361), human beings had acquired a set of instincts during the long evolutionary march to modernity. Because so much of man's past had been spent in "active" pursuit of food—e.g., hunting, fishing, etc.—and territory, he developed very aggressive instincts—e.g., war—that were now out of line with a technological and sedentary society. Recreation and leisure must continue to serve as outlets for these instincts, and therefore they must require strenuous physical activity. Ogburn thus defined as good all forms of recreation that were based on motor activity and allowed for release of instinctual urges. Included in this list were hunting, fishing, camping, and all forms of body sports. Bad forms of recreation were those that stirred up the instincts but did not allow for their complete release in activity. Appeals to the sex instinct were particularly troublesome because they did not provide for the completion of the act. Dancing was therefore a dysfunctional leisure activity according to Ogburn. Other bad forms of recreation included card-playing, gambling, and talking, because Ogburn (1922:360) was not sure "what happens psychologically when one takes part in them." Novels and movies would have also been suspect because of their vicarious participation without activity by readers or viewers. Thus Ogburn's list of "good" and "evil" forms of recreation was nearly identical to Ellwood's. In a statement that one would probably more readily attribute to Ellwood, Ogburn (1933:ii) said that "leisure should be graceful and wholesome, and not evocative of temptation." One can only conclude that Ogburn's sociology was far from being value free.

Another of Ogburn's objectives was to replace "careless" sociological research with an objective positivistic mathematical technique known as statistical analysis. This was the only way that Ogburn felt he could assure American sociology's respectability. This would mean jettisoning the empathic case study method that many sociologists were employing, especially at Chicago. Ogburn brought his vision of sociology to the University of Chicago in 1927, but even before that he had been an active participant in the Social Science Research Council (S.S.R.C.), an organization dedicated to quantifiable research. The council had been founded in 1923 with money supplied by the Rockefeller Foundation and the Laura Spellman Rockefeller Memorial Fund. (For an analysis of the influence of the Rockefeller family in social science in America revealing the Foundation's attempts to secularize "good stewardship," see Collier and Horowitz [1976:51– 64, 100–108, 143–151].) Ogburn joined the council in 1924 and remained a member until 1941, serving as its chairman from 1933 to 1936. After an early debate about whether the organization should be primarily concerned with social reform or improving the methodology of the social sciences, Ogburn's faction, which espoused the latter position, became dominant (Sibley, 1974:8–10). The following statements were typical of the S.S.R.C.'s goals under Ogburn's leadership:

> That a sounder empirical method of research had to be achieved in
> political science if it were to assist in the development of a scientific
> political method (Sibley, 1974:8).

The low average level of mathematical competence among social scientists has been a perennial impediment to the use of the most advanced methods of analyzing and interpreting social data (Sibley, 1974:20).

The graduate schools have been inundated with vast numbers of students neither capable of nor interested in creative scholarship or scientific research (Sibley, 1974:77).

In 1931 the S.S.R.C. set up a scholarship fund to provide the opportunity for "some talented social scientists to obtain unusual training"; basically this meant to learn statistical methodology. The purpose of the fellowships was to promote the development of research workers, rather than to support research itself (Sibley, 1974:78). The S.S.R.C.'s goal was "to produce scientists, not welfare workers" and focused its energies on teaching the proper methods of research, rather than funding actual research. In 1933 Ogburn (p. xxiii) praised the S.S.R.C. for its commitment to objective methodology, arguing that the council was now ready to take on social planning:

The Social Science Research Council may prove an instrumentality of great value in the broader view of complex social problems, the integration of social knowledge, and in the initiative toward social planning on a high level.

In 1927 Ogburn moved from Columbia to the University of Chicago. There he was to directly attack the sociological traditions of Small, Henderson, Ellwood, Thomas, and Park, which he felt must be dispensed with so that the era of statistical analysis could commence. A book published in 1929 entitled *Chicago: An Experiment in Social Science Research* clearly showed Ogburn's influence on the department (Smith and White, 1968). In comparison to the studies undertaken prior to Ogburn's arrival such as Thomas and Znaniecki's (1927) *The Polish Peasant in Europe and America*, Shaw's (1930) *The Jack-Roller*, or Zorbaugh's (1929) *The Gold Coast and the Slum*, which rely heavily on letters, autobiographies, and other human documents, Smith and White's *Chicago: An Experiment in Social Science Research* concentrates on statistical research methods, data collection, "objective" analysis, and applied research.

Ogburn also used his graduate students to attack the Chicago tradition of qualitative research. One of Ogburn's most famous students, Samuel Stouffer, did his doctoral dissertation in 1930 comparing case history methods and statistical analysis. Although Stouffer (1980:7, 50, 52) found that the results garnered from his case study material and his statistical findings were similar, he insisted that statistical data had a brighter future. The goal of the statistical method was to devise a simple test that could be taken in ten or fifteen minutes, scored rapidly and objectively, producing a valid measure of attitudes. A researcher could test several thousand subjects on a large number of background factors using this method, gathering an amount of data that could not be as easily collected with the time-consuming case study approach. During World War II, Stouffer would serve as the director of the Research Branch of the Information and Education Division of the War Department, where he would use his statistical skills to study combat morals, hoping to turn American soldiers into more efficient fighting machines. American sociology seized this opportunity to prove to the government that it could indeed be a useful science, one willing to aid in defeating America's wartime enemies (Parsons and Barber, 1948).

In 1929 Ogburn was elected president of the American Sociological Society. In his presidential address, "The Folkways of a Scientific Sociology," he predicted that positivistic methodology would not only become predominant within the discipline but would also spell the end for grand sociological theory.

> In the past the great names in sociology have been social theorists and social philosophers. But this will not be the case in the future. For social theory and social philosophy will decline, that is, in the field of scientific sociology. Social theory will have no place in a scientific sociology, for it is not built upon sufficient data. Or course, certain syntheses of broader researches may be called theory, a new meaning for an old term. But such syntheses will be based on evidence (quoted in Odum, 1951:152).

Elsewhere in the same address, Ogburn claimed that sociology was to have no interest in social reform.

> Sociology as a science is not interested in making the world a better place in which to live, in encouraging beliefs, in spreading information, in dispensing news, in setting forth impressions of life, in leading the multitudes, or in guiding the ship of state. Science is interested directly in only one thing, to wit, discovering new knowledge (quoted in Becker, 1971:28).

Of course, new knowledge could only be discovered using a statistical methodology.

In 1930 President Hoover appointed Ogburn as director of the President's Research Committee on Social Trends, to which on Ogburn's behalf the Rockefeller Foundation gave a $500,000 grant (Odum, 1951:148). All studies undertaken for this project were to be based upon statistical findings, Ogburn insisted.

> The idea was that as a multiplication table should be reliable both for the Tory and the Communist, so the conclusion of social trends should be valid alike for the radical and the conservative (quoted in Odum, 1951:151).

The statistical methodology employed in *Recent Social Trends* would aid sociology not only to document the past and present but to predict the future as well. Ogburn believed that sociology could predict at least a decade or two into the future with a probability of being correct nine times out of ten (Jaffe, 1968:280). Contributors to *Recent Social Trends* included Howard Odum, Charles Merriam, Robert Lynd, Edwin Sutherland, and Ogburn, who personally contributed chapters on the family and recent inventions. Topics included demography, occupations, education, urban life, rural life, minority groups, family, women, children, labor, leisure, the arts, religion, medicine, crime, welfare, law, and government. The chapter on the arts in social life by Frederick P. Keppel provides a good example of how a complex cultural form, such as is represented by the aesthetic side of human nature, can be trivialized through the use of statistics. Keppel simply counts everything: the number of books published in drama, literature, poetry, etc., and the student enrollments in music and arts schools (Ogburn, 1933:958–1008). Another example of the limited usefulness of this approach appears in Keppel's discussion of Black culture. While

Keppel lists the names of a few prominent Black artists and writers, there is no discussion of the content or meaning of their works or of the race question in the arts.

Albion Small's worry over the future of sociology now appears to have been prescient. Small's concern was that as sociology sought to become objective it might reduce itself to a single technique, such as the one advocated by Ogburn (Becker, 1971:24). Ogburn, who came to Chicago only one year after Small's death, sought to turn sociology away from both grand theory and qualitative methodology toward a single, comprehensive positivistic methodology that could be employed to study all aspects of culture.

In the 1930s, as the Ogburn men attempted to reclaim sociology, one of the few dissenting voices was that of Charles Ellwood, who was finishing out his lengthy career at Duke University. Ellwood (1907:590), who had always advocated an eclectic methodological approach—e.g., personal observations, statistical methods, comparative methods, and deductions—authored his only work specifically on methods in 1933. In it he attempted to counter the claims made by Ogburn and his followers that the only way sociology could be made scientific was through the use of the statistical method. Ellwood (1933:104) held that statistical methods must be seen as ancillary and not as essential in the social sciences. The social sciences could not borrow the method of the natural sciences because human social behavior must be placed in a class by itself among the objects of scientific investigation. There is no analogue of human culture in the rest of nature, Ellwood (1933:101–104) stated, and he believed that the "subjective elements of reality" could not be studied quantitatively. Ellwood (1933:74), instead of concentrating on statistics, advocated the case study method or participant observation stressing "empathy" and "sympathetic understanding" between sociologist and the group he was studying. But Ellwood's advocacy of a Weberian *verstehen* approach could not halt the trend toward statistical positivism, which had taken over American sociology.

By 1930, the era of overt Christian sociology had come to an end. With much of its support from the church gone as the result of the revival of Fundamentalist theologies, its ties to reformist social work severed as that profession became psychologized, and secular positivism now reigning at the major universities, social gospel sociology had neither backers nor an audience. It disappeared from the American sociological scene with the deaths of Small, Ely, Ellwood, and Ross. Not only was their program for a Christian social science no longer a part of American sociology, but the discipline decided to forget about its religious origins as well.

However, the question must once again be raised as to whether the demise of Christian sociology meant the end of "religion" in American social science. Was sociology no longer left with a god(s) to serve? Did American sociology cease being moralistic? Ogburn and the positivists claimed that it had, that sociology was becoming objective and value free, and that it would serve no god but the pursuit of scientific knowledge. Ogburn and his generation, although they claimed to be rejecting the religious heritage of their mentors, in reality secularized or transvalued their thought. Ogburn's vision of sociology included a "kingdom" run by a technocratic elite, a variant of Ely's and Ross's moral-intellectual elite who had helped rule the state of Wisconsin. Also, Ogburn continued the social gospel's tradition of moralism, although he claimed all of his ideas were objective truth. While the Christian sociologists admitted that their values originated from their religious faith and were then put to the test through social scientific analysis, Ogburn claimed his values were generated solely from scientific roots. Ogburn remained a moralist despite his claims to the contrary.

However, in the years since Ogburn, the full acceptance of positivist methodology has led most to conclude that sociology as a discipline has now purged itself of religious moralism. Nevertheless, American sociological positivism can itself still be interpreted as a religious faith, based upon the transvalued Christianity of Giddings and Ogburn. Positivism seeks to complete the soteriological mission which the social gospelers began. While the ameliorative methods of the social gospelers, such as "love," sacrifice, and stewardship, have been replaced by a new form of scientific salvation—bureau-cratic/technocratic societal planning—empirical sociologists represent the prophets and missionaries of the discipline's current inner-worldly gospel.

Even the language currently employed by positivists was first selected by scientists for its sacred quality. Of course, the language that positivism speaks is mathematics. The religious significance of the usage of mathematics within positivism has often been overlooked. Both Pascal and Galileo, attempting to answer a question that has often plagued Christianity, "What language does God speak?," concluded that the language of God is mathematics. God's language must be mathematics, they argued, because it alone is universal and not subject to cultural relativism, as is vernacular language. In their first modern usage, mathematical formulas served to sacralize scientific endeavors. In the centuries that separate Pascal's and Galileo's formulation of the sacredness of mathematics from the social gospelers' decision to employ mathematics and statistics for purposes of inner-worldly salvation, mathematics had lost its initial sacred character and become the autonomous icon of mundane science. Ironically, then, secular positivism appropriated the erstwhile language of God in order to assure itself of its emancipation from religious doctrines. Through the use of statistics, positivism hoped to give its claims the weight of scientific authority.

However, once sociology rejected the Christian God as its ultimate authority, and positivism turned to the world and its institutions for support, how was the discipline to find a higher purpose for its activities? In the modern world, science, business, and government have replaced God as the source for moral authority and social legitimation. Rather than being a religion in service to one God, positivism's faith has been placed in a number of institutions that serve as God's surrogates on earth. Ogburn's 1930s' proposal that the state institute the statistical social science advocated by the S.S.R.C. as the basis for social reconstruction was the single most important attempt to legitimate the "religion" or positivism by political means. However, President Roosevelt rejection of Ogburn's proposal forced positivism into a struggle for its legitimation that continues to the present day.

But ever since Ogburn's assertion of a value-free and hence nonreligious sociology, positivists have sought the discipline's legitimation through identification with the aims of industrial elites and public administration. Positivist industrial sociologists, before they could be employed, had to reject the critical stance that the social gospelers had held concerning business and industry. Seeking the support of the business establishment, sociologists offered to aid management in its pursuit of "using labor more efficiently."

In order to serve its new gods, positivist social science declared it had no ultimate goals or standards of its own, only a value-neutral technique that anyone could use. Even before Ogburn had developed his value-free approach, the separation of sociological means from societal ends had been enunciated in the writings on industrial relations by Harvard's Hugo Munsterberg. Munsterberg believed that industrial social scientists should concern themselves only with means and never with ends. To specify ends would violate the social scientist's claim to objectivity, since ends were always normative and therefore outside the boundaries of objective science. Ends would be supplied by whoever was employing the social scientist's services. Industrial psychology's technique was to be put at the disposal of business, to be employed as the managers saw fit (Baritz, 1960:1990).

Through aligning itself with the business establishment, positivist sociology sought to legitimate its ameliorative aspirations. The outstanding example, and the one that was to set the tone for sociology's contribution to industrial sociology for the next forty years, was the research conducted jointly by the Harvard Business School, the Massachusetts Institute of Technology, and the National Research Council—another Rockefeller-backed organization—at Western Electric's Hawthorne works. The central thrust of these studies was the translation of labor-management conflicts into problems of social engineering that could be solved by benevolent and technoscientific management policies. Refusing to identify with the grievances of labor, the sociologists sought to clothe their authoritative judgments about the solutions to industrial problems in the authority and within the ideology of capitalist management (Roethlisberger and Dickson, 1939).

Sociologists continued to volunteer their services to societal elites in order to give their discipline legitimacy through the Second World War, during which some of the same researchers who had worked on the Hawthorne studies were hired to resolve the problems of absenteeism and worker morale in behalf of the aims of industrial efficiency and the war effort. It was in this period that positivist sociologists ingratiated themselves and established respect for their brand of sociology with both big business and government. Building upon their successes during the Great Depression and the Second World War, positivist sociologists forged an alliance with Parsonian functionalists—who advocated a secularized variant of the Protestant covenant conceived as a social system—and contributed their research and scientific services to the administrators of the "Cold War." In the 1950s and 1960s, monies for sponsored research increased tremendously.

Government sponsorship of sociological research began to decrease in the 1980s for a number of reasons, most important being the growing disillusionment with the results of positivist social science. Because of declining student enrollments and federal cutbacks in the funding of both public welfare and academic social research, a crisis was declared by sociology's positivist leaders. Applied sociology emerged as the solution.

It now appears that money alone has become a significant symbol in and of itself of legitimation within the sociological enterprise. In Rossi and Whyte's recent essay, "The Applied Side of Sociology," appeared a call to seek out those who will supply the one material resource that will legitimate their activities—money (in Freeman et al., 1983:5–31). Rossi and Whyte (pp. 10, 17) freely admit that applied sociology will be used primarily in support of the business and political status quo. Business and government are institutions that have the money to pay for sociological research.

> Of course, it is generally more difficult to find funds for projects designed to serve the interests of organizations claiming to represent the poor and the powerless; however, such practical distinctions should not obscure the similarities in the roles and activities of sociologists involved in social engineering projects designed to serve establishment and antiestablishment organizations.
>
> This close tie between applied work and the political status quo is the source of much criticism of applied sociology, especially applied social research and clinical work. The criticism is well taken.

However, it is directed at the consequence of the usual sources of financial support for applied work. It is not aimed at the intrinsic features of applied work. That is, the current sources for the support of work in applied sociology are concerned with what they conceive to be their policy spaces. Alternative sources might conceive of different policy spaces and if demand were to arise from such sources, one might see applied sociology in support of, say, labor and socialist movements as well as of public bureaucracies and current political regimes.

Reprising Ogburn's thesis about the irrelevance of sociological theory, Rossi and Whyte (pp. 15–16) argue that applied sociologists must be willing to concentrate their efforts on the "manipulation" of only those policy variables that are relevant to their employers' interests. Sociological theory will have very little role to play in this version of applied sociology because the "truth" discovered by theory points to aspects of social reality that are beyond the "manipulations" of sociologists. Implicit in this statement is a recognition of man's frailty and the awesome power of that which is beyond man. A religious sociology would have recognized this power as that of God. Secular positivism, having ejected God from social science, in effect, readmits Him by the back door of its own impotence.

American sociology has been and continues to be a largely religious undertaking, though its practitioners no longer recognize this to be the case. While the first generation were clearly cognizant of the fact that sociology in America was an elaboration and application of Christian theology, the second generation claimed to have developed a secular value-free social science that rejected religious moralism. In reality the latter's version of social science, positivism, remained a transvalued form of the first generation's social gospel. Much of the moralistic and ameliorative orientation of the social gospelers was continued within the value-free language of the sociological perspective adopted by positivism. However, like the descendants of the Puritans described by Max Weber in *The Protestant Ethic*, who continued to work long after the religious significance of their endeavors had been forgotten, sociologists persist in their efforts to serve American society while having forgotten the original Christian impetus to do so.

Epilogue

This book does not purport to be a history of all of early American sociology, only of its forgotten religious roots and their later secularization in the applied side of the discipline. There were of course other important influences upon American sociology during its inception. One of the most important was European social thought, in particular German social science. Almost all of the founders of American sociology spent at least one year undertaking graduate studies in German universities. Some combined their German scholarship with their social gospel theology. For example, Richard T. Ely found in the economic ideas of Roscher and Knies theories compatible with his own attempt to create a Christian economics. However, German and French sociology did not take on an ameliorative orientation to the same degree that American sociology did because they did not share America's religious mission.

A number of early sociologists have not been discussed in depth in this work: among them are Lester Ward, George Herbert Mead, William Isaac Thomas, and Robert Park. Although Ward's philosophy of social amelioration was frequently referred to by religiously motivated sociologists such as Small and Ross, Ward's avid atheism kept him from becoming a leading figure in Christian sociology. Thomas and Park both had no interest in creating or supporting a religiously inspired social science. A discussion of how Thomas fit into the University of Chicago's sociology department while it was under Small's control appears in the work of Diner (1975). Park tended to show little interest in social reform once he arrived at Chicago. George Herbert Mead, although he was an advocate of social reform, tended to avoid publication of what would become his major legacy to American sociology, his pragmatically influenced theory of symbolic interactionism—so named by his student, Herbert Blumer. The influence that American pragmatic philosophy and psychology—e.g., through the works of Beard, Dewey, Royce, James, Pierce—had upon American sociology is beyond the scope of this book, although such an analysis would indeed be important.

Theoretical trends in American sociology after 1930 have not been analyzed because once applied sociology adopted a positivistic statistical methodology, it claimed to have little need for social theory. Ogburn's predicted demise of sociological theory has come true, at least within applied sociology. Except for functionalism, applied sociology seems to have made very little use of the theories which emerged in the post–World War II era such as neo-Marxian or phenomenological sociologies. Merton's "theories of the middle range" fit nicely with applied sociology, because such theories were both subject to statistical analysis and often contained manipulatable factors that applied sociologists could use as proof that their rendered services indeed produced quantifiable results.

The tension between applied sociology and theoretical sociology is fated to continue. One hopes this thesis will be helpful to those interested in the history of American sociology's long-term fascination with social problems and their cure. According to Stephen Turner (1991), sociology's unwillingness to examine its own historical origins is quite remarkable. Other disciplines, such as psychology, have extensive archival materials to which scholars have had access for a number of years.

However, since this essay was first written in 1983, several books have been published reevaluating the role that religion played in the history of early American sociology. The most important was Vidich and Lyman's (1985) *American Sociology*. In actuality, there is a great deal of similarity between my work and theirs, given that they were simultaneously writing their own history of early American sociology while directing my doctoral dissertation at the New School for Social Research, the origin of this book. Although I never read their manuscript while it was still being prepared, their work certainly influenced mine, particularly as a result of the many stimulating conversations between Stanford Lyman and myself on these issues. As a result there are several points of overlap between the two works. Vidich and Lyman, though, cover many more theorists than I attempted to discuss here. In addition, they located the true origins of the first nonreligious American sociology in the work of Herbert Blumer, who throughout his career opposed the quantification of the discipline advocated by Ogburn and his colleagues (Lyman and Vidich, 1985). My work differs from theirs in its greater emphasis on: (1) the origins of the social gospel in nineteenth century American Protestantism; (2) reasons given for why the social gospel needed sociology if it were to complete its inner-worldly religious mission; and (3) focus on the study of deviance and criminology among the first generation sociologists.

The only other study published since 1983 that specifically attempted to examine the religious nature of early American sociology was Swatos's (1984) *Faith of Our Fathers.* Far too brief to cover the topic adequately, Swatos never really analyzed the "sociology" of the founding fathers and mothers but instead focused on their methodological debates and philosophies of science. Had Swatos discussed the actual topics early sociologists researched and the theories they developed to explain such phenomena his treatise would have been more valuable.

The most thorough reexamination of nineteenth-century social science since Vidich and Lyman is Dorothy Ross's (1991) *The Origins of American Social Science.* Ross makes a strong argument for American exceptionalism—the belief that America had a unique millennial path to follow—but does not discuss, except in the work of Small, the importance of the social gospel for early American sociology. However, her discussion of the Small and Giddings factions within early sociology is informative as is the discussion of the role of Ogburn and the S.S.R.C. in turning the discipline toward quantification. Another book that dealt with the latter topic of the move toward positivism was Robert Bannister's (1987) *Sociology and Scientism.* In addition to covering Small, Giddings, and Ogburn, Bannister also discussed the important role played by L.L. Bernard in the early development of the discipline.

Dennis Smith (1988) included chapters on Small and Ogburn in his *The Chicago School*. Both Small and Ogburn appear in the book, because according to Smith they represented strands of the University of Chicago sociology department's liberal critique of capitalism. However, neither of the works attempts to discuss how the religious backgrounds of these sociologists shaped their work. Bulmer's (1984) history of the Chicago school of sociology concentrates primarily on Thomas and Park rather than Small and Henderson, although the latter two are discussed briefly.

The relationship between first-wave feminism and Christian sociology has been discussed by Mary Jo Deegan (1988), who included the chapter, "Jane Addams, Social Reform, and the Religious Men," in her book *Jane Addams and the Men of the Chicago School, 1892–1918*. Addams's relationship to Small, Henderson, Vincent, and Charles Zeublin is covered. According to Deegan there was considerable interplay between Hull House and the University of Chicago, and she details how both influenced the other. Kathleen McCarthy (1982) also discusses Jane Addams in her book on the charity movement in Chicago entitled *Noblesse Oblige*. While Wolf Lepenies's (1988) *Between Literature and Science: The Rise of Sociology* does not directly address itself to the American debate over whether sociology should be largely descriptive—i.e., literary—or mathematical, his work can be applied to an analysis of the largely gender-based splits that emerged in early American sociology over reform vs. theory, social work vs. sociology, domestic science vs. urban sociology, etc.

Marlene Shore (1987) has written an important history of early sociology in Canada, demonstrating the direct links between social scientific redemptionism at the University of Chicago and sociology at McGill University. Particularly important was Carl Dawson, who returned to McGill after attending the University of Chicago's Divinity School, thereafter rejecting the ministry for sociology. Dawson wholeheartedly adopted Park's ecological approach to urbanization and combined it with McGill's "tradition of utility." The result was a hybrid form of ecological reformism.

Another topic that has received little attention is the relationship between early American sociology and criminology. While criminology/penology existed in America prior to sociology, the new discipline attempted to subsume the old. Like sociology, criminology in the United States was, in the nineteenth century, largely the realm of religiously motivated reformers (McHugh, 1978). The relationship between sociology and criminology is briefly mentioned in Hartsfield's (1985) *The American Response to Professional Crime, 1870–1917* and in Jones's (1986) *History of Criminology*. In addition, the hereditarian attitudes in early criminology have been discussed by Haller (1984) and Rafter (1988). However, no one has made the link between the Kingdom vision of early sociology and the social gospel's need to develop means to rehabilitate, control, or, if need be, eliminate deviant and criminal populations in order to prepare the society for Christ's return.

The need for additional research on the early history of American sociology is self-evident. Until the discipline seriously reevaluates its own religious origins rather than ignoring them, it will continue to be unable to grapple with the moral and ethical problems which currently plague our society. By rejecting the unique critical theory—sin—developed by early American sociologists the discipline has been bifurcated: those who continue the "prophetic tradition" are left with various brands of Marxism to employ as critical theories, even though Marxian models mistakenly, in my opinion, see class rather than race as the key to understanding societal conflict in the United States, while those who seek legitimation of sociology through research and policy reforms have chosen to rely upon an atheoretical positivism which latently supports the status quo.

Bibliography

Abbott, Lyman. 1869. *Jesus of Nazareth*. New York: Harper.

Abbott, Lyman. 1887. *Henry Ward Beecher: A Sketch of His Career.* Hartford: American Publishing Co.

Abbott, Lyman. 1897. *The Theology of a Evolutionist.* New York: Houghton, Mifflin & Co.

Abbott, Lyman. 1925 (1892). *The Evolution of Christianity.* New York: The Outlook Company.

Abel, Theodore. 1933. *Protestant Home Missions to Catholic Immigrants.* New York: Institute of Social and Religious Research.

Abell, Aaron (editor). 1968. *American Catholic Thought on Social Questions.* New York: Bobbs-Merrill.

Addams, Jane. 1899a. "A Belated Industry," *American Journal of Sociology.* Vol. 4, No. 4, Jan., pp. 536–550.

Addams, Jane. 1899b. "Trade Unions and Public Duty," *American Journal of Sociology.* Vol. 4, No. 4, Jan., pp. 448–462.

Addams, Jane. 1905. "Problems of Municipal Administration," *American Journal of Sociology.* Vol. 10, No. 4, Jan., pp. 425–444.

Addams, Jane. 1909. *The Spirit of Youth and City Streets.* New York: Macmillan.

Addams, Jane. 1912a. "Recreation as a Public Function in Urban Communities," *American Journal of Sociology.* Vol. 17, No. 5, Mar., pp. 615–619.

Addams, Jane. 1912b. *A New Conscience and an Ancient Evil.* New York: Macmillan.

Addams, Jane. 1914. "A Modern Devil-Baby," *American Journal of Sociology.* Vol. 20, No. 1, July, pp. 117–118.

Ahlstrom, Sidney. 1975. *A Religious History of the American People.* Garden City, N.Y.: Doubleday. Two volumes.

Andrews, Edward Deming. 1963. *The People Called Shakers.* New York: Dover Books.

Banfield, Edward. 1974. *The Unheavenly City Revisited.* Boston: Little, Brown.

Bannister, Robert. 1987. *Sociology and Scientism: The American Quest for Objectivity, 1880–1940.* Chapel Hill: University of North Carolina Press.

Barbour, Ian. 1971. *Issues in Science and Religion.* New York: Harper Torchbooks.

Baritz, Loren. 1960. *The Servants of Power: A History of the Use of Social Science in American Industry.* Middletown, Conn.: Wesleyan University Press.

Barnes, Gilbert Hobbes. 1973. *The Anti-Slavery Impulse, 1830–1844.* Gloucester: Peter Smith.

Barnes, Harry Elmer. 1968. "Charles A. Ellwood," in Sills, David (editor). *Encyclopedia of the Social Sciences*. New York: Free Press. Vol. 5, pp. 31–33.

Bascom, John. 1883. *The Words of Christ*. New York: G.P. Putman's Sons.

Bascom, John. 1897. *Evolution and Religion; or, Faith as a Part of a Complete Cosmic System*. New York: G.P. Putman's Sons.

Batten, Samuel Z. 1902. "The Church as the Maker of Conscience," *American Journal of Sociology*. Vol. 7, No. 5, Mar., pp. 611–628.

Batten, Samuel Z. 1908. "The Redemption of the Unfit," *American Journal of Sociology*. Vol. 14, No. 2, Sept., pp. 233–260.

Becker, Ernest. 1971. *The Lost Science of Man*. New York: George Braziller.

Beecher, Catherine. 1841. *A Treatise on Domestic Economy*. Boston: T.H. Webb and Co.

Beecher, Henry Ward. 1884. *Evolution and Religion*. New York: Fords, Howard & Hulbert.

Beecher, Lyman. 1828. *Six Sermons on the Nature, Occasions, Signs, Evils, and Remedy of Intemperance*. Boston: T.R. Marvin (6th edition).

Beecher, Lyman. 1835. *A Plea for the West*. New York: Leavitt, Lord, and Co. (2nd edition).

Beecher, Lyman. 1884. *The Practicability of Suppressing Vice by Means of Societies Instituted for that Purpose*. New London, Conn.: Samuel Green.

Bellamy, Edward. 1888. *Looking Backward, 2000–1887*. New York: Houghton, Mifflin and Co.

Bernard, L.L. 1909. "The Teaching of Sociology in the United States," *American Journal of Sociology*. Vol. 15, No. 2, Sept., pp. 164–213.

Bestor, Arthur. 1967. *Backwoods Utopia*. Philadelphia: University of Pennsylvania Press.

Bierstedt, Robert. 1981. *American Sociological Theory*. New York: Academic Press.

Bliss, William D.P. (editor). 1898. *Encyclopedia of Social Reform*. New York: Funk & Wagnalls (2nd edition).

Blumer, Herbert. 1971. "Social Problems as Collective Behavior," *Social Problems*. Vol. 18, No. 3, Winter, pp. 298–306.

Bodo, John R. 1954. *The Protestant Clergy and Public Issues, 1812–1848*. Princeton, N.J.: Princeton University Press.

Bordin, Ruth. 1981. *Women and Temperance*. Philadelphia: Temple University Press.

Brown, Ira V. 1953. *Lyman Abbott, Christian Evolutionist*. Cambridge: Harvard University Press.

Brown, William Adams. 1906. *Christian Theology in Outline*. New York: Charles Scribner's Sons.

Buck, Paul (editor). 1965. *Social Sciences at Harvard, 1860–1920*. Cambridge: Harvard University Press.

Bulmer, Martin. 1984. *The Chicago School of Sociology*. Chicago: University of Chicago Press.

Bury, J.B. 1955. *The Idea of Progress.* New York: Dover Press.

Bushnell, Horace. 1839. *A Discourse on the Slavery Question.* Hartford, Conn.: Case, Tiffany, & Co. (3rd edition).

Bushnell, Horace. 1863. *Nature and the Supernatural, as Together Constituting the One System of God.* New York: Charles Scribner (3rd edition).

Bushnell, Horace. 1975 (1847). *Views of Christian Nurture.* Delmar, N.Y.: Scholar's Facsimiles and Reprints.

Carns, Donald. 1971. Introduction to the reprint of Small and Vincent. *An Introduction to the Study of Society.* Dubuque, Iowa: Wm. C. Brown Reprint Library.

Carter, Paul A. 1971. *The Decline and Revival of the Social Gospel.* Hamden, Conn.: Archon Books.

Church, Robert. 1965. "The Economists Study Society: Sociology at Harvard, 1891–1902," in Buck (editor), pp. 18–90.

Clark, Clifford. 1978. *Henry Ward Beecher: Spokesman for a Middle-Class America.* Urbana: University of Illinois Press.

Cole, Charles. 1950. "Horace Bushnell and the Slavery Question," *New England Quarterly.* Vol. 23, No. 1, Mar., pp. 19–30.

Cole, Charles. 1954. *The Social Ideas of the Northern Evangelicals, 1826–1860.* New York: Columbia University Press.

Coleman, James Melville. 1903. *Social Ethics.* New York: The Baker & Taylor Co.

Coleman, James Melville. No date. "Psychology of the Social Redemption." Privately published essay.

Collier, Peter, and David Horowitz. 1976. *The Rockefellers.* New York: Holt, Rinehart, and Winston.

Commons, John R. 1897. "The Junior Republic," *American Journal of Sociology.* Vol. 3, No. 1, Nov., pp. 281–296.

Commons, John R. 1898. "The Junior Republic II," *American Journal of Sociology.* Vol. 3, No. 2, Jan., pp. 433–448.

Commons, John R. 1899a. "A Sociological View of Sovereignty," *American Journal of Sociology.* Vol. 5, No. 1, July, pp. 1–15.

Commons, John R. 1899b. "A Sociological View of Sovereignty. Part II," *American Journal of Sociology.* Vol. 5, No. 2, Sept., pp. 155–171.

Commons, John R. 1899c. "A Sociological View of Sovereignty. Part III," *American Journal of Sociology.* Vol. 5, No. 3, Nov., pp. 347–366.

Commons, John R. 1900a. "A Sociological View of Sovereignty. Part IV," *American Journal of Sociology.* Vol. 5, No. 4, Jan., pp. 544–552.

Commons, John R. 1900b. "A Sociological View of Sovereignty. Part V," *American Journal of Sociology.* Vol. 5, No. 5, Mar., pp. 683–695.

Commons, John R. 1900c. "A Sociological View of Sovereignty. Part VI," *American Journal of Sociology.* Vol. 5, No. 6, May, pp. 814–825.

Commons, John R. 1900d. "A Sociological View of Sovereignty. Part VII," *American Journal of Sociology.* Vol. 6, No. 1, July, pp. 67–89.

Commons, John R. 1908. "Is Class Conflict in America Growing and Is It Inevitable?," *American Journal of Sociology.* Vol. 13, No. 6, May, pp. 756–783.

Conrad, Peter, and Joseph W. Schneider. 1980. *Deviance and Medicalization.* St. Louis: C.V. Mosby Co.

Cooley, Charles Horton. 1964 (1909). *Social Organization.* New York: Schocken Books.

Cross, Barbara. 1958. *Horace Bushnell: Minister to a Changing America.* Chicago: University of Chicago Press.

Cross, Whitney. 1965. *The Burned-Over District.* New York: Harper Torchbooks.

Curti, Merle. 1980. *Human Nature in American Thought.* Madison: University of Wisconsin Press.

Darwin, Charles. 1975. *The Origin of Species.* London: Dent.

Davie, Maurice R. (editor). 1963. *William Graham Sumner.* New York: Thomas Y. Crowell Co.

Davis, Allen F. 1967. *Spearheads for Reform: The Social Settlements and the Progressive Movement, 1890–1914.* New York: Oxford University Press.

Davis, Allen F. 1973. *American Heroine: The Life and Legend of Jane Addams.* New York: Oxford University Press.

Davis, Lawrence B. 1973. *The Immigrants, Baptists, and the Protestant Mind in America.* Urbana: University of Illinois Press.

Dayton, Donald W. 1976. *Discovering an Evangelical Heritage.* New York: Harper & Row.

Deegan, Mary Jo. 1988. *Jane Addams and the Men of the Chicago School, 1892–1918.* New Brunswick, N.J.: Transaction Books.

Dibble, Vernon K. 1975. *The Legacy of Albion Small.* Chicago: University of Chicago Press.

Diner, Steven J. 1975. "Department and Discipline: The Department of Sociology at the University of Chicago, 1892–1920," *Minerva.* Vol. 13, No. 4, Winter, pp. 514–553.

Douglas, Ann. 1977. *The Feminization of American Culture.* New York: Avon Books.

Dubbert, Joe. 1979. *A Man's Place.* Englewood Cliffs, N.J.: Prentice-Hall.

Dubois, W.E.B. 1967 (1899). *The Philadelphia Negro.* New York: Schocken Books.

Dubois, W.E.B. 1970 (1903). *The Souls of Black Folk.* New York: Washington Square Press.

Edwards, Jonathan. 1879. "A History of the Work of Redemption," in *The Works of President Edwards.* New York: Robert Caster and Brothers. Vol. I, pp. 297–516.

Ellwood, Charles E. 1907. "How Should Sociology Be Taught as a College or University Subject?," *American Journal of Sociology.* Vol. 12, No. 5, Mar., pp. 588–606.

Ellwood, Charles A. 1913 (1910). *Sociology and Modern Social Problems.* New York: American Book Company.

Ellwood, Charles. 1923. *Christianity and Social Science.* New York: Macmillan.

Ellwood, Charles A. 1925 (1922). *The Reconstruction of Religion: A Sociological View.* New York: Macmillan.

Ellwood, Charles A. 1929. *Man's Social Destiny.* Nashville: Cokesbury Press.

Ellwood, Charles A. 1933. *Methods in Sociology.* Durham: Duke University Press.

Ely, Richard T. 1884. *The Past and Present of Political Economy.* Baltimore: Johns Hopkins University Press.

Ely, Richard T. 1885. *Recent American Socialism.* Baltimore: Johns Hopkins University Press.

Ely, Richard T. 1889. *Social Aspects of Christianity.* New York: Thomas Y. Crowell & Co.

Ely, Richard T. 1894. *Socialism.* New York: Thomas Y. Crowell & Co.

Ely, Richard T. 1937. *Outline of Economics.* New York: Macmillan (6th edition).

Everett, John R. 1946. *Religion in Economics.* New York: King's Crown Press.

Fairbanks, Arthur. 1903. "Aristophanes as a Student of Society," *American Journal of Sociology.* Vol. 8, No. 5, Mar., pp. 655–666.

Faris, Robert E.L. 1970. *Chicago Sociology, 1920–1932.* Chicago: University of Chicago Press.

Fiske, John. 1884. *The Destiny of Man Viewed in the Light of His Origin.* New York: Houghton, Mifflin and Co.

Fiske, John. 1899. *From Nature to God*. Boston: Houghton, Mifflin.

Fleming, Daniel Johnson. 1925. *Whither Bound in Missions*. New York: Association Press.

Foucault, Michel. 1972. *The Archaeology of Knowledge*. New York: Pantheon Books.

Freeman, Howard E., Russell R. Dynes, Peter H. Rossi, and William Foote Whyte (editors). 1983. *Applied Sociology*. San Francisco: Jossey-Bass Publishers.

Gans, Herbert (editor). 1990. *Sociology in America*. Newbury Park, Calif.: Sage.

Geneva College Catalogue. Beaver Falls, Pa.: Geneva College. 1895–1896, 1897–1898, 1900–1901, 1901–1902 editions.

George, Henry. 1945 (1879). *Progress and Poverty*. New York: Robert Schalkenbach Foundation.

Gerth, Hans, and C. Wright Mills (editors). 1946. *From Max Weber*. New York: Oxford University Press.

Giddings, Franklin. 1893. "The Ethics of Social Progress," in Henry C. Adams (editor), *Philanthropy and Social Progress*. Freeport: Books for Libraries Press. pp. 203–248. (Reprinted 1969.)

Giddings, Franklin. 1898. "Sociology," in Bliss (editor), pp. 1277–1281.

Giddings, Franklin. 1899. *The Elements of Sociology*. New York: Macmillan.

Gillispie, Charles. 1959. *Genesis and Geology: The Impact of Scientific Discoveries upon Religious Beliefs in the Decades Before Darwin.* New York: Harper Torchbooks.

Gladden, Washington. 1886. *Applied Christianity.* Boston: Houghton, Mifflin & Co.

Gladden, Washington. 1888 (1885). *Working People and Their Employees.* New York: Funk & Wagnalls.

Gladden, Washington. 1891. *Burning Questions.* New York: The Century Co.

Gladden, Washington. 1902. *Social Salvation.* Boston: Houghton, Mifflin.

Gladden, Washington. 1905. *Christianity and Socialism.* New York: Eaton & Mains.

Glasgow, William. 1908. *The Geneva Book.* Philadelphia: Westbrook Publishing Co.

Gordon, Michael. 1978. "From an Unfortunate Necessity to the Cult of Mutual Orgasm: Sex in American Marital Education Literature, 1830–1940," in James Henslin and Edward Sagarin (editors), *The Sociology of Sex.* New York: Schocken Books.

Grover, Norman L. 1957. "The Church and Social Action: The Idea of the Church and Its Relation to Christian Social Strategy in Charles G. Finney, Horace Bushnell, and Washington Gladden." Unpublished Ph.D. Dissertation, Yale University.

Gusfield, Joseph. 1963. *Symbolic Crusade.* Urbana: University of Illinois Press.

Haller, Mark. 1984. *Eugenics: Hereditarian Attitudes in American Thought.* New Brunswick, N.J.: Rutgers University Press.

Harding, Vincent. 1965. "Lyman Beecher and the Transformation of American Protestantism, 1775–1863." Unpublished Ph.D. Dissertation, University of Chicago.

Harding, William Henry (editor). 1943. *Finney's Life and Lectures.* Grand Rapids: Zondervan Publishing House.

Hartsfield, Larry. 1985. *The American Response to Professional Crime, 1870–1917.* Wesport, Conn.: Greenwood Press.

Henderson, Charles. 1895a. "The Place and Functions of Voluntary Associations," *American Journal of Sociology.* Vol. 1, No. 3, Nov., pp. 327–334.

Henderson, Charles. 1895b. "Sociology and Theology," *American Journal of Sociology.* Vol. 1, No. 3, Nov., pp. 381–383.

Henderson, Charles. 1896a. "Business Men and Social Theorists," *American Journal of Sociology.* Vol. 1, No. 4, Jan., pp. 385–397.

Henderson, Charles. 1896b. "Rise of the German Inner Mission," *American Journal of Sociology.* Vol. 1, No. 5, Mar., pp. 583–595.

Henderson, Charles. 1896c. "The German Inner Mission," *American Journal of Sociology.* Vol. 1, No. 6, May, pp. 674–684.

Henderson, Charles. 1896d. "The German Inner Mission," *American Journal of Sociology.* Vol. 2, No. 1, July, pp. 58–73.

Henderson, Charles. 1898. "Politics in Public Institutions of Charity and Corrections," *American Journal of Sociology.* Vol. 4, No. 2, Sept., pp. 202–234.

Henderson, Charles. 1899. *Social Settlements.* New York: Lentilhan & Co.

Henderson, Charles. 1900. "Prison Laboratories," *American Journal of Sociology.* Vol. 6, No. 3, Nov., pp. 316–323.

Henderson, Charles. 1901. "The Scope of Social Technology," *American Journal of Sociology.* Vol. 6, No. 4, Jan., pp. 465–486.

Henderson, Charles. 1904. "Definition of a Social Policy Relating to the Dependent Group," *American Journal of Sociology.* Vol. 10, No. 3, Nov., pp. 315–334.

Henderson, Charles. 1905. "Social Solidarity in France," *American Journal of Sociology.* Vol. 17, No. 2, Sept., pp. 168–182.

Henderson, Charles. 1906 (1893). *An Introduction to the Study of the Dependent, Defective, and Delinquent Classes.* Boston: D.C. Heath & Co.

Henderson, Charles. 1907a. "Industrial Insurance Part I," *American Journal of Sociology.* Vol. 12, No. 4, Jan., pp. 470–486.

Henderson, Charles. 1907b. "Industrial Insurance Part II," *American Journal of Sociology.* Vol. 12, No. 5, Mar., pp. 717–734.

Henderson, Charles. 1907c. "Industrial Insurance Part III," *American Journal of Sociology.* Vol. 12, No. 6, May, pp. 756–778.

Henderson, Charles. 1907d. "Industrial Insurance Part IV," *American Journal of Sociology.* Vol. 13, No. 1, July, pp. 34–47.

Henderson, Charles. 1907e. "Industrial Insurance Part V," *American Journal of Sociology.* Vol. 13, No. 2, Sept., pp. 183–199.

Henderson, Charles. 1907f. "Industrial Insurance Part VI," *American Journal of Sociology.* Vol. 13, No. 3, Nov., pp. 349–379.

Henderson, Charles. 1908a. "Industrial Insurance Part VII," *American Journal of Sociology.* Vol. 13, No. 4, Jan., pp. 489–507.

Henderson, Charles. 1908b. "Industrial Insurance Part VIII," *American Journal of Sociology.* Vol. 13, No. 5, Mar., pp. 584–616.

Henderson, Charles. 1908c. "Industrial Insurance Part IX," *American Journal of Sociology.* Vol. 13, No. 6, May, pp. 841–854.

Henderson, Charles. 1908d. "Industrial Insurance Part X," *American Journal of Sociology.* Vol. 14, No. 1, July, pp. 64–77.

Henderson, Charles. 1908e. "Industrial Insurance Part XI," *American Journal of Sociology.* Vol. 14, No. 2, Sept., pp. 197–212.

Henderson, Charles. 1909a. "Industrial Insurance Part XII," *American Journal of Sociology.* Vol. 14, No. 4, Jan., pp. 451–464.

Henderson, Charles. 1909b. "Are Modern Industry and City Life Unfavorable to the Family?," *American Journal of Sociology.* Vol. 14, No. 5, Mar., pp. 668–680.

Henderson, Charles. 1910. "Improvements in Industrial Life Insurance," *American Journal of Sociology.* Vol. 15, No. 4, Jan., pp. 478–501.

Henderson, Charles. 1911. "Infant Welfare: Method of Organization and Administration in Italy," *American Journal of Sociology.* Vol. 17, No. 3, Nov., pp. 289–302.

Henderson, Charles. 1912a. "Infant Welfare: France," *American Journal of Sociology*. Vol. 17, No. 4, Jan., pp. 458–477.

Henderson, Charles. 1912b. "Infant Welfare: Germany," *American Journal of Sociology*. Vol. 17, No. 5, Mar., pp. 669–684.

Henderson, Charles. 1912c. "Infant Welfare in Germany and Belgium," *American Journal of Sociology*. Vol. 17, No. 6, May, pp. 783–803.

Henderson, Charles. 1912d. "Applied Sociology (or Social Technology)," *American Journal of Sociology*. Vol. 18, No. 2, Sept., pp. 215–221.

Henderson, Charles. 1914. "Social Assimilation: America and China," *American Journal of Sociology*. Vol. 19, No. 5, Mar., pp. 640–648.

Henderson, Charles. 1915a. "How Chicago Met the Unemployment Problem of 1915," *American Journal of Sociology*. Vol. 20, No. 6, May, pp. 721–730.

Henderson, Charles. 1915b. "The Everlasting Kingdom of Righteousness," in Soares (editor), pp. 21–36.

Herbst, Jurgen. 1961. "Francis Greenwood Peabody: Harvard's Theologian of the Social Gospel," *Harvard Theological Review*. Pp. 45–69.

Herron, George D. 1893. *The New Redemption*. New York: Thomas Y. Crowell & Co.

Herron, George D. 1894. *The Christian Society*. New York: Fleming H. Revell Co.

Herron, George D. 1895. *The Christian State.* New York: Thomas Y. Crowell & Co.

Hine, Lewis. 1974. *Lewis W. Hine, 1874–1940.* New York: Grossman Publishers.

Hine, Lewis. 1981. *Women at Work.* New York: Dover Press.

Hinkle, Roscoe, and Gisela Hinkle. 1954. *The Development of Modern Sociology: Its Nature and Growth in the United States.* New York: Random House.

Hodge, Charles. 1874. *What Is Darwinism?* New York: Scribner, Armstrong, & Co.

Hofstadter, Richard. 1955. *Social Darwinism in American Thought.* Boston: Beacon Press.

Hofstadter, Richard. 1963. *The Progressive Movement.* Englewood Cliffs, N.J.: Prentice-Hall.

Holloway, Mark. 1966. *Heavens on Earth.* New York: Dover Press.

Hopkins, Charles Howard. 1940. *The Rise of the Social Gospel in American Protestantism, 1865–1915.* New Haven: Yale University Press.

Hopkins, Samuel. 1852 (1793). *A Treatise on the Millennium. The Works of Samuel Hopkins.* Boston: Doctrinal Tract and Book Society. Pp. 224–366.

Howerth, Ira W. 1894. "Present Condition of Sociology in the U.S.," *Annals of the American Academy of Political and Social Science.* Vol. 5, Sept., pp. 112–121.

Jaffe, A.J. 1968. "William Fielding Ogburn," in *Encyclopedia of the Social Sciences*. Vol. 11, pp. 271–281.

Jones, David. 1986. *History of Criminology*. Westport, Conn.: Greenwood Press.

Kelly, Florence. 1896. "The Working Boy," *American Journal of Sociology*. Vol. 2, No. 3, Nov., pp. 358–368.

Kelly, Florence. 1898a. "The Illinois Child-Labor Law," *American Journal of Sociology*. Vol. 3, No. 4, Jan., pp. 490–501.

Kelly, Florence. 1898b. "The U.S. Supreme Court and the Utah Eight-Hours Law," *American Journal of Sociology*. Vol. 4, No. 1, July, pp. 21–34.

Kelly, Florence. 1899. "The Aims and Principles of the Consumers' League," *American Journal of Sociology*. Vol. 5, No. 3, Nov., pp. 289–304.

Kelly, Florence. 1904. "Has Illinois the Best Laws in the Country for the Protection of Children?," *American Journal of Sociology*. Vol. 10, No. 3, Nov., pp. 299–314.

Kelly, Florence. 1911. "Minimum-Wage Boards," *American Journal of Sociology*. Vol. 17, No. 3, Nov., pp. 303–314.

Kett, Joseph. 1977. *Rites of Passage*. NY: Harper & Row.

Lasch, Christopher (editor). 1965. *The Social Thought of Jane Addams*. Indianapolis: Bobbs-Merrill.

LeConte, Joseph. 1897. *Evolution: Its Nature, Its Evidences, and Its Relation to Religious Thought*. New York: D. Appleton & Co.

Lepenies, Wolf. 1988. *Between Literature and Science: The Rise of Sociology*. New York: Cambridge University Press.

Lubove, Roy. 1965. *The Professional Altruist: The Emergence of Social Work as a Career, 1880–1930*. Cambridge: Harvard University Press.

Lyman, Stanford M. 1978a. *The Seven Deadly Sins: Society and Evil*. New York: St. Martin's Press.

Lyman, Stanford M. 1978b. "The Acceptance, Rejection, and Reconstruction of Histories," in Richard Harvey Brown and Stanford M. Lyman (editors), *Structure, Consciousness, and History*. New York: Cambridge University Press. Pp. 53–105.

Lyman, Stanford, and Arthur Vidich. 1988. *Social Order and Public Philosophy: An Analysis and Interpretation of the Work of Herbert Blumer*. Fayettville: University of Arkansas Press.

Machen, John Gresham. 1922. *Christianity and Liberalism*. New York: Macmillan.

Magnuson, Norris. 1977. *Salvation in the Slums: Evangelical Social Work, 1865–1920*. Metuchen, N.J.: Scarecrow Press.

Mathews, Donald G. 1977. *Religion in the Old South*. Chicago: University of Chicago Press.

Mathews, Shailer. 1895a. "Christian Sociology: Introduction," *American Journal of Sociology*. Vol. 1, No. 1, July, pp. 69–78.

Mathews, Shailer. 1895b. "Christian Sociology: Man," *American Journal of Sociology*. Vol. 1, No. 2, Sept., pp. 182–194.

Mathews, Shailer. 1895c. "Christian Sociology: Society," *American Journal of Sociology*. Vol. 1, No. 3, Nov., pp. 359–380.

Mathews, Shailer. 1896a. "Christian Sociology: The Family," *American Journal of Sociology.* Vol. 1, No. 4, Jan., pp. 457–472.

Mathews, Shailer. 1896b. "Christian Sociology: The State," *American Journal of Sociology.* Vol. 1, No. 5, Mar., pp. 604–617.

Mathews, Shailer. 1896c. "Christian Sociology: Wealth," *American Journal of Sociology.* Vol. 1, No. 6, May, pp. 771–784.

Mathews, Shailer. 1896d. "Christian Sociology: Social Life," *American Journal of Sociology.* Vol. 2, No. 1, July, pp. 108–117.

Mathews, Shailer. 1896e. "Christian Sociology: The Forces of Human Progress," *American Journal of Sociology.* Vol. 2, No. 2, Sept., pp. 274–287.

Mathews, Shailer. 1896f. "Christian Sociology: The Process of Social Regeneration," *American Journal of Sociology.* Vol. 2, No. 3, Nov., pp. 416–432.

Mathews, Shailer. 1899. "The Significance of the Church to the Social Movement," *American Journal of Sociology.* Vol. 4, No. 5, Mar., pp. 603–620.

Mathews, Shailer. 1900. "The Christian Church and Social Unity," *American Journal of Sociology.* Vol. 5, No. 4, Jan., pp. 450–469.

Mathews, Shailer. 1910. *The Social Gospel.* Boston: The Griffith and Rowland Press.

Mathews, Shailer. 1912. "The Social Origin of Theology," *American Journal of Sociology.* Vol. 18, No. 3, Nov., pp. 289–317.

Mathews, Shailer. 1918. *Patriotism and Religion*. New York: Macmillan.

Mathews, Shailer. 1927. "The Development of Social Christianity in America during the Past Twenty-Five Years," *The Journal of Religion*. Pp. 376–386.

McCarthy, Kathleen. 1982. *Noblesse Oblige: Charity and Cultural Philanthropy in Chicago, 1849–1929*. Chicago: University of Chicago Press.

McCosh, James. 1888. *The Religious Aspect of Evolution*. New York: G.P. Putnam's Sons.

McHugh, Gerald Austin. 1978. *Christian Faith and Criminal Justice*. New York: Paulist Press.

McLoughlin, William. 1959. *Modern Revivalism*. New York: Ronald Press Co.

McLoughlin, William G. (editor). 1968. *The American Evangelicals, 1800–1900*. New York: Harper Torchbooks.

McLoughlin, William G. 1978. *Revivals, Awakenings, and Reform*. Chicago: University of Chicago Press.

Miller, Perry. 1949. *Jonathan Edwards*. New York: William Sloane Associates.

Mills, C. Wright. 1943. "The Professional Ideology of Social Pathologists," *American Journal of Sociology*. Vol. 49, No. 2, Sept., pp. 165–180.

Moberg, David O. 1977. *The Great Reversal: Evangelism and Social Concern*. Philadelphia: J.B. Lippincott. (Revised edition.)

Morgan, Edmund S. 1966. *The Puritan Family.* New York: Harper & Row.

Morgan, J. Graham. 1969. "The Development of Sociology and the Social Gospel in America," *Sociological Analysis.* Vol. 30, No. 1, Spring, pp. 42–53.

Morgan, J. Graham. 1980. "Women in American Sociology in the Nineteenth Century," *Journal for the History of Sociology.* Vol. 2, No. 1, pp. 1–34.

Morrison, Theodore. 1974. *Chautauqua.* Chicago: University of Chicago Press.

Niebuhr, H. Richard. 1936. "The Attack on the Social Gospel," *Religion in Life.* Vol. 5, Spring, pp. 176–181.

Niebuhr, H. Richard. 1959 (1937). *The Kingdom of God in America.* New York: Harper Torchbooks.

Niebuhr, Reinhold. 1932. *Moral Man and Immoral Society.* New York: C. Scribner's Sons.

Nordhoff, Charles. 1966. *The Communistic Societies of the United States.* New York: Dover Press.

Odum, Howard W. 1951. *American Sociology.* Westport, Conn.: Greenwood Press.

Ogburn, William. 1922. *Social Change.* New York: B.W. Huebsch, Inc.

Ogburn, William F. (editor). 1933. *Recent Social Trends.* New York: McGraw-Hill Book Co. Two volumes.

Page, Charles H. 1969. *Class and American Sociology.* New York: Schocken Books.

Parsons, Talcott, and Bernard Barber. 1948. "Sociology, 1941–46," *American Journal of Sociology.* Vol. 53, No. 4, Jan., pp. 245–257.

Patterson, Bob E. 1977. *Reinhold Niebuhr.* Waco, Tex.: Word Books.

Peabody, Francis Greenwood. 1900. *Jesus Christ and the Social Question.* New York: Macmillan.

Peabody, Francis G. 1913. "The Socialization of Religion," *American Journal of Sociology.* Vol. 18, No. 5, Mar., pp. 694–705.

Persons, Stow (editor). 1950. *Evolutionary Thought in America.* New Haven: Yale University Press.

Porterfield, Amanda. 1980. *Feminine Spirituality in America.* Philadelphia: Temple University Press.

Rader, Benjamin. 1966. *The Academic Mind and Reform: The Influence of Richard T. Ely in American Life.* Lexington: University of Kentucky Press.

Rafter, Nicole (editor). 1988. *White Trash: The Eugenic Family Studies, 1877–1919.* Boston: Northeastern University Press.

Rauschenbusch, Walter. 1896. "Ideals of Social Reformers," *American Journal of Sociology.* Vol. 2, No. 2, Sept., pp. 202–219.

Rauschenbusch, Walter. 1897. "The Stake of the Church in the Social Movement," *American Journal of Sociology.* Vol. 3, No. 1, July, pp. 18–30.

Rauschenbusch, Walter. 1907. *Christianity and the Social Crisis*. New York: Macmillan Co.

Rauschenbusch, Walter. 1910. *For God and the People: Prayers of the Social Awakening*. Boston: Pilgrim Press.

Rauschenbusch, Walter. 1912. *Christianizing the Social Order*. Boston: Pilgrim Press.

Rauschenbusch, Walter. 1916. *The Social Principles of Jesus*. New York: Association Press.

Rauschenbusch, Walter. 1945 (1917). *A Theology for the Social Gospel*. Nashville: Abingdon Press.

Rauschenbusch, Walter. 1950. *A Gospel for the Social Awakening*. New York: Association Press.

Richmond, Mary. 1917. *Social Diagnosis*. New York: Russell Sage Foundation.

Richmond, Rebecca. 1953. *Invitation to Chautauqua*. Published privately.

Riis, Jacob. 1906 (1890). *How the Other Half Lives*. New York: Scribner's.

Robinson, Virginia. 1930. *A Changing Psychology in Social Case Work*. Philadelphia: University of Pennsylvania Press.

Roethlisberger, Fritz J., and William J. Dickson. 1939. *Management and the Worker*. Cambridge: Harvard University Press.

Rosebush, Judson G. 1923. *The Ethics of Capitalism*. New York: Association Press.

Rosenberg, Carroll Smith. 1971. *Religion and the Rise of the American City.* Ithaca: Cornell University Press.

Rosenberg, Rosalind. 1982. *Beyond Separate Spheres: Intellectual Roots of Modern Feminism.* New Haven: Yale University Press.

Ross, Dorothy. 1991. *The Origins of American Social Science.* New York: Cambridge University Press.

Ross, E.A. 1914. *The Old World in the New.* New York: The Century Co.

Ross, E.A. 1969 (1901). *Social Control.* Cleveland: Case Western Reserve University.

Ross, E.A. 1973 (1907). *Sin and Society.* New York: Harper Torchbooks.

Russett, Cynthia. 1976. *Darwin in America: The Intellectual Response, 1865–1912.* San Francisco: W.H. Freeman & Co.

Savage, M.J. 1893. *The Evolution of Christianity.* Boston: George H. Ellis.

Sharpe, Dores R. 1942. *Walter Rauschenbusch.* New York: Macmillan.

Shaw, Clifford R. 1966 (1930). *The Jack-Roller.* Chicago: University of Chicago Press.

Sheldon, Charles M. 1978 (1896). *In His Steps.* Grand Rapids: Baker Book House.

Shore, Marlene. 1987. *The Science of Social Redemption: McGill, the Chicago School, and the Origins of Social Research in Canada.* Toronto: University of Toronto Press.

Sibley, Elbridge. 1974. *Social Science Research Council: The First Fifty Years*. New York: Social Science Research Council.

Simpson, Ida Harper. 1988. *The First Fifty Years of the Southern Sociological Society*. Athens: University of Georgia Press.

Sizer, Sandra. 1978. *Gospel Hymns and Social Religion*. Philadelphia: Temple University Press.

Small, Albion. 1895a. "The Era Of Sociology," *American Journal of Sociology*. Vol. 1, No. 1, July, pp. 1–15.

Small, Albion. 1895b. "The Civic Federation of Chicago," *American Journal of Sociology*. Vol. 1, No. 1, July, pp. 76–103.

Small, Albion, 1895c. "Static and Dynamic Sociology," *American Journal of Sociology*. Vol. 1, No. 2, Sept., pp. 195–209.

Small, Albion. 1895d. "Christian Sociology," *American Journal of Sociology*. Vol. 1, No. 2, Sept., pp. 215–216.

Small, Albion. 1895e. "Private Business as a Public Trust," *American Journal of Sociology*. Vol. 1, No. 3, Nov., pp. 276–289.

Small, Albion. 1896a. "The State and Semi-Public Corporation," *American Journal of Sociology*. Vol. 1, No. 4, Jan., pp. 398–410.

Small, Albion. 1896b. "The Limits of Christian Sociology," *American Journal of Sociology*. Vol. 1, No. 4, Jan., pp. 509–511.

Small, Albion. 1896c. "Scholarship and Social Agitation," *American Journal of Sociology*. Vol. 1, No. 5, Mar., pp. 564–582.

Small, Albion. 1896d. "Review of Franklin Giddings' *The Principles of Sociology*," *American Journal of Sociology*. Vol. 2, No. 2, Sept., pp. 288–305.

Small, Albion. 1897a. "The Sociologists' Point of View," *American Journal of Sociology*. Vol. 3, No. 2, Sept., pp. 145–170.

Small, Albion. 1897b. "The Meaning of the Social Movement," *American Journal of Sociology*. Vol. 3, No. 3, Nov., pp. 340–354.

Small, Albion. 1898a. "The Methodology of the Social Problem," *American Journal of Sociology*. Vol. 4, No. 1, July, pp. 113–144.

Small, Albion. 1898b. "Sanity in Social Agitation," *American Journal of Sociology*. Vol. 4, No. 3, Nov., pp. 335–351.

Small, Albion. 1900. "The Scope of Sociology," *American Journal of Sociology*. Vol. 6, No. 2, Sept., pp. 177–203.

Small, Albion. 1903a. "What Is a Sociologist?," *American Journal of Sociology*. Vol. 8, No. 4, Jan., pp. 468–477.

Small, Albion. 1903b. "The Significance of Sociology for Ethics," in *Decennial Publications of the University of Chicago*. Chicago: University of Chicago Press. First Series, Vol. 4, pp. 111–149.

Small, Albion. 1904. "The Scope of Sociology: Premises of Practical Sociology," *American Journal of Sociology*. Vol. 10, No. 1, July, pp. 26–46.

Small, Albion. 1908a. "Ratzenhofer's Sociology," *American Journal of Sociology*. Vol. 13, No. 4, Jan., pp. 433–438.

Small, Albion. 1908b. "The Meaning of Sociology," *American Journal of Sociology.* Vol. 14, No. 1, July, pp. 1–14.

Small, Albion. 1910. "The Sociological Stage in the Evolution of the Social Sciences," *American Journal of Sociology.* Vol. 15, No. 5, Mar., pp. 681–697.

Small, Albion. 1912. "Socialism in the Light of Social Science," *American Journal of Sociology.* Vol. 17, No. 6, May, pp. 804–819.

Small, Albion. 1913a. "Review of Walter Rauschenbusch's *Christianizing the Social Order,*" *American Journal of Sociology.* Vol. 18, No. 6, May, pp. 808–811.

Small, Albion. 1913b. *Between Eras: From Capitalism to Democracy.* Kansas City: Inter-Collegiate Press.

Small, Albion. 1914. "The Ford Motor Company Incident," *American Journal of Sociology.* Vol. 19, No. 5, Mar., pp. 656–658.

Small, Albion. 1915. "The Life," in Soares (editor), pp. 181–199.

Small, Albion. 1916. "Fifty Years of Sociology in the U.S. (1865–1915)," *American Journal of Sociology.* Vol. 21, No. 6, May, pp. 721–864.

Small, Albion. 1919a. "The Church and Class Conflicts," *American Journal of Sociology.* Vol. 24, No. 5, Mar., pp. 481–501.

Small, Albion. 1919b. "Material for the Ideal Democracy," *American Journal of Sociology.* Vol. 25, No. 3, Nov., pp. 257–297.

Small, Albion. 1920a. "Christianity and Industry," *American Journal of Sociology.* Vol. 25, No. 6, May, pp. 673–694.

Small, Albion. 1920b. "A Prospectus on Sociological Theory," *American Journal of Sociology.* Vol. 26, No. 1, July, pp. 22–59.

Small, Albion. 1923a. "Review of Ellwood's *The Reconstruction of Religion,*" *American Journal of Sociology.* Vol. 29, No. 2, Sept., pp. 236–237.

Small, Albion. 1923b. "Review of Ellwood's *Christianity and Social Science,*" *American Journal of Sociology.* Vol. 29, No. 3, Nov., p. 363.

Small, Albion, and George E. Vincent. 1894. *An Introduction to the Study of Society.* Chicago: American Book Co.

Smith, Dennis. 1988. *The Chicago School: A Liberal Critique of Capitalism.* New York: St. Martin's Press.

Smith, T.V., and Leonard D. White. 1968 (1929). *Chicago: An Experiment in Social Science Research.* Westport, Conn.: Greenwood Press.

Smith, Timothy L. 1952. *Revivalism and Social Reform.* Nashville: Abington Press.

Soares, Theodore (editor). 1915. *University of Chicago Sermons.* Chicago: University of Chicago Press.

Spector, Malcolm, and John Kitsuse. 1977. *Constructing Social Problems.* Menlo Park, Calif.: Benjamin Cummings Publishing.

Stelzle, Charles. 1903. *The Working Man and Social Problems.* Chicago: Fleming H. Revell Co.

Stocking, George W., Jr. 1968. "Lamarckianism in American Social Science, 1890–1915" in Stocking (editor), *Race, Culture, and Evolution*. New York: Free Press, pp. 234–269.

Stonequist, Everett. 1961 (1937). *The Marginal Man*. New York: Russell & Russell.

Stouffer, Samuel. 1980 (1930). *An Experimental Comparison of Statistical and Case History Methods of Attitude Research*. New York: Arno Press.

Strong, Josiah. 1893. *The New Era or the Coming Kingdom*. New York: Baker & Taylor Co.

Strong, Josiah. 1895. "Local Alliances," *American Journal of Sociology*. Vol. 1, No. 2, Sept., pp. 170–181.

Strong, Josiah. 1898. *The Twentieth Century City*. New York: Baker and Taylor Co.

Strong, Josiah. 1902. *The Next Great Awakening*. New York: Baker & Taylor Co.

Strong, Josiah (editor). 1904. *Social Progress: A Year Book and Encyclopedia of Economic, Industrial, Social, and Religious Statistics*. New York: Baker & Taylor Co. (Also 1905 and 1906 editions.)

Strong, Josiah. 1914. *Our World: The New World-Life*. Garden City, N.Y.: Doubleday, Page, & Co.

Strong, Josiah. 1915. *The New World-Religion*. Garden City, N.Y.: Doubleday, Page, & Co.

Strong, Josiah. 1963 (1886). *Our Country: Its Possible Future and Its Present Crisis*. Cambridge: Harvard University Press.

Stuckenberg, J.H.W. 1893. *The Age and the Church.* Hartford: The Student Publishing Co.

Stuckenberg, J.H.W. 1897. *Introduction to the Study of Sociology.* New York: A.C. Armstrong & Son.

Sudermann, Elmer F. 1976. "Religion in the Popular American Novel: 1870–1900," *Journal of Popular Culture.* Vol. IX, No. 4, Spring, pp. 1003–1009.

Sumner, William Graham. 1883. *What Social Classes Owe to Each Other.* New York: Harper & Brothers.

Sumner, William Graham. 1959 (1906). *Folkways.* New York: Dover Press.

Sumner, William Graham. 1963. *Social Darwinism.* Englewood Cliffs, N.J.: Prentice-Hall.

Sutherland, Edwin. 1973. *On Analyzing Crime.* Chicago: University of Chicago Press.

Swatos, William. 1984. *Faith of Our Fathers.* Bristol, Ind.: Wyndham Hall Press.

Taft, Jessie. 1916. *The Women's Movement from the Point of View of Social Consciousness.* Chicago: University of Chicago Press.

Taylor, Graham. 1899. "The Social Function of the Church," *American Journal of Sociology.* Vol. 5, No. 3, Nov., pp. 305–321.

Teggart, Frederick J. 1972. *Theory and Processes of History.* Gloucester, N.J.: Peter Smith.

Thomas, W.I., and Florian Znaniecki. 1927. *The Polish Peasant in Europe and America.* New York: Alfred A. Knopf.

de Tocqueville, Alexis. 1954. *Democracy in America.* New York: Vintage Books. Two volumes.

Torrey, R.A., and A.C. Dixon. 1970 (1917). *The Fundamentals.* Grand Rapids: Baker Book House.

Turner, Stephen. 1991. "Salvaging Sociology's Past," *Footnotes.* May, p. 6.

Tuveson, Ernest Lee. 1968. *Redeemer Nation.* Chicago: University of Chicago Press.

Vidich, Arthur. 1982. "The Moral, Economic, and Political Status of Labor in American Society," *Social Research.* Vol. 49, No. 3, Autumn, pp. 752–790.

Vidich, Arthur J., and Stanford M. Lyman. 1982. "Secular Evangelism at the University of Wisconsin," *Social Research.* Vol. 49, No. 4, Winter, pp. 1047–1072.

Vidich, Arthur J., and Stanford M. Lyman. 1985. *American Sociology.* New Haven: Yale University Press.

Vincent, George. 1896. "The Province of Sociology," *American Journal of Sociology.* Vol. 1, No. 4, Jan., pp. 473–491.

Vincent, George. 1898. "A Retarded Frontier," *American Journal of Sociology.* Vol. 4, No. 1, July, pp. 1–20.

Vincent, George. 1904a. "Spencer, the Man," *American Journal of Sociology.* Vol. 9, No. 5, Mar., pp. 709–711.

Vincent, George. 1904b. "The Laws of Hammurabi," *American Journal of Sociology.* Vol. 9, No. 6, May, pp. 737–754.

Vincent, George. 1904c. "The Development of Sociology," *American Journal of Sociology*. Vol. 10, No. 2, Sept., pp. 145–160.

Vincent, George. 1905. "A Laboratory Experiment in Journalism," *American Journal of Sociology*. Vol. 11, No. 3, Nov., pp. 297–311.

Vincent, George. 1906. "Varieties of Sociology," *American Journal of Sociology*. Vol. 12, No. 1, July, pp. 1–10.

Vincent, George. 1907. "Review of Sumner's *Folkways*," *American Journal of Sociology*. Vol. 13, No. 3, Nov., pp. 414–419.

Vincent, George. 1911. "The Rivalry of Social Groups," *American Journal of Sociology*. Vol. 16, No. 4, Jan., pp. 469–484.

Visser 'T Hooft, Willem A. 1928. *The Background of the Social Gospel in America*. St. Louis: Bethany Press.

Vulgamore, Melvin. 1963. "Social Reform in the Theology of Charles Finney." Unpublished Ph.D. Dissertation, Boston University.

Walters, Ronald G. 1978. *American Reformers, 1815–1860*. New York: Hill and Wang.

Weber, Max. 1930. *The Protestant Ethic and the Spirit of Capitalism*. New York: Scribner.

Weber, Max. 1963. *The Sociology of Religion*. Boston: Beacon Press.

Weld, Theodore Dwight. 1969 (1839). *American Slavery As It Is*. New York: Arno Press.

Wesley, John. 1966. *A Plain Account of Christian Perfection*. Kansas City: Beacon Hill Press.

White, Ronald C., Jr., and C. Howard Hopkins. 1976. *The Social Gospel*. Philadelphia: Temple University Press.

Woods, Robert. 1914. "The Neighborhood in Social Reconstruction," *American Journal of Sociology*. Vol. 19, No. 5, Mar., pp. 577–591.

Wooley, Helen Thompson. 1903. *The Mental Traits of Sex*. Chicago: University of Chicago Press.

Wright, Carroll D. 1895. "Contributions of the U.S. Government to Social Science," *American Journal of Sociology*. Vol. 1, No. 3, Nov., pp. 241–275.

Wright, Carroll. 1899. *Outline of Practical Sociology*. New York: Longman Green (2nd edition).

Wyatt-Brown, Bertram. 1969. *Lewis Tappan and the Evangelical War against Slavery*. Cleveland: Case Western Reserve University Press.

Zorbaugh, Harvey. 1929. *The Gold Coast and the Slum*. Chicago: University of Chicago Press.

About the Author

Cecil Greek was born in 1953 in Latrobe, Pennsylvania. Raised as a member of the Churches of God in North America (headquartered in Findley, Ohio), he studied sociology at Eastern College in St. Davids, Pennsylvania. There he was taught by Tony Campolo, a modern "social gospeler." While attending the New School for Social Research in New York City (from which he received both an M.A. and a Ph.D.), he began to investigate the links between social gospel theology and early American sociology after discovering that social gospel preachers regularly published articles in the *American Journal of Sociology* during the 1890s. He was particularly encouraged to continue pursuit of this topic by Stanford Lyman, who became Greek's doctoral supervisor. The eventual result was this treatise.

Greek is currently teaching in the criminology department at the University of South Florida in St. Petersburg. He previously held positions at the University of Central Oklahoma (Edmond, Oklahoma) and Minot State University (Minot, North Dakota).

He has continued his research interest in the social constructionist perspective on deviance and social problems. Among the topics he has published are the history of forfeiture and seizure penalties in England and the American colonies, the history of juvenile corrections in the United States, and contemporary religiously inspired antipornography crusades in the United States and England.